MARVEL

THE THING AND THE HUMAN TORCH

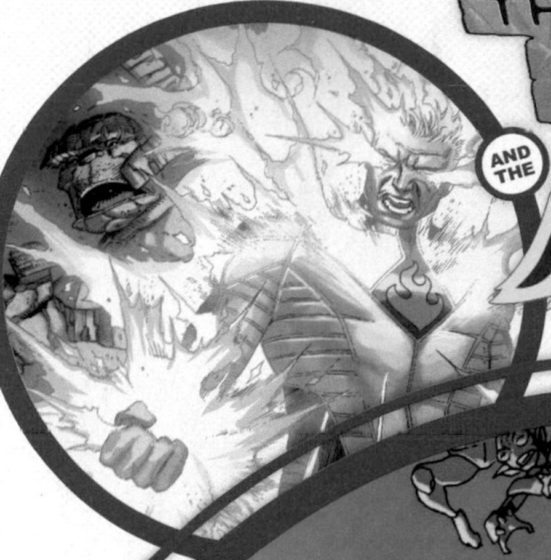

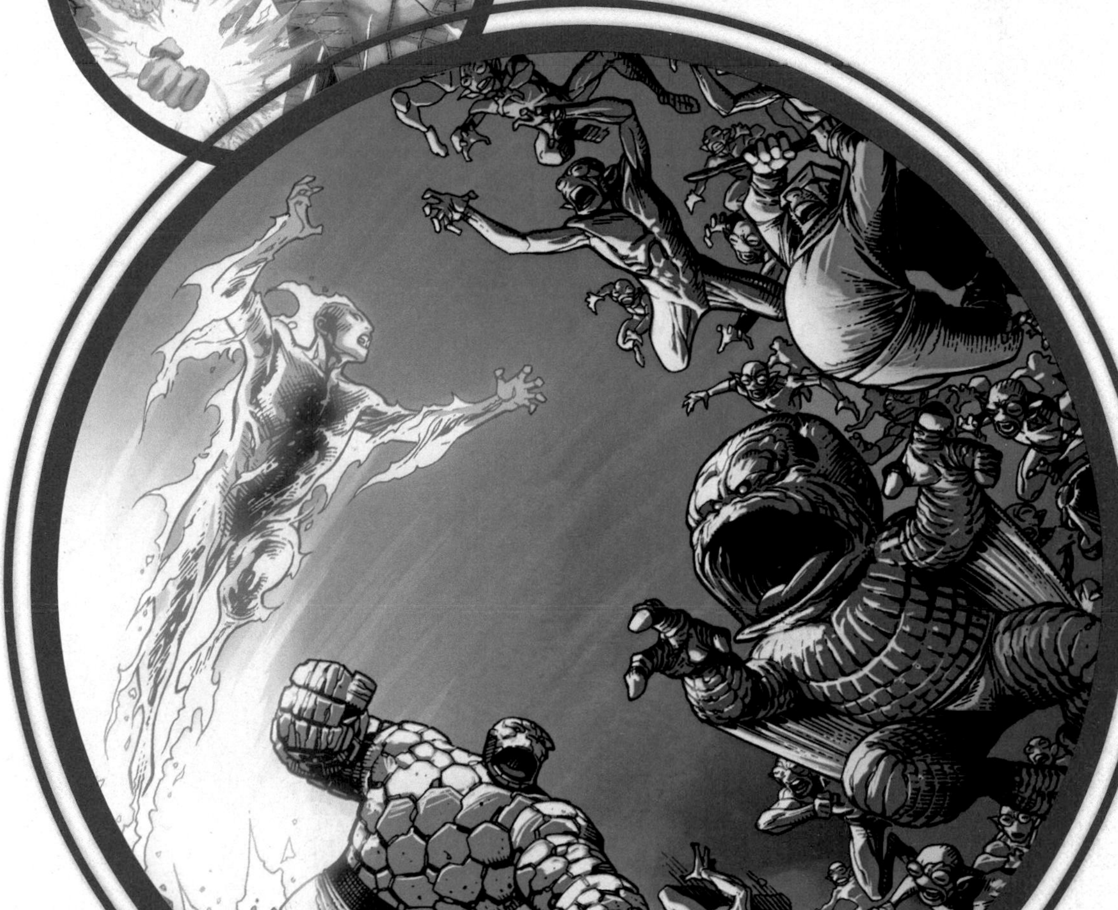

Fate of the Four

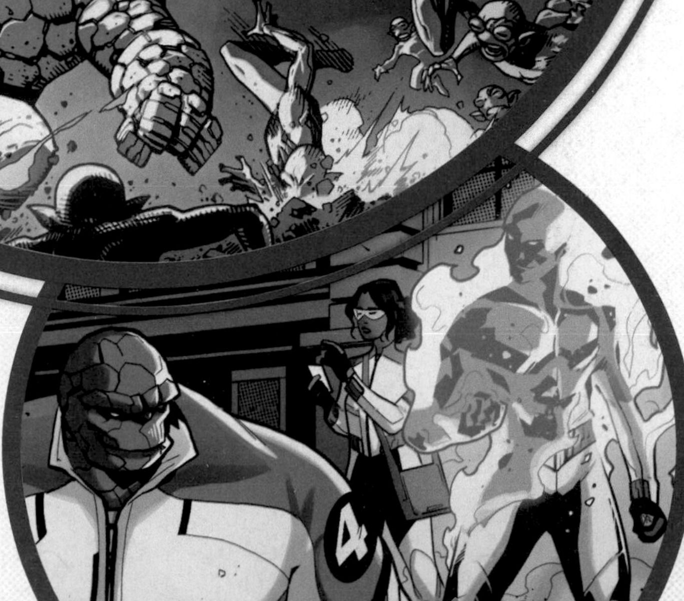

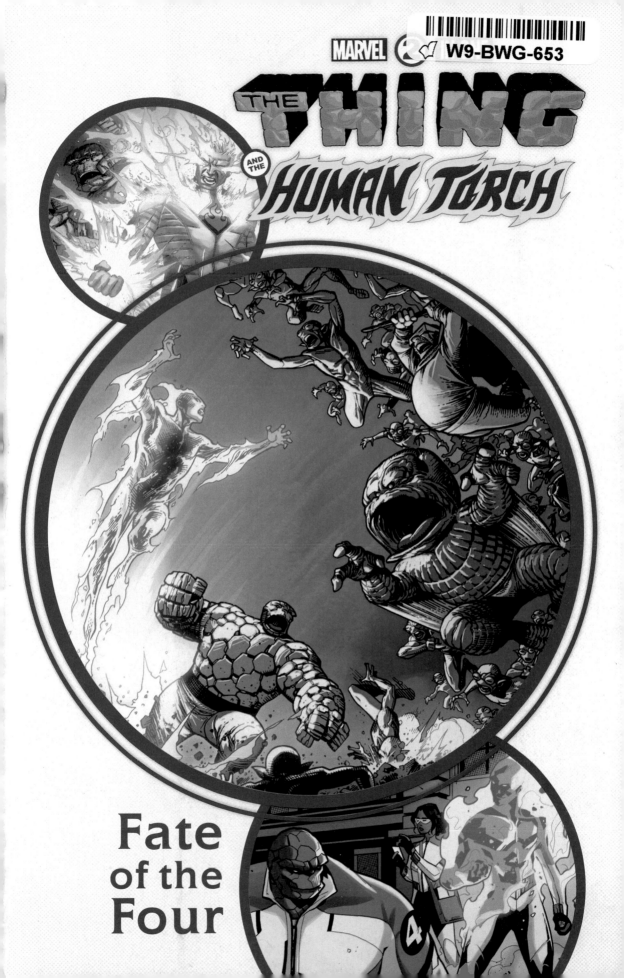

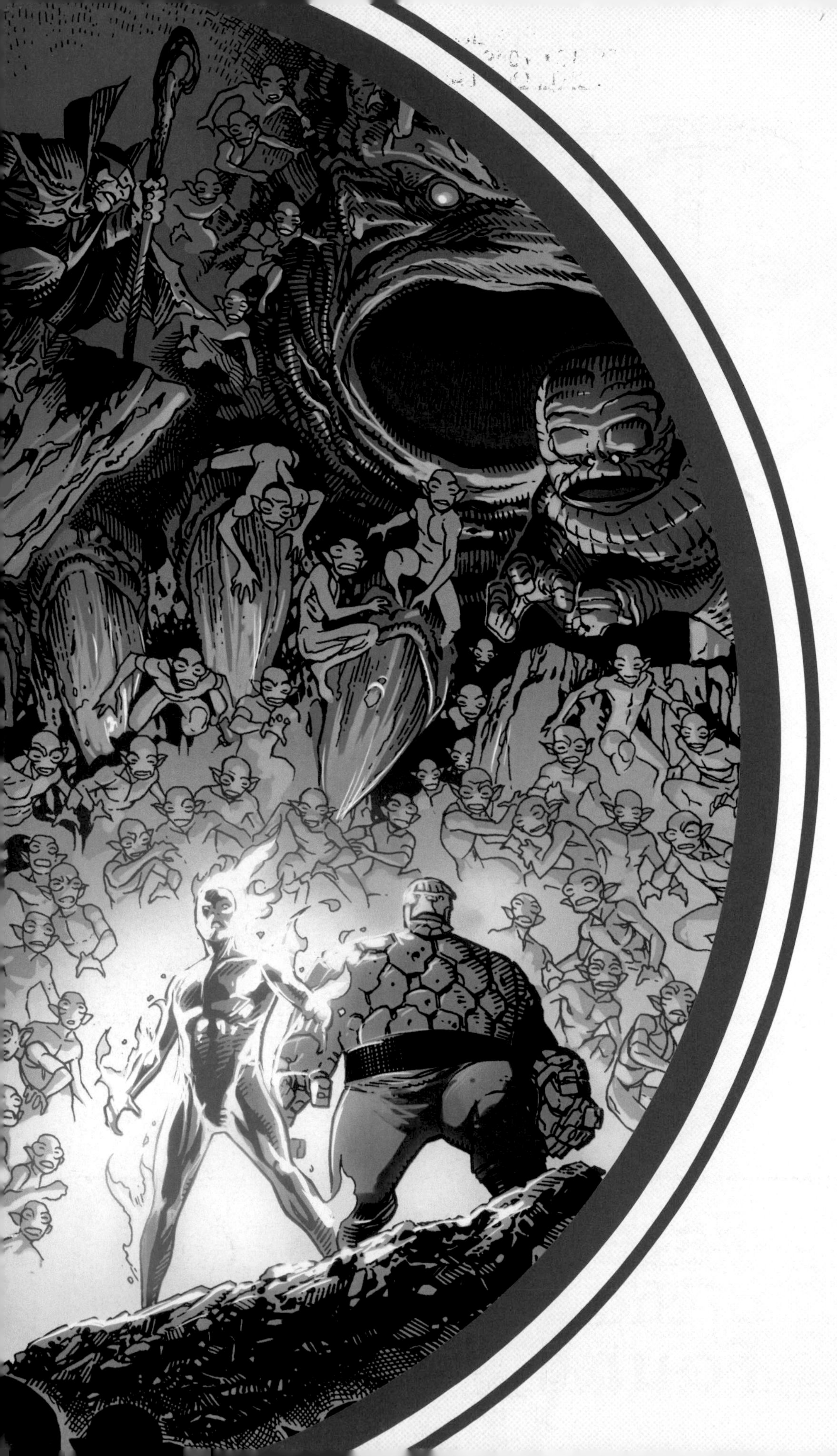

2 IN ONE

THE THING and the HUMAN TORCH

Fate of the Four

Chip Zdarsky
writer

Jim Cheung [#1-2 & #6] & Valerio Schiti [#3-5]
pencilers

John Dell with Walden Wong & Jim Cheung [#1-2], Valerio Schiti [#3-5] and Walden Wong [#6]
inkers

Frank Martin
color artist

VC's Joe Caramagna
letterer

Jim Cheung & Justin Ponsor [#1-2], Jim Cheung & Frank Martin [#3 & #6] and Nick Bradshaw & Morry Hollowell [#4-5]
cover art

Alanna Smith
assistant editor

Tom Brevoort
editor

— **Fantastic Four** created by **Stan Lee** & **Jack Kirby** —

collection editor **Mark D. Beazley**
assistant editor **Caitlin O'Connell**
associate managing editor **Kateri Woody**
senior editor, special projects **Jennifer Grünwald**

vp production & special projects **Jeff Youngquist**
svp print, sales & marketing **David Gabriel**
book designer **Adam Del Re**

editor in chief **C.B. Cebulski**
chief creative officer **Joe Quesada**
president **Dan Buckley**
executive producer **Alan Fine**

MARVEL 2-IN-ONE VOL. 1: FATE OF THE FOUR. Contains material originally published in magazine form as MARVEL 2-IN-ONE #1-6. First printing 2018. ISBN 978-1-302-91092-1. Published by MARVEL WORLDWIDE, INC., a subsidiary of MARVEL ENTERTAINMENT, LLC. OFFICE OF PUBLICATION: 135 West 50th Street, New York, NY 10020. Copyright © 2018 MARVEL No similarity between any of the names, characters, persons, and/or institutions in this magazine with those of any living or dead person or institution is intended, and any such similarity which may exist is purely coincidental. **Printed in the U.S.A.** DAN BUCKLEY, President, Marvel Entertainment; JOHN NEE, Publisher; JOE QUESADA, Chief Creative Officer; TOM BREVOORT, SVP of Publishing; DAVID BOGART, SVP of Business Affairs & Operations, Publishing & Partnership; DAVID GABRIEL, SVP of Sales & Marketing, Publishing; JEFF YOUNGQUIST, VP of Production & Special Projects; DAN CARR, Executive Director of Publishing Technology; ALEX MORALES, Director of Publishing Operations; DAN EDINGTON, Managing Editor; SUSAN CRESPI, Production Manager; STAN LEE, Chairman Emeritus. For information regarding advertising in Marvel Comics or on Marvel.com, please contact Vit DeBellis, Custom Solutions & Integrated Advertising Manager, at vdebellis@marvel.com. For Marvel subscription inquiries, please call 888-511-5480. **Manufactured between 5/25/2018 and 6/26/2018 by QUAD GRAPHICS SARATOGA, SARATOGA SPRINGS, NY, USA.**

10 9 8 7 6 5 4 3 2 1

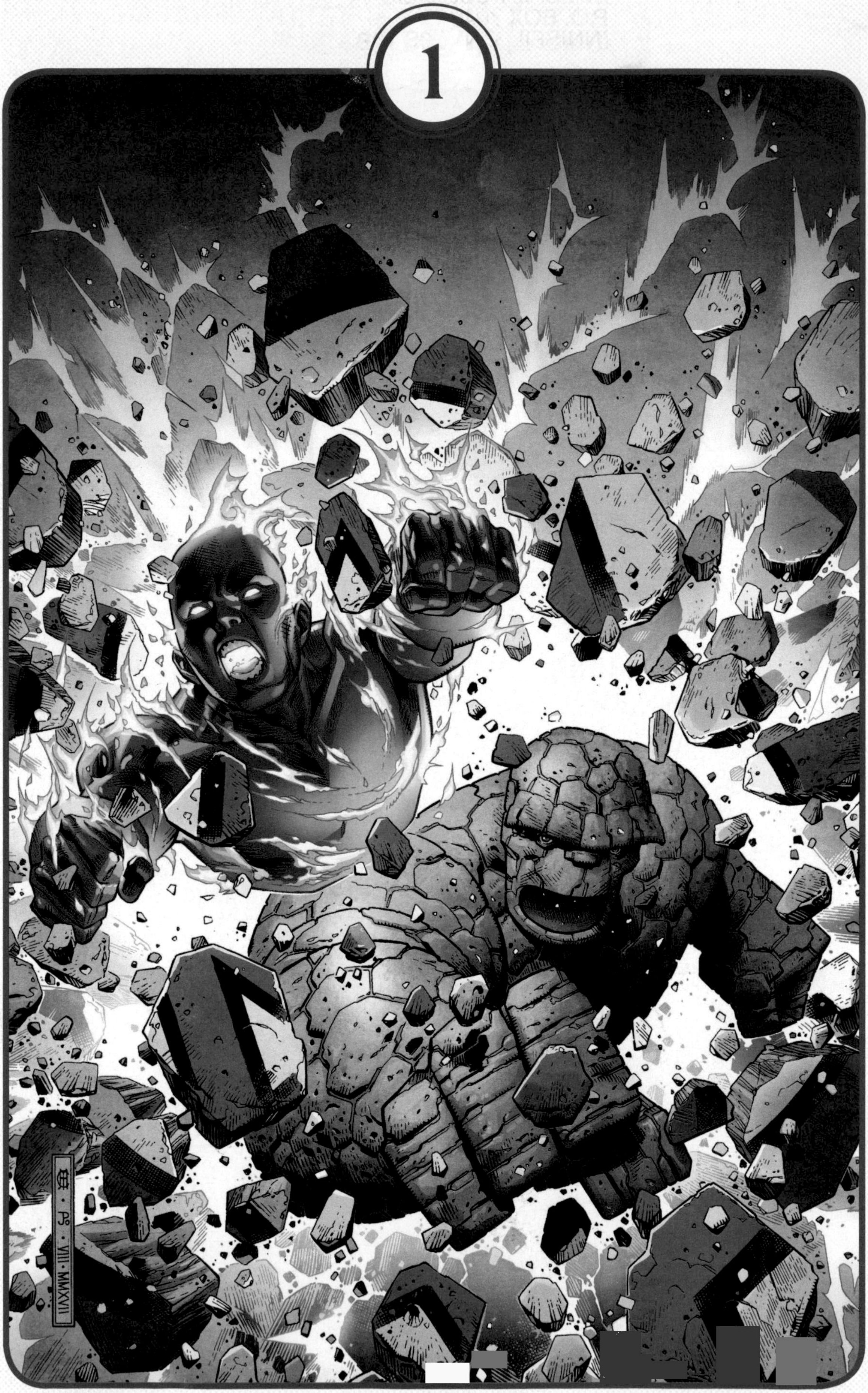
1

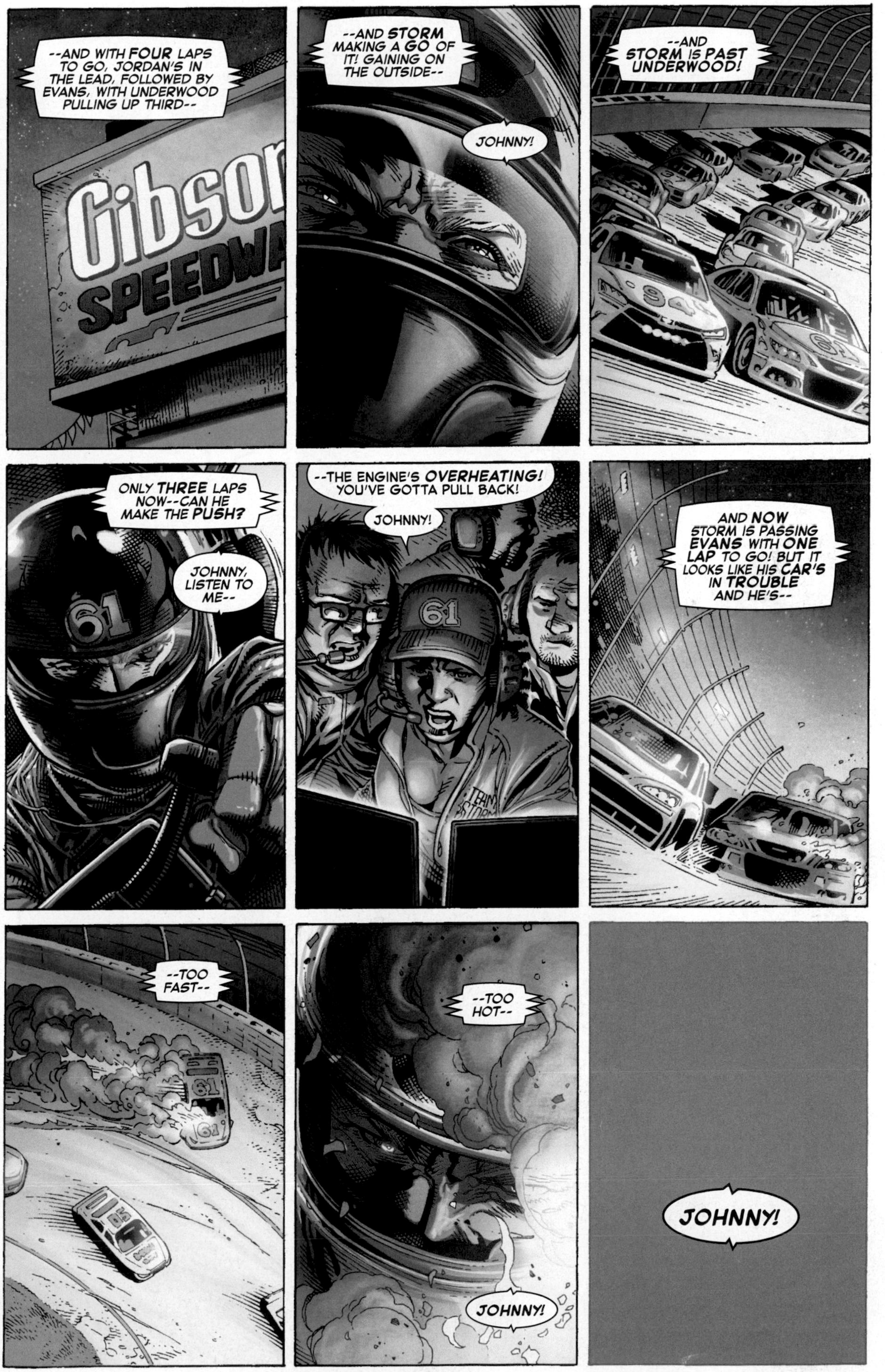
--AND WITH FOUR LAPS TO GO, JORDAN'S IN THE LEAD, FOLLOWED BY EVANS, WITH UNDERWOOD PULLING UP THIRD--
Gibson
SPEEDWA
--AND STORM MAKING A GO OF IT! GAINING ON THE OUTSIDE--
JOHNNY!
--AND STORM IS PAST UNDERWOOD!
ONLY THREE LAPS NOW--CAN HE MAKE THE PUSH?
JOHNNY, LISTEN TO ME--
--THE ENGINE'S OVERHEATING! YOU'VE GOTTA PULL BACK!
JOHNNY!
AND NOW STORM IS PASSING EVANS WITH ONE LAP TO GO! BUT IT LOOKS LIKE HIS CAR'S IN TROUBLE AND HE'S--
--TOO FAST--
--TOO HOT--
JOHNNY!
JOHNNY!

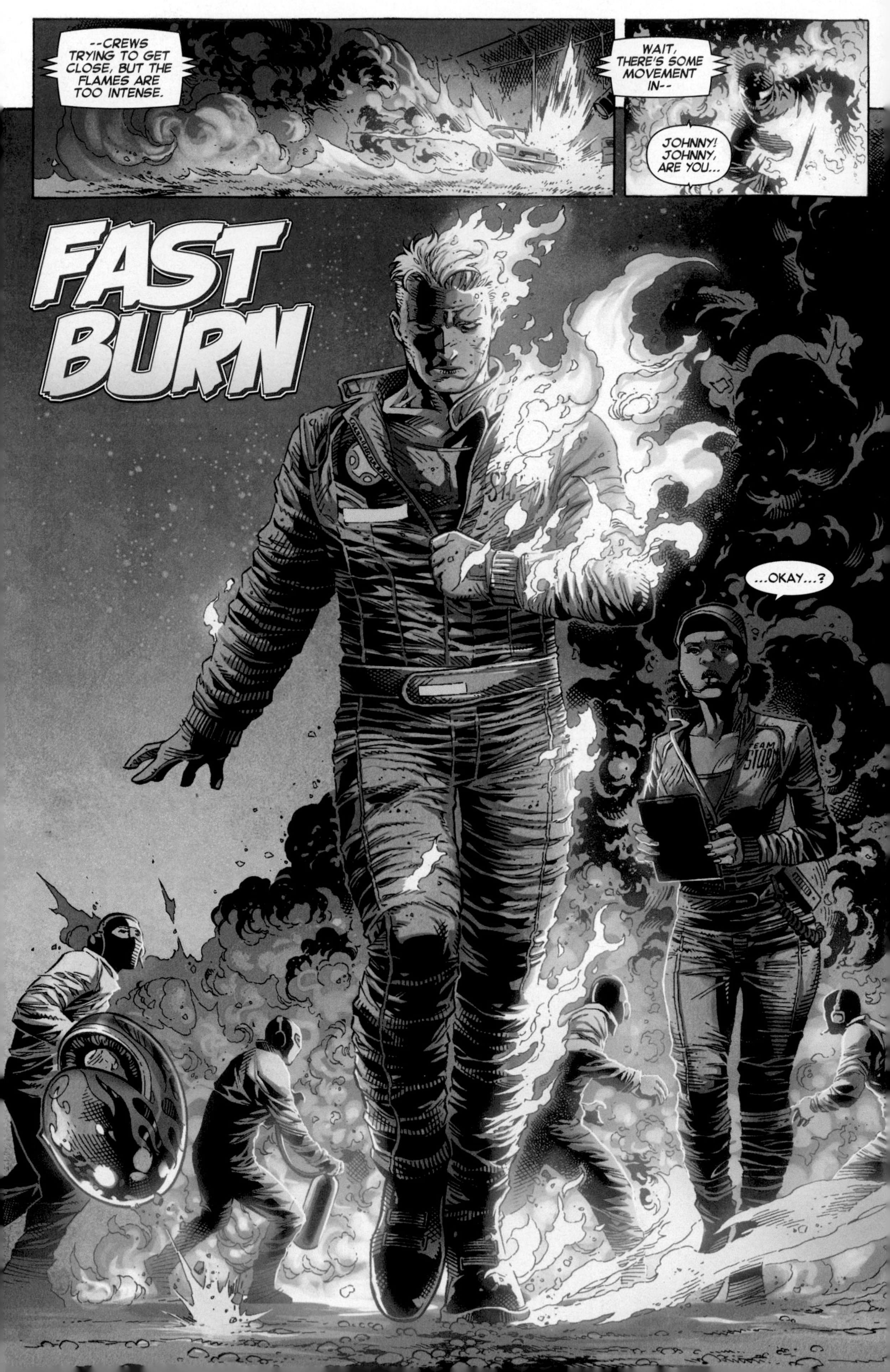
--CREWS TRYING TO GET CLOSE, BUT THE FLAMES ARE TOO INTENSE.
WAIT, THERE'S SOME MOVEMENT IN--
JOHNNY! JOHNNY, ARE YOU...
FAST BURN
...OKAY...?

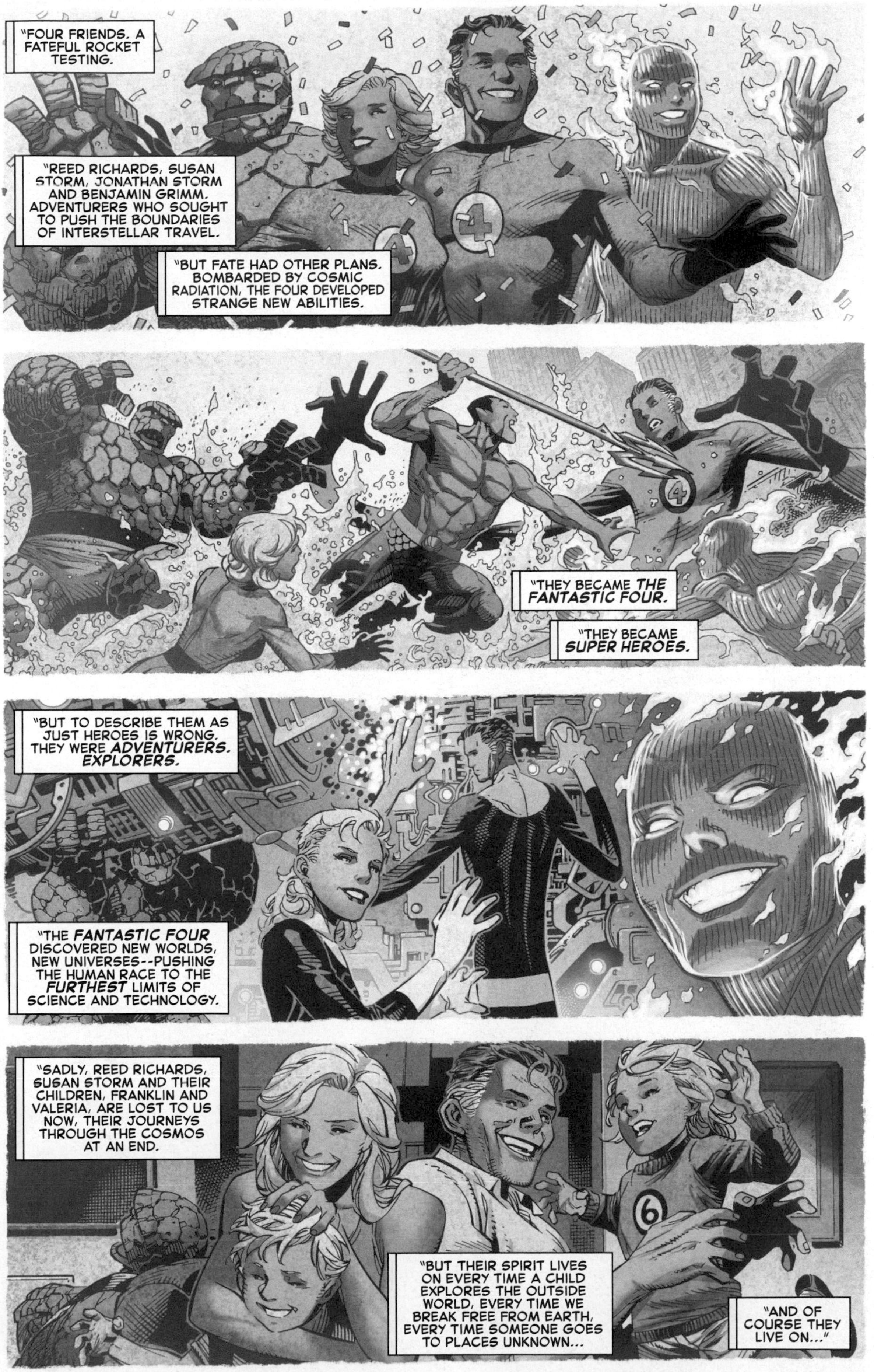
"FOUR FRIENDS. A FATEFUL ROCKET TESTING.
"REED RICHARDS, SUSAN STORM, JONATHAN STORM AND BENJAMIN GRIMM. ADVENTURERS WHO SOUGHT TO PUSH THE BOUNDARIES OF INTERSTELLAR TRAVEL.
"BUT FATE HAD OTHER PLANS. BOMBARDED BY COSMIC RADIATION, THE FOUR DEVELOPED STRANGE NEW ABILITIES.
"THEY BECAME *THE FANTASTIC FOUR.*
"THEY BECAME *SUPER HEROES.*
"BUT TO DESCRIBE THEM AS JUST HEROES IS WRONG. THEY WERE *ADVENTURERS. EXPLORERS.*
"THE *FANTASTIC FOUR* DISCOVERED NEW WORLDS, NEW UNIVERSES--PUSHING THE HUMAN RACE TO THE *FURTHEST* LIMITS OF SCIENCE AND TECHNOLOGY.
"SADLY, REED RICHARDS, SUSAN STORM AND THEIR CHILDREN, FRANKLIN AND VALERIA, ARE LOST TO US NOW, THEIR JOURNEYS THROUGH THE COSMOS AT AN END.
"BUT THEIR SPIRIT LIVES ON EVERY TIME A CHILD EXPLORES THE OUTSIDE WORLD, EVERY TIME WE BREAK FREE FROM EARTH, EVERY TIME SOMEONE GOES TO PLACES UNKNOWN...
"AND OF COURSE THEY LIVE ON..."

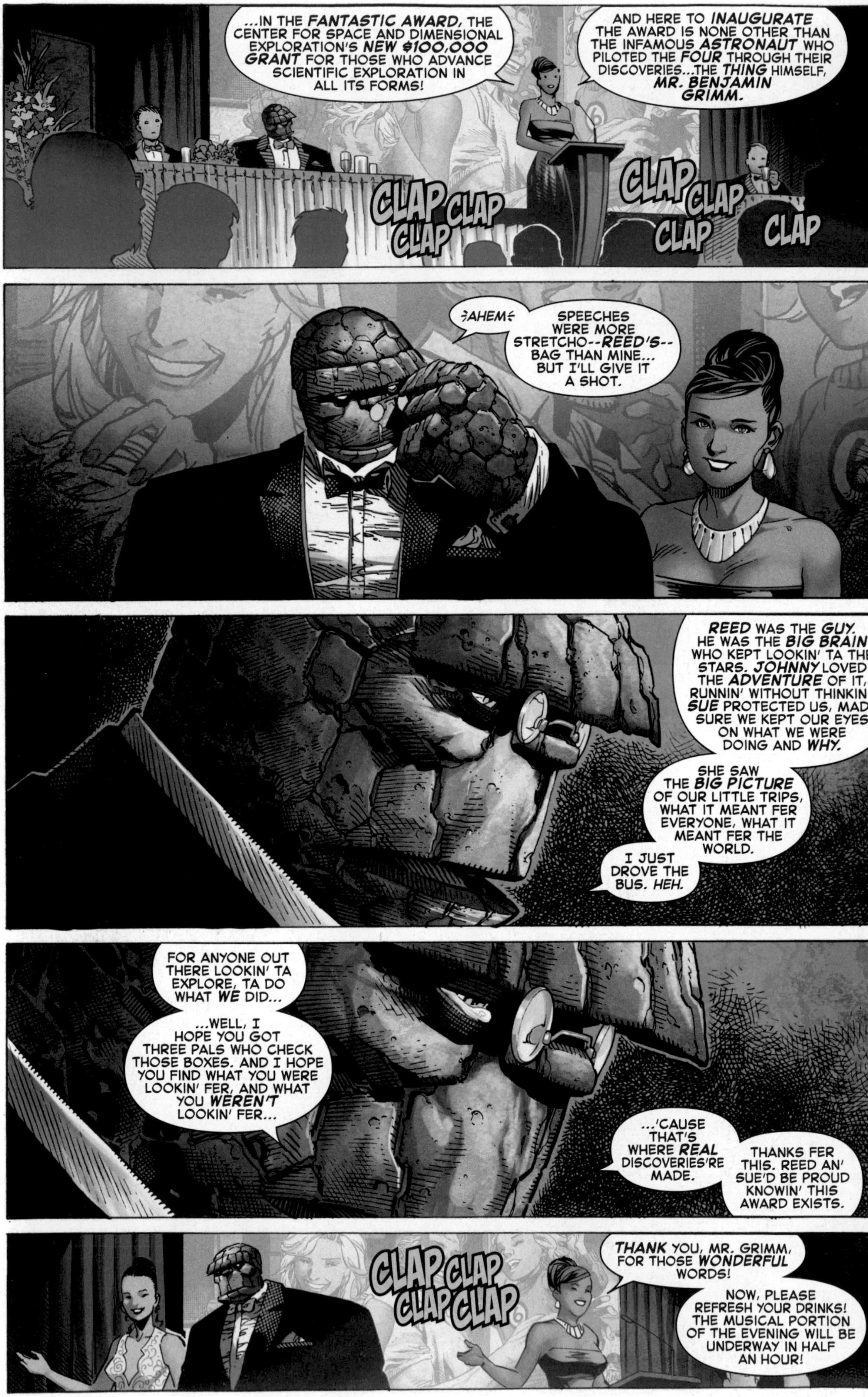
...IN THE FANTASTIC AWARD, THE CENTER FOR SPACE AND DIMENSIONAL EXPLORATION'S NEW $100,000 GRANT FOR THOSE WHO ADVANCE SCIENTIFIC EXPLORATION IN ALL ITS FORMS!
AND HERE TO INAUGURATE THE AWARD IS NONE OTHER THAN THE INFAMOUS ASTRONAUT WHO PILOTED THE FOUR THROUGH THEIR DISCOVERIES...THE THING HIMSELF, MR. BENJAMIN GRIMM.
CLAP CLAP CLAP
CLAP CLAP CLAP
CLAP
AHEM
SPEECHES WERE MORE STRETCHO--REED'S--BAG THAN MINE... BUT I'LL GIVE IT A SHOT.
REED WAS THE GUY. HE WAS THE BIG BRAIN WHO KEPT LOOKIN' TA THE STARS. JOHNNY LOVED THE ADVENTURE OF IT, RUNNIN' WITHOUT THINKIN'. SUE PROTECTED US, MADE SURE WE KEPT OUR EYES ON WHAT WE WERE DOING AND WHY.
SHE SAW THE BIG PICTURE OF OUR LITTLE TRIPS, WHAT IT MEANT FER EVERYONE, WHAT IT MEANT FER THE WORLD.
I JUST DROVE THE BUS. HEH.
FOR ANYONE OUT THERE LOOKIN' TA EXPLORE, TA DO WHAT WE DID...
...WELL, I HOPE YOU GOT THREE PALS WHO CHECK THOSE BOXES. AND I HOPE YOU FIND WHAT YOU WERE LOOKIN' FER, AND WHAT YOU WEREN'T LOOKIN' FER...
...'CAUSE THAT'S WHERE REAL DISCOVERIES'RE MADE.
THANKS FER THIS. REED AN' SUE'D BE PROUD KNOWIN' THIS AWARD EXISTS.
CLAP CLAP CLAP CLAP
THANK YOU, MR. GRIMM, FOR THOSE WONDERFUL WORDS!
NOW, PLEASE REFRESH YOUR DRINKS! THE MUSICAL PORTION OF THE EVENING WILL BE UNDERWAY IN HALF AN HOUR!

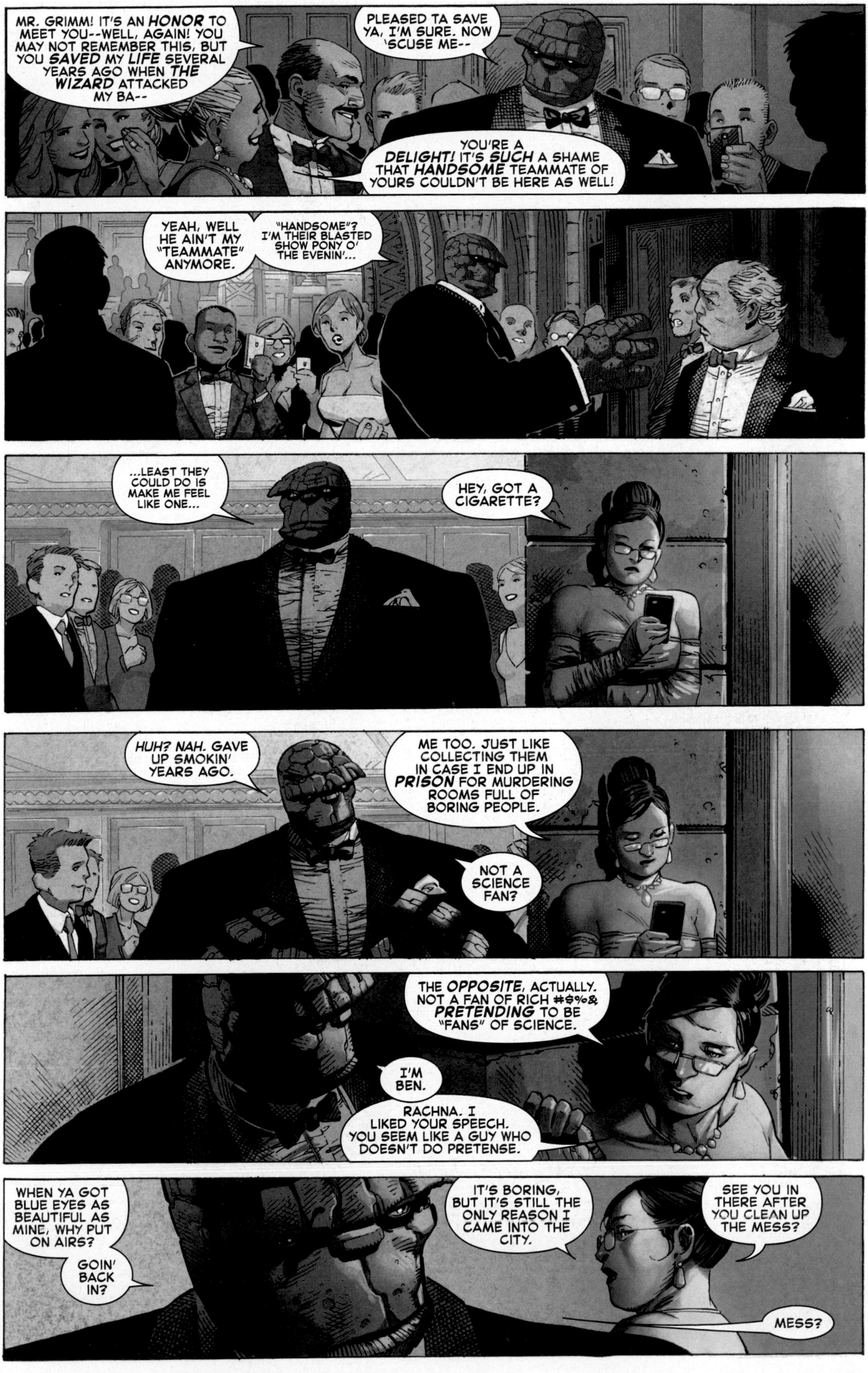
MR. GRIMM! IT'S AN HONOR TO MEET YOU--WELL, AGAIN! YOU MAY NOT REMEMBER THIS, BUT YOU SAVED MY LIFE SEVERAL YEARS AGO WHEN THE WIZARD ATTACKED MY BA--
PLEASED TA SAVE YA, I'M SURE. NOW 'SCUSE ME--
YOU'RE A DELIGHT! IT'S SUCH A SHAME THAT HANDSOME TEAMMATE OF YOURS COULDN'T BE HERE AS WELL!
YEAH, WELL HE AIN'T MY "TEAMMATE" ANYMORE.
"HANDSOME"? I'M THEIR BLASTED SHOW PONY O' THE EVENIN'...
...LEAST THEY COULD DO IS MAKE ME FEEL LIKE ONE...
HEY, GOT A CIGARETTE?
HUH? NAH. GAVE UP SMOKIN' YEARS AGO.
ME TOO. JUST LIKE COLLECTING THEM IN CASE I END UP IN PRISON FOR MURDERING ROOMS FULL OF BORING PEOPLE.
NOT A SCIENCE FAN?
THE OPPOSITE, ACTUALLY. NOT A FAN OF RICH #$%& PRETENDING TO BE "FANS" OF SCIENCE.
I'M BEN.
RACHNA. I LIKED YOUR SPEECH. YOU SEEM LIKE A GUY WHO DOESN'T DO PRETENSE.
WHEN YA GOT BLUE EYES AS BEAUTIFUL AS MINE, WHY PUT ON AIRS?
GOIN' BACK IN?
IT'S BORING, BUT IT'S STILL THE ONLY REASON I CAME INTO THE CITY.
SEE YOU IN THERE AFTER YOU CLEAN UP THE MESS?
MESS?

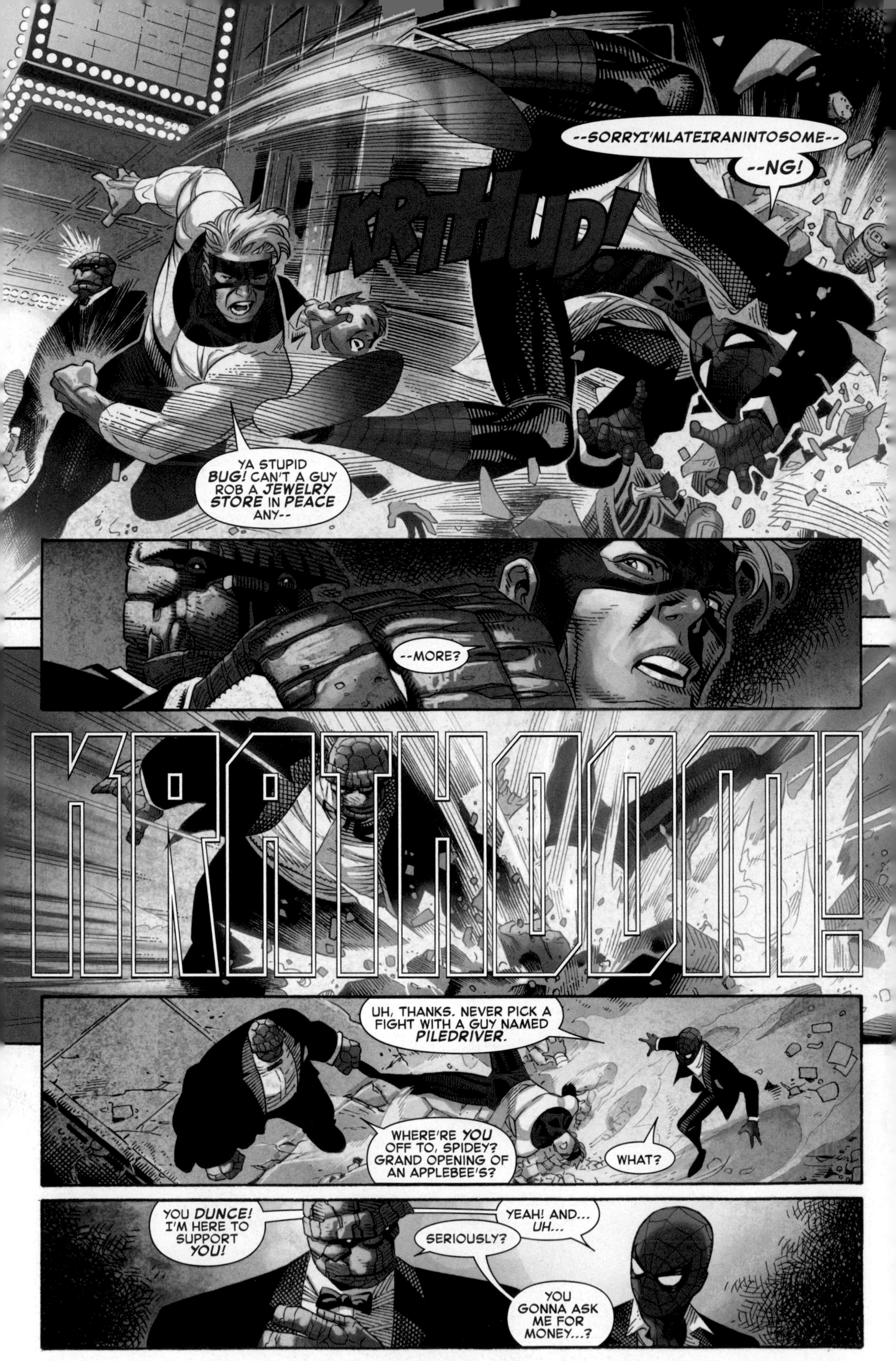
--SORRYI'MLATEIRANINTOSOME--
--NG!
KRTHUD!
YA STUPID BUG! CAN'T A GUY ROB A JEWELRY STORE IN PEACE ANY--
--MORE?
KRTHOOM!
UH, THANKS. NEVER PICK A FIGHT WITH A GUY NAMED PILEDRIVER.
WHERE'RE YOU OFF TO, SPIDEY? GRAND OPENING OF AN APPLEBEE'S?
WHAT?
YOU DUNCE! I'M HERE TO SUPPORT YOU!
YEAH! AND... UH...
SERIOUSLY?
YOU GONNA ASK ME FOR MONEY...?

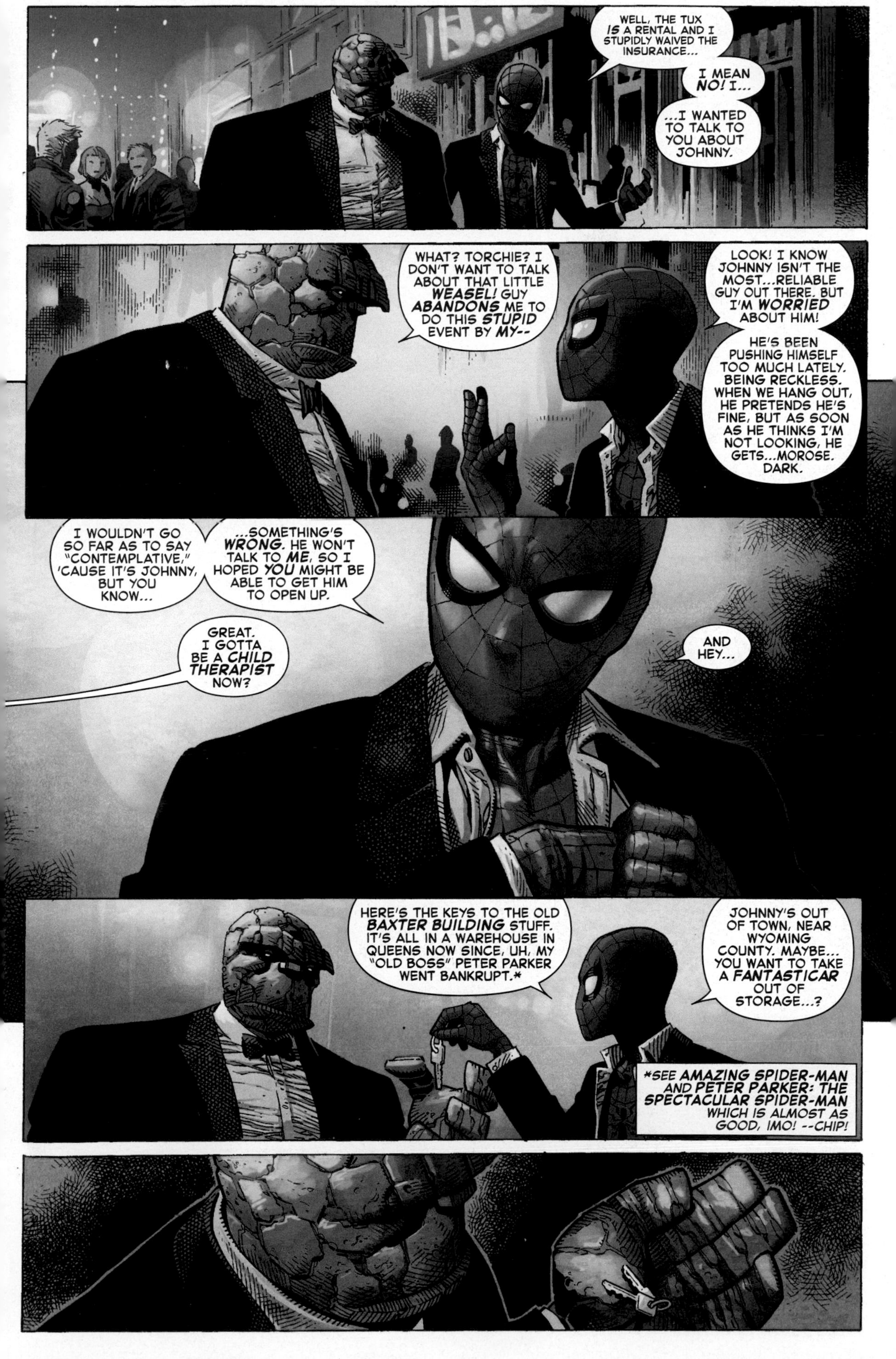

WELL, THE TUX IS A RENTAL AND I STUPIDLY WAIVED THE INSURANCE...
I MEAN NO! I...
...I WANTED TO TALK TO YOU ABOUT JOHNNY.
WHAT? TORCHIE? I DON'T WANT TO TALK ABOUT THAT LITTLE WEASEL! GUY ABANDONS ME TO DO THIS STUPID EVENT BY MY--
LOOK! I KNOW JOHNNY ISN'T THE MOST...RELIABLE GUY OUT THERE. BUT I'M WORRIED ABOUT HIM!
HE'S BEEN PUSHING HIMSELF TOO MUCH LATELY. BEING RECKLESS. WHEN WE HANG OUT, HE PRETENDS HE'S FINE, BUT AS SOON AS HE THINKS I'M NOT LOOKING, HE GETS...MOROSE. DARK.
I WOULDN'T GO SO FAR AS TO SAY "CONTEMPLATIVE," 'CAUSE IT'S JOHNNY, BUT YOU KNOW...
...SOMETHING'S WRONG. HE WON'T TALK TO ME, SO I HOPED YOU MIGHT BE ABLE TO GET HIM TO OPEN UP.
GREAT. I GOTTA BE A CHILD THERAPIST NOW?
AND HEY...
HERE'S THE KEYS TO THE OLD BAXTER BUILDING STUFF. IT'S ALL IN A WAREHOUSE IN QUEENS NOW SINCE, UH, MY "OLD BOSS" PETER PARKER WENT BANKRUPT.*
JOHNNY'S OUT OF TOWN, NEAR WYOMING COUNTY. MAYBE... YOU WANT TO TAKE A FANTASTICAR OUT OF STORAGE...?
*SEE AMAZING SPIDER-MAN AND PETER PARKER: THE SPECTACULAR SPIDER-MAN WHICH IS ALMOST AS GOOD, IMO! --CHIP!

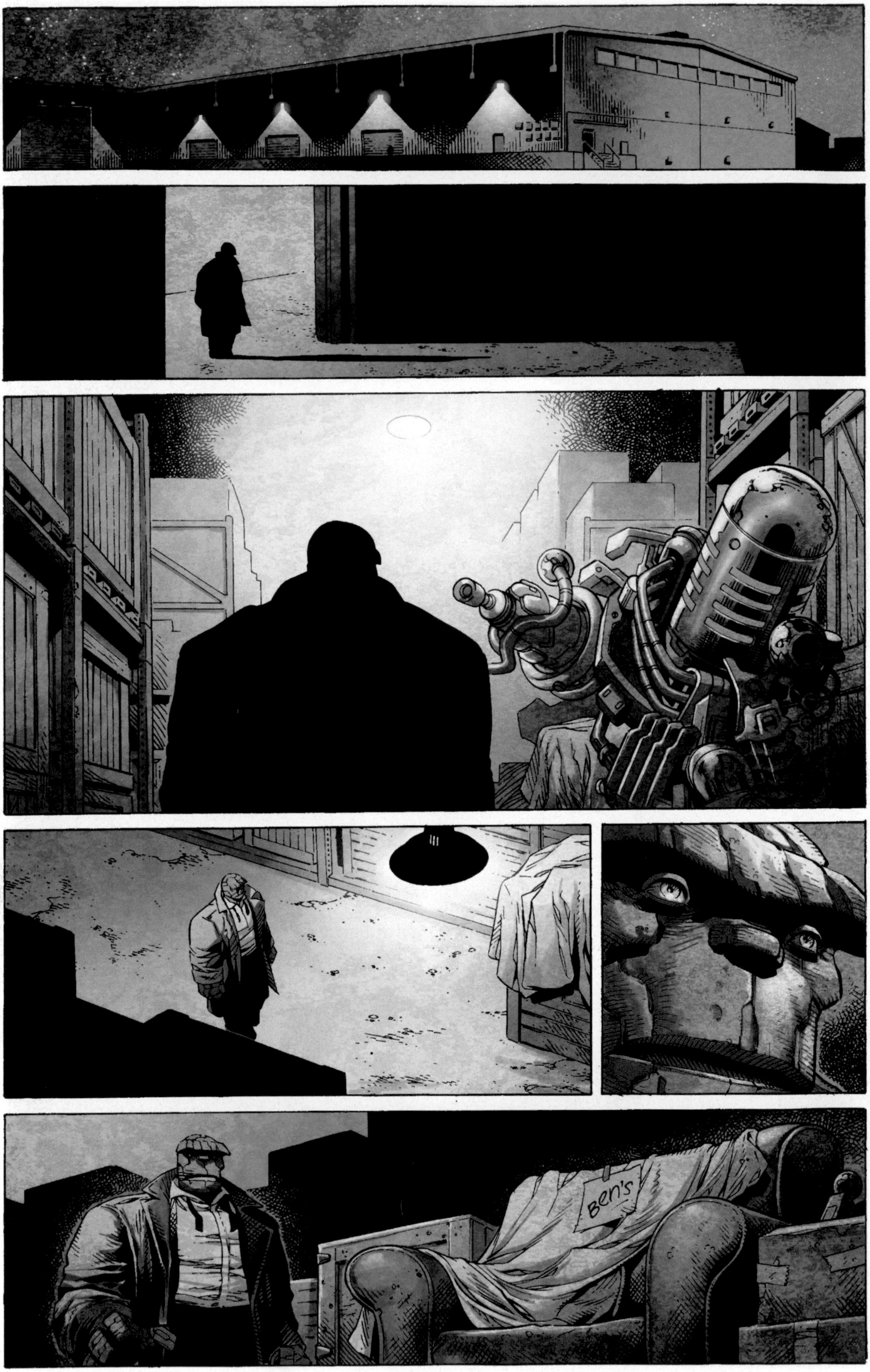
Ben's

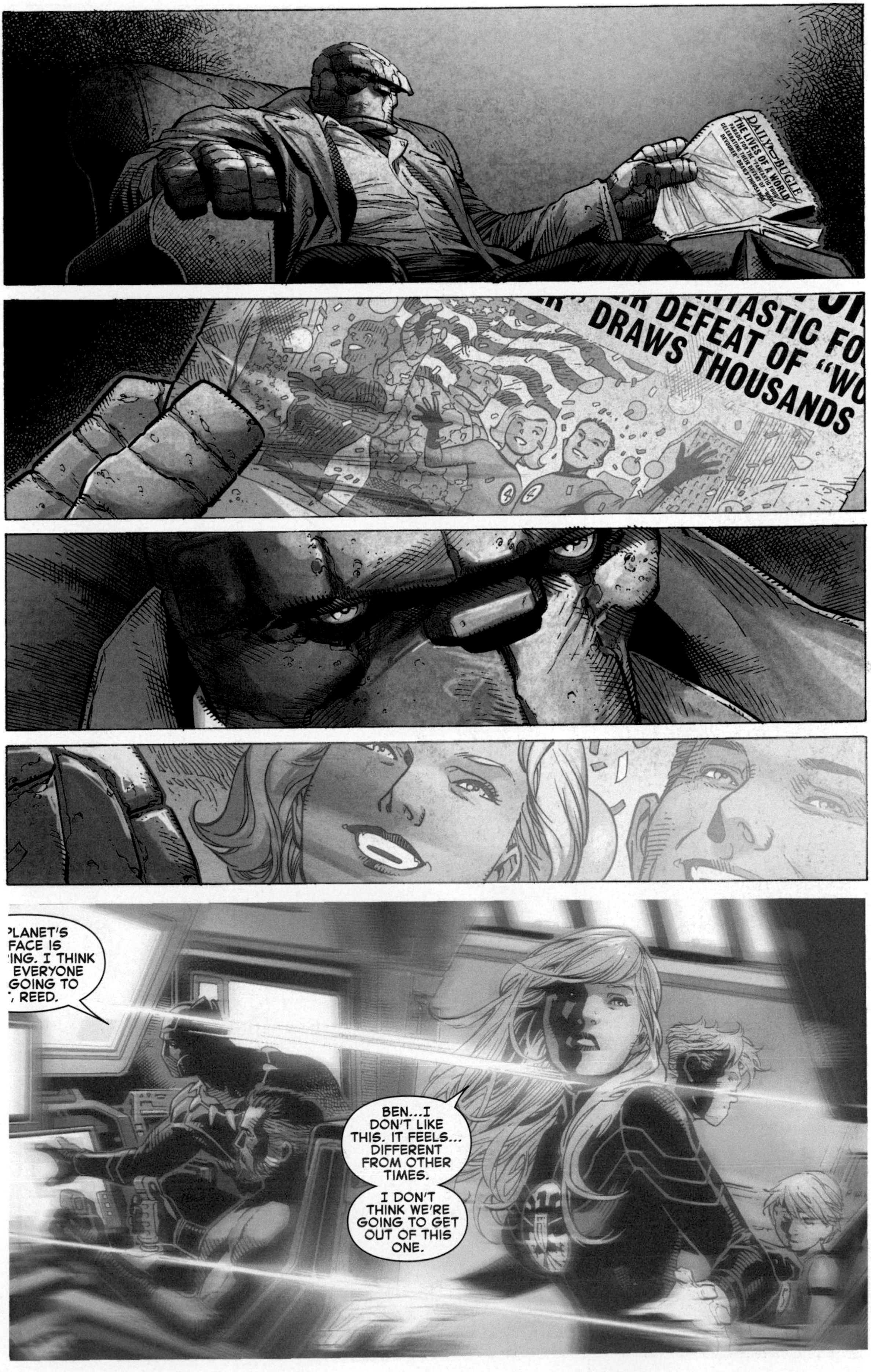

DAILY BUGLE
THE LIVES OF A WORLD
DEFEAT OF "WO
DRAWS THOUSANDS
PLANET'S FACE IS ING. I THINK EVERYONE GOING TO , REED.
BEN...I DON'T LIKE THIS. IT FEELS... DIFFERENT FROM OTHER TIMES.
I DON'T THINK WE'RE GOING TO GET OUT OF THIS ONE.

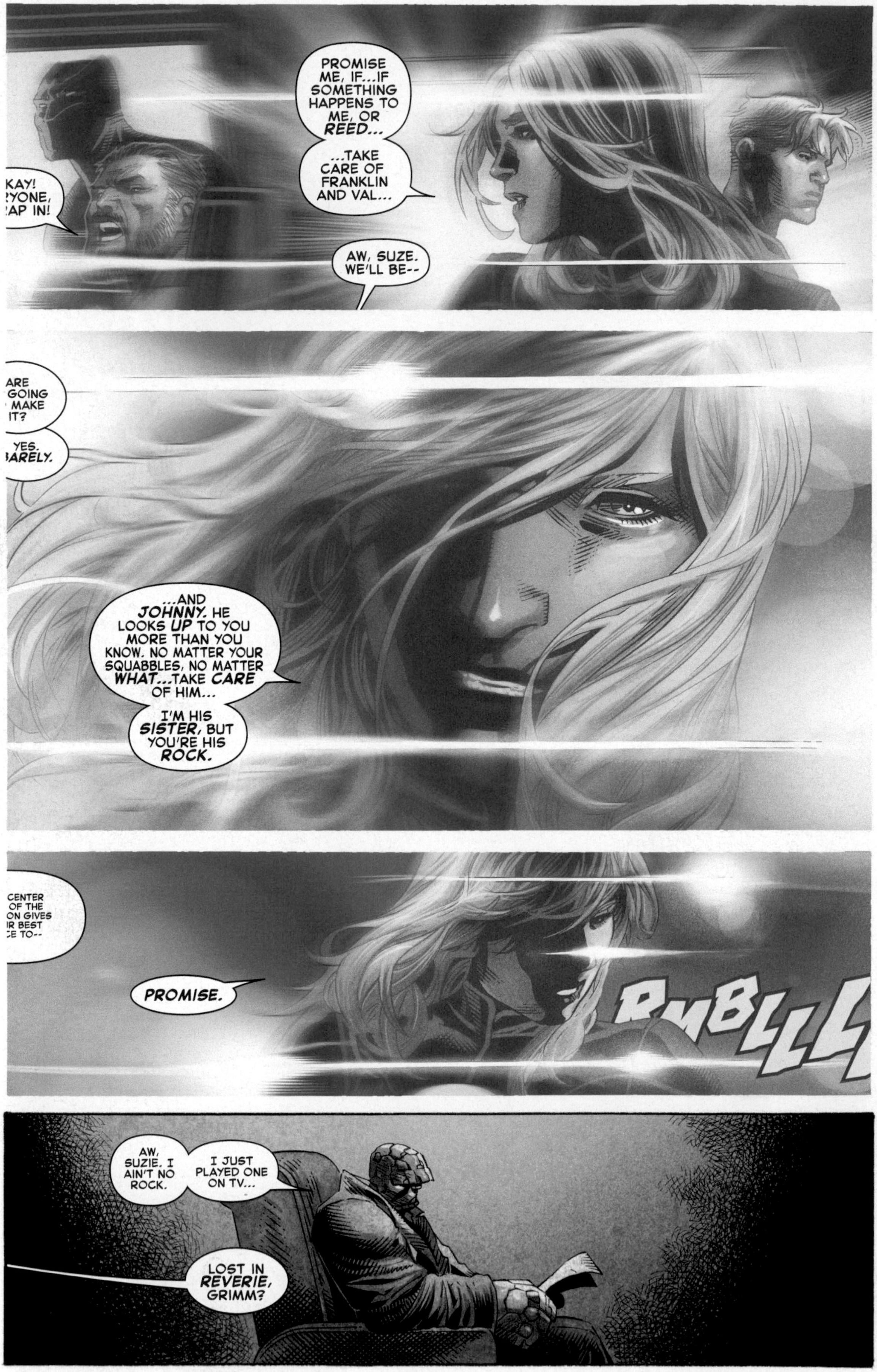

KAY! RYONE, RAP IN!
PROMISE ME, IF...IF SOMETHING HAPPENS TO ME, OR REED...
...TAKE CARE OF FRANKLIN AND VAL...
AW, SUZE. WE'LL BE--
ARE GOING MAKE IT?
YES. BARELY.
...AND JOHNNY. HE LOOKS UP TO YOU MORE THAN YOU KNOW. NO MATTER YOUR SQUABBLES, NO MATTER WHAT...TAKE CARE OF HIM...
I'M HIS SISTER, BUT YOU'RE HIS ROCK.
CENTER OF THE ON GIVES R BEST CE TO--
PROMISE.
RUBLLL
AW, SUZIE. I AIN'T NO ROCK.
I JUST PLAYED ONE ON TV...
LOST IN REVERIE, GRIMM?

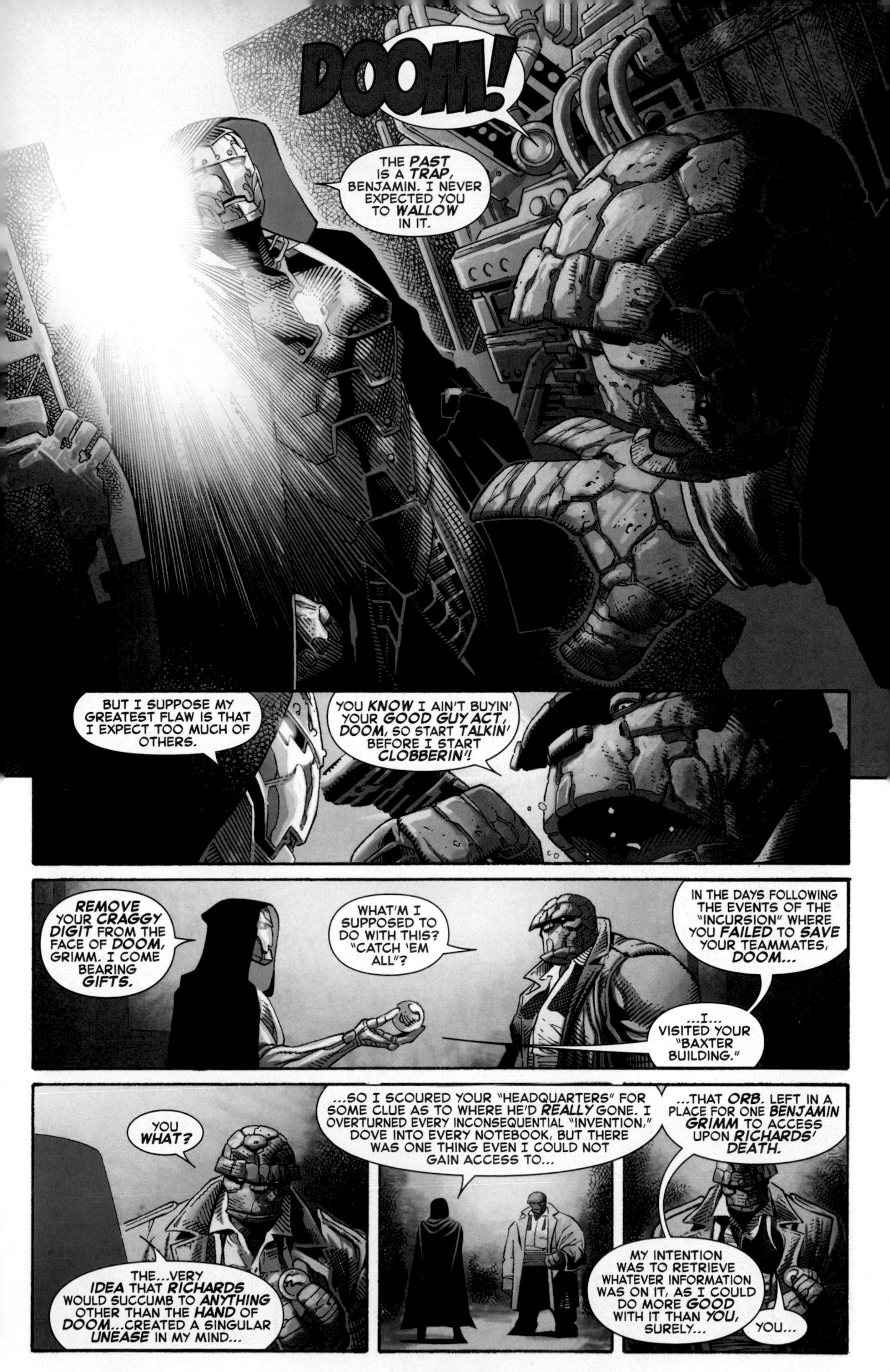
DOOM!
THE PAST IS A TRAP, BENJAMIN. I NEVER EXPECTED YOU TO WALLOW IN IT.
BUT I SUPPOSE MY GREATEST FLAW IS THAT I EXPECT TOO MUCH OF OTHERS.
YOU KNOW I AIN'T BUYIN' YOUR GOOD GUY ACT, DOOM, SO START TALKIN' BEFORE I START CLOBBERIN'!
REMOVE YOUR CRAGGY DIGIT FROM THE FACE OF DOOM, GRIMM. I COME BEARING GIFTS.
WHAT'M I SUPPOSED TO DO WITH THIS? "CATCH 'EM ALL"?
IN THE DAYS FOLLOWING THE EVENTS OF THE "INCURSION" WHERE YOU FAILED TO SAVE YOUR TEAMMATES, DOOM...
...I... VISITED YOUR "BAXTER BUILDING."
YOU WHAT?
THE...VERY IDEA THAT RICHARDS WOULD SUCCUMB TO ANYTHING OTHER THAN THE HAND OF DOOM...CREATED A SINGULAR UNEASE IN MY MIND...
...SO I SCOURED YOUR "HEADQUARTERS" FOR SOME CLUE AS TO WHERE HE'D REALLY GONE. I OVERTURNED EVERY INCONSEQUENTIAL "INVENTION," DOVE INTO EVERY NOTEBOOK, BUT THERE WAS ONE THING EVEN I COULD NOT GAIN ACCESS TO...
...THAT ORB. LEFT IN A PLACE FOR ONE BENJAMIN GRIMM TO ACCESS UPON RICHARDS' DEATH.
MY INTENTION WAS TO RETRIEVE WHATEVER INFORMATION WAS ON IT, AS I COULD DO MORE GOOD WITH IT THAN YOU, SURELY...
YOU...

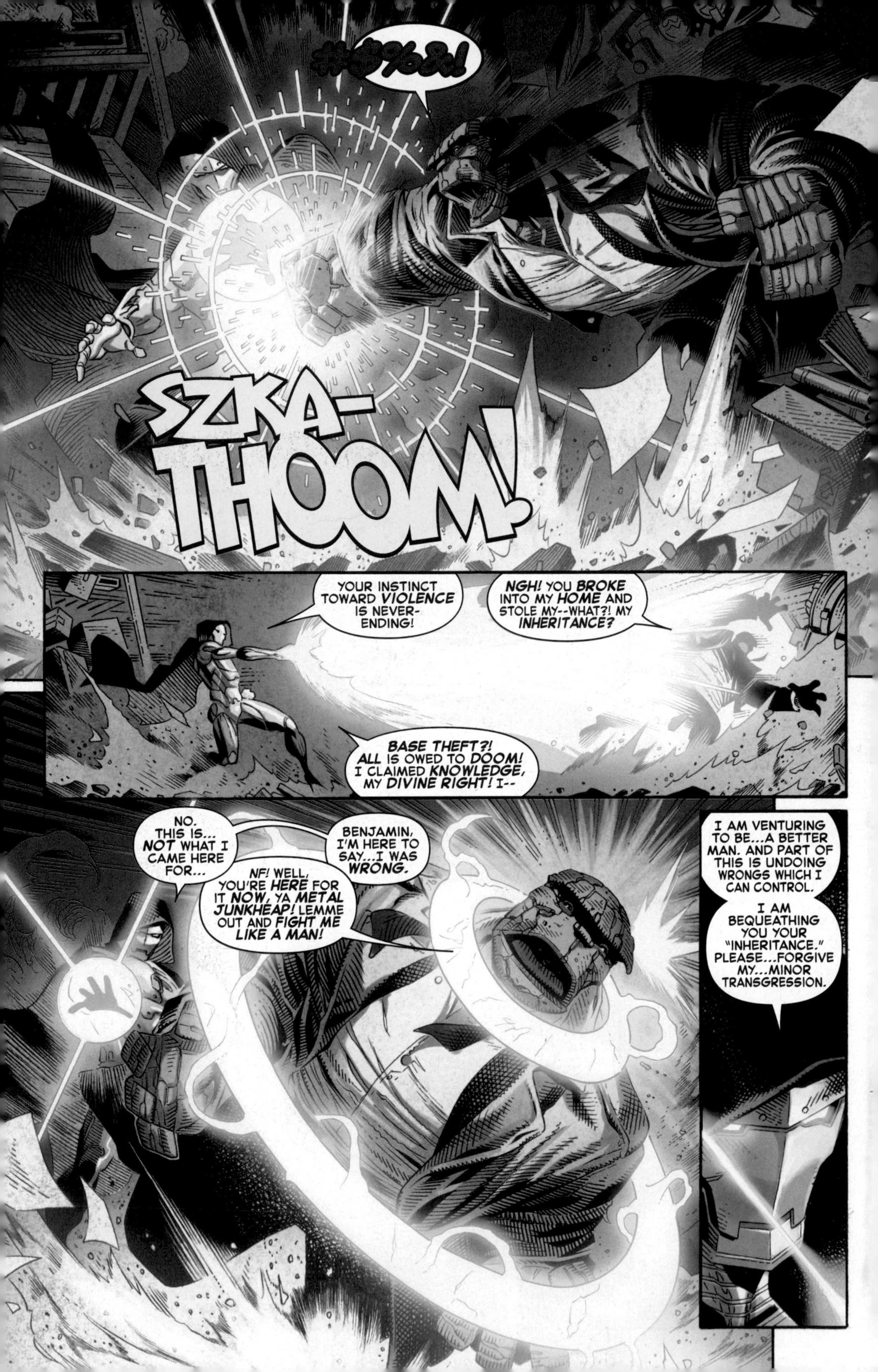
#@%&!
SZKA-THOOM!
YOUR INSTINCT TOWARD VIOLENCE IS NEVER-ENDING!
NGH! YOU BROKE INTO MY HOME AND STOLE MY--WHAT?! MY INHERITANCE?
BASE THEFT?! ALL IS OWED TO DOOM! I CLAIMED KNOWLEDGE, MY DIVINE RIGHT! I--
NO. THIS IS... NOT WHAT I CAME HERE FOR...
BENJAMIN, I'M HERE TO SAY...I WAS WRONG.
NF! WELL, YOU'RE HERE FOR IT NOW, YA METAL JUNKHEAP! LEMME OUT AND FIGHT ME LIKE A MAN!
I AM VENTURING TO BE...A BETTER MAN. AND PART OF THIS IS UNDOING WRONGS WHICH I CAN CONTROL.
I AM BEQUEATHING YOU YOUR "INHERITANCE." PLEASE...FORGIVE MY...MINOR TRANSGRESSION.

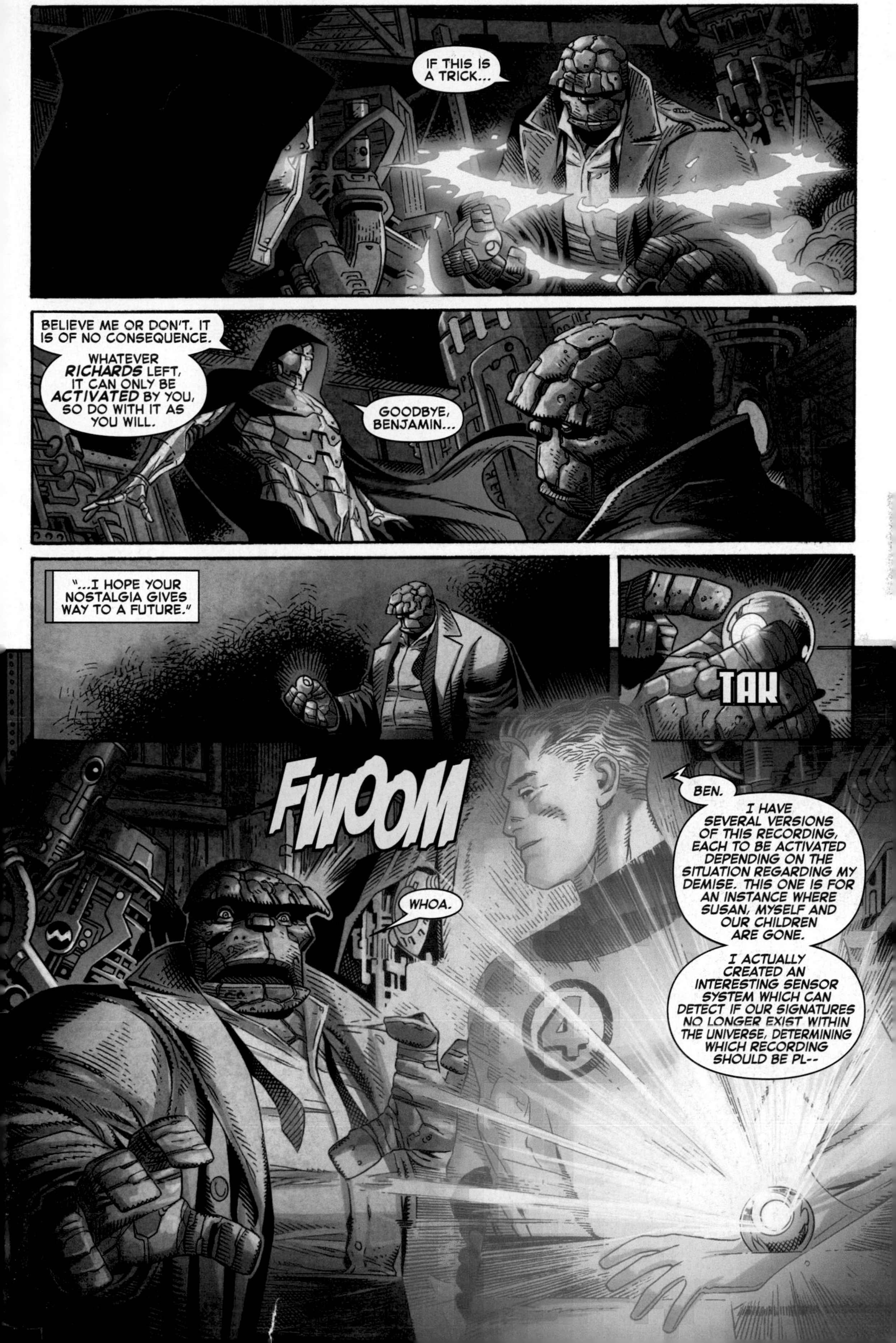
IF THIS IS A TRICK...
BELIEVE ME OR DON'T. IT IS OF NO CONSEQUENCE.
WHATEVER RICHARDS LEFT, IT CAN ONLY BE ACTIVATED BY YOU, SO DO WITH IT AS YOU WILL.
GOODBYE, BENJAMIN...
"...I HOPE YOUR NOSTALGIA GIVES WAY TO A FUTURE."
TAK
FWOOM
BEN.
I HAVE SEVERAL VERSIONS OF THIS RECORDING, EACH TO BE ACTIVATED DEPENDING ON THE SITUATION REGARDING MY DEMISE. THIS ONE IS FOR AN INSTANCE WHERE SUSAN, MYSELF AND OUR CHILDREN ARE GONE.
WHOA.
I ACTUALLY CREATED AN INTERESTING SENSOR SYSTEM WHICH CAN DETECT IF OUR SIGNATURES NO LONGER EXIST WITHIN THE UNIVERSE, DETERMINING WHICH RECORDING SHOULD BE PL--

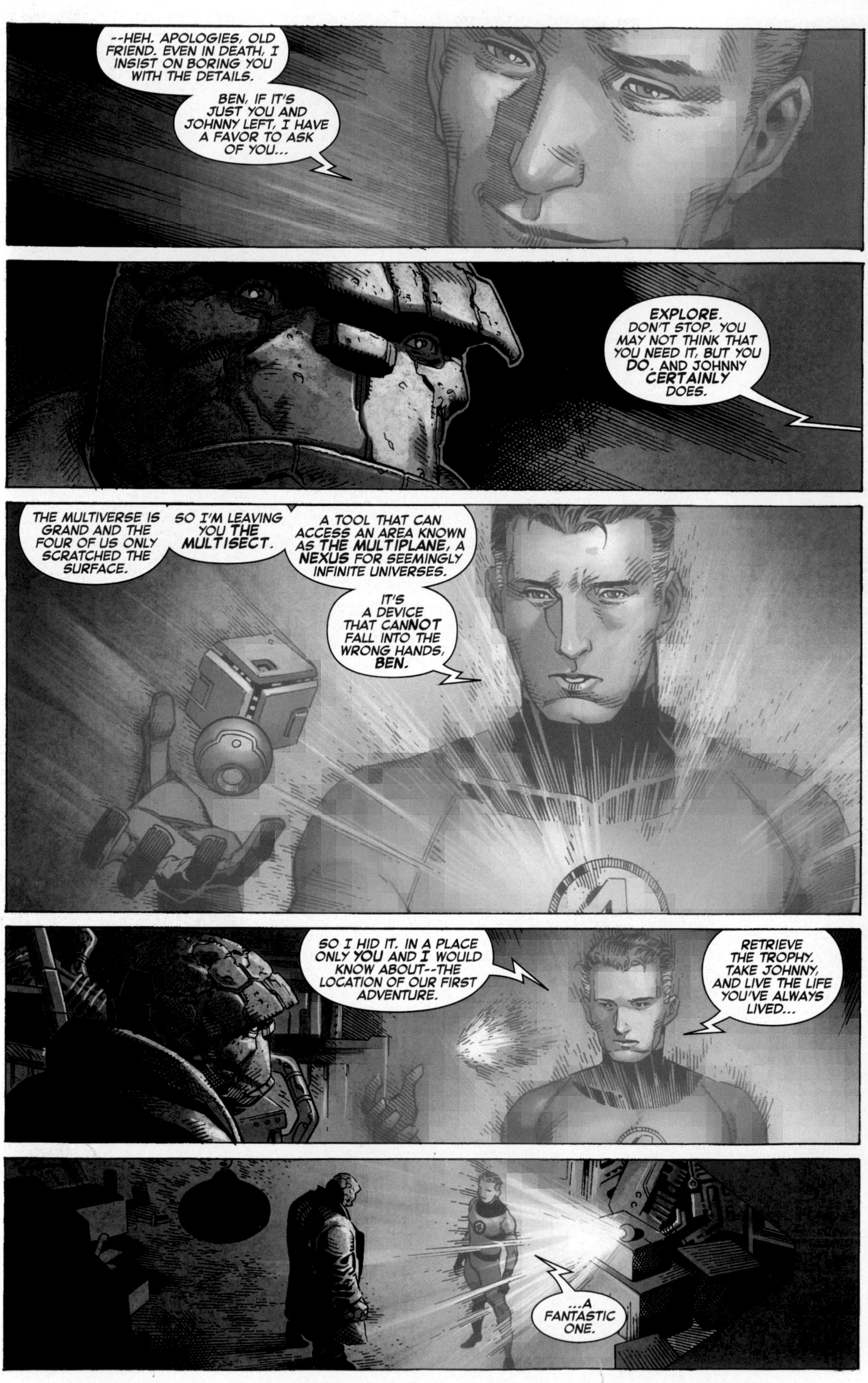
--HEH. APOLOGIES, OLD FRIEND. EVEN IN DEATH, I INSIST ON BORING YOU WITH THE DETAILS.
BEN, IF IT'S JUST YOU AND JOHNNY LEFT, I HAVE A FAVOR TO ASK OF YOU...
EXPLORE. DON'T STOP. YOU MAY NOT THINK THAT YOU NEED IT, BUT YOU DO. AND JOHNNY CERTAINLY DOES.
THE MULTIVERSE IS GRAND AND THE FOUR OF US ONLY SCRATCHED THE SURFACE.
SO I'M LEAVING YOU THE MULTISECT.
A TOOL THAT CAN ACCESS AN AREA KNOWN AS THE MULTIPLANE, A NEXUS FOR SEEMINGLY INFINITE UNIVERSES.
IT'S A DEVICE THAT CANNOT FALL INTO THE WRONG HANDS, BEN.
SO I HID IT. IN A PLACE ONLY YOU AND I WOULD KNOW ABOUT--THE LOCATION OF OUR FIRST ADVENTURE.
RETRIEVE THE TROPHY. TAKE JOHNNY, AND LIVE THE LIFE YOU'VE ALWAYS LIVED...
...A FANTASTIC ONE.

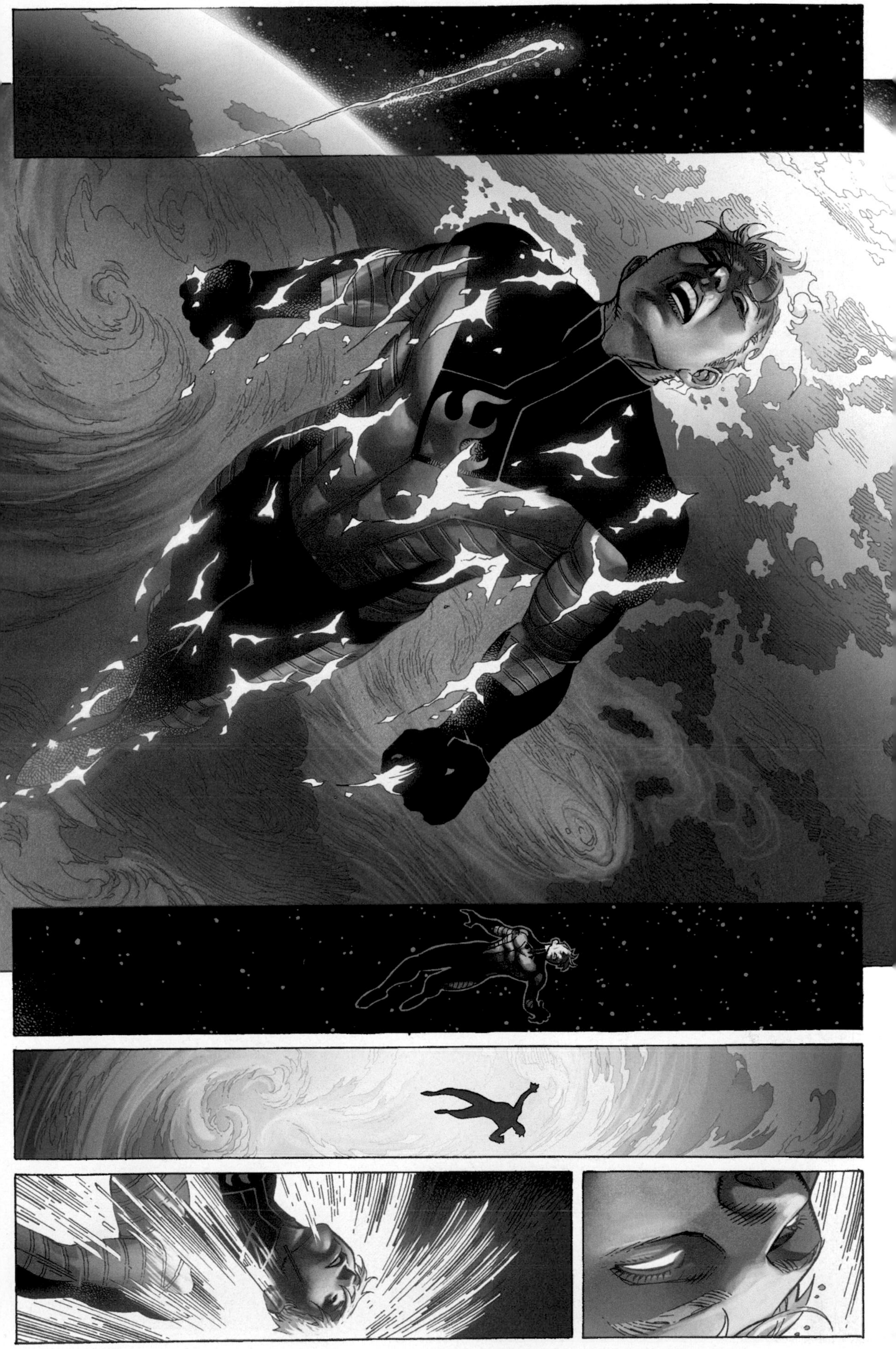

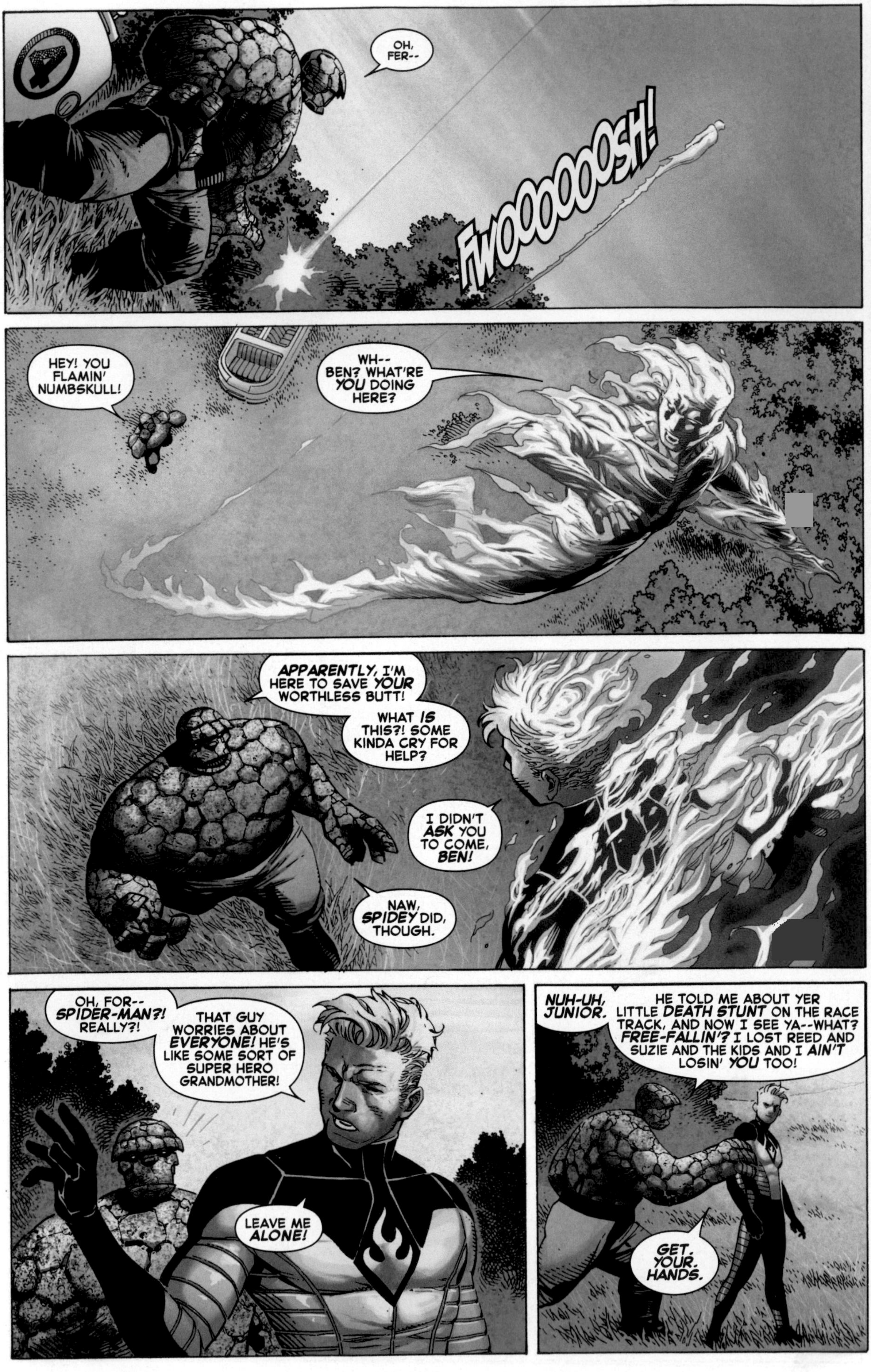

OH, FER--
FWOOOOOOSH!
HEY! YOU FLAMIN' NUMBSKULL!
WH-- BEN? WHAT'RE YOU DOING HERE?
APPARENTLY, I'M HERE TO SAVE YOUR WORTHLESS BUTT!
WHAT IS THIS?! SOME KINDA CRY FOR HELP?
I DIDN'T ASK YOU TO COME, BEN!
NAW, SPIDEY DID, THOUGH.
OH, FOR-- SPIDER-MAN?! REALLY?!
THAT GUY WORRIES ABOUT EVERYONE! HE'S LIKE SOME SORT OF SUPER HERO GRANDMOTHER!
LEAVE ME ALONE!
NUH-UH, JUNIOR.
HE TOLD ME ABOUT YER LITTLE DEATH STUNT ON THE RACE TRACK, AND NOW I SEE YA--WHAT? FREE-FALLIN'? I LOST REED AND SUZIE AND THE KIDS AND I AIN'T LOSIN' YOU TOO!
GET. YOUR. HANDS.

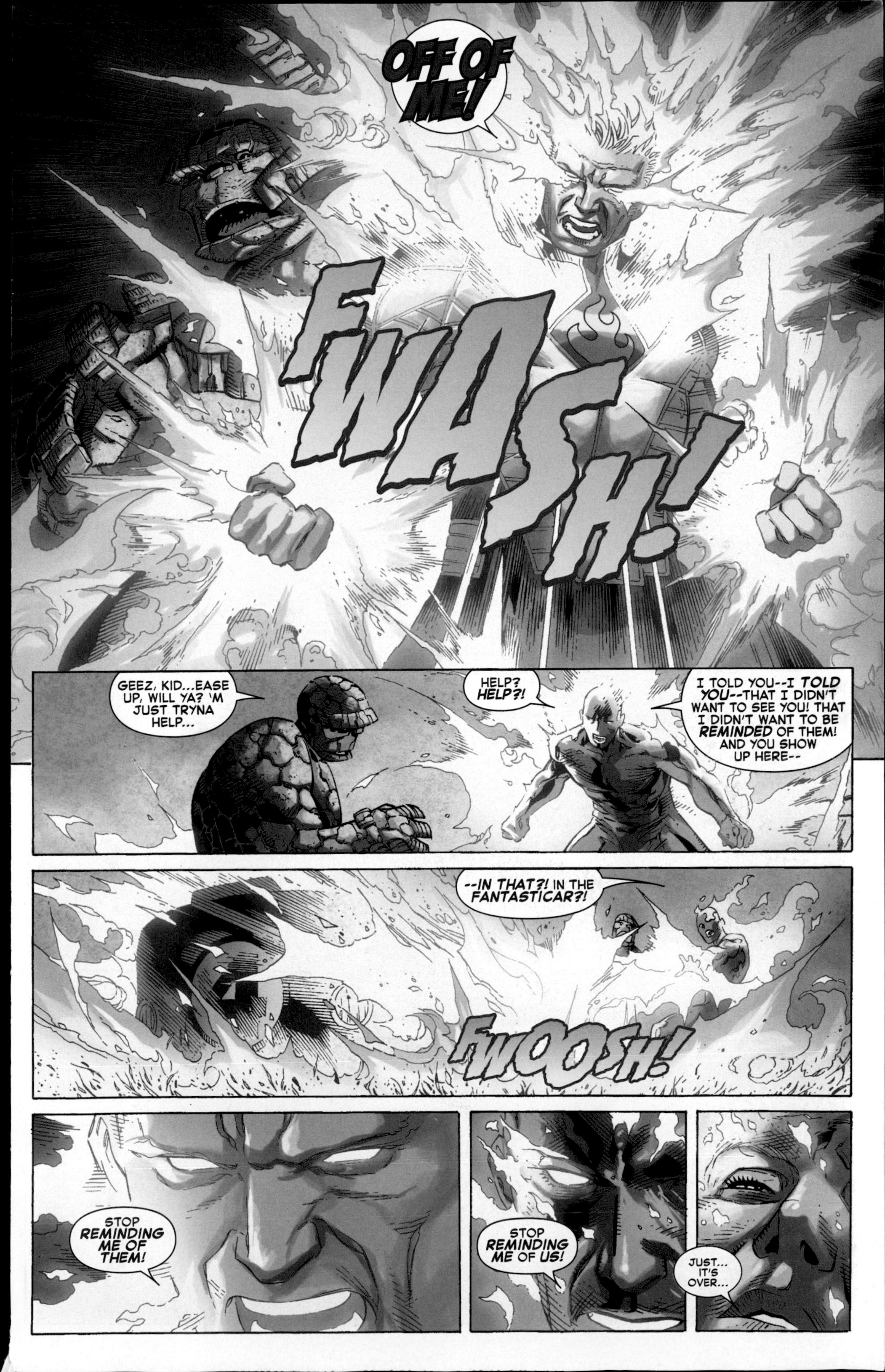
OFF OF ME!
FWASH!
GEEZ, KID...EASE UP, WILL YA? 'M JUST TRYNA HELP...
HELP? HELP?!
I TOLD YOU--I TOLD YOU--THAT I DIDN'T WANT TO SEE YOU! THAT I DIDN'T WANT TO BE REMINDED OF THEM! AND YOU SHOW UP HERE--
--IN THAT?! IN THE FANTASTICAR?!
FWOOSH!
STOP REMINDING ME OF THEM!
STOP REMINDING ME OF US!
JUST... IT'S OVER...

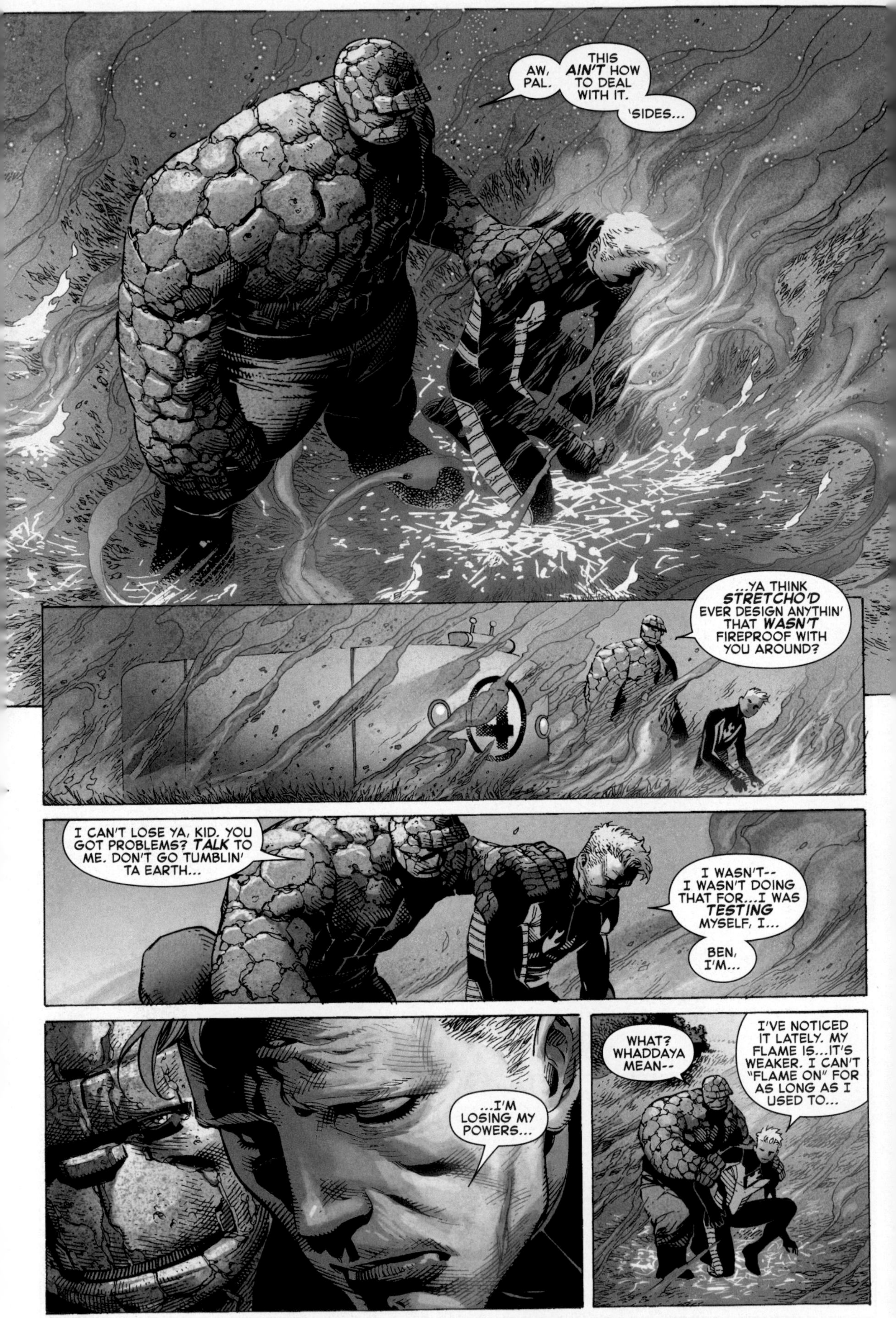
AW, PAL.
THIS AIN'T HOW TO DEAL WITH IT.
'SIDES...
...YA THINK STRETCHO'D EVER DESIGN ANYTHIN' THAT WASN'T FIREPROOF WITH YOU AROUND?
I CAN'T LOSE YA, KID. YOU GOT PROBLEMS? TALK TO ME. DON'T GO TUMBLIN' TA EARTH...
I WASN'T-- I WASN'T DOING THAT FOR...I WAS TESTING MYSELF, I...
BEN, I'M...
...I'M LOSING MY POWERS...
WHAT? WHADDAYA MEAN--
I'VE NOTICED IT LATELY. MY FLAME IS...IT'S WEAKER. I CAN'T "FLAME ON" FOR AS LONG AS I USED TO...

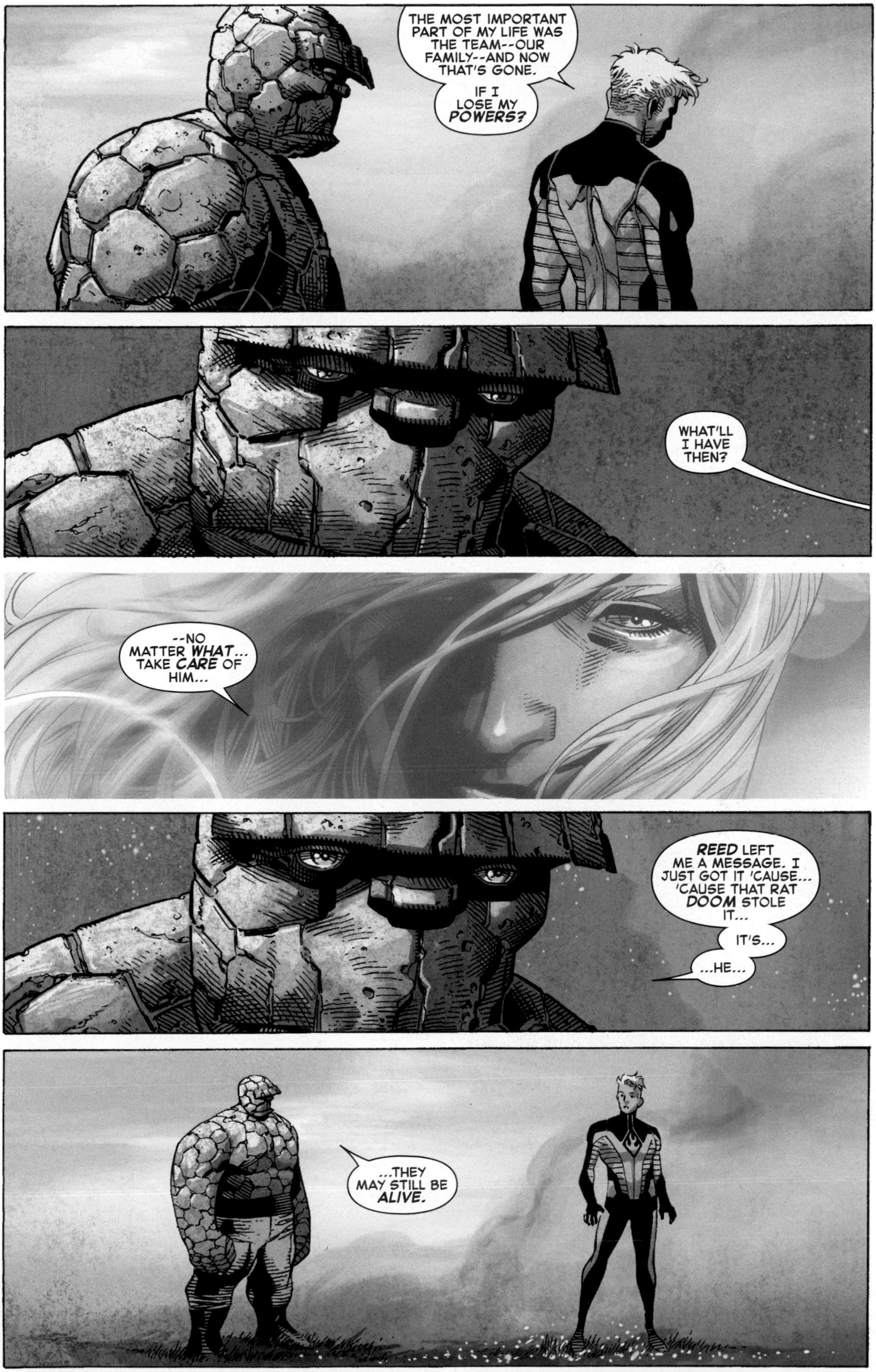
THE MOST IMPORTANT PART OF MY LIFE WAS THE TEAM--OUR FAMILY--AND NOW THAT'S GONE.
IF I LOSE MY POWERS?
WHAT'LL I HAVE THEN?
--NO MATTER WHAT... TAKE CARE OF HIM...
REED LEFT ME A MESSAGE. I JUST GOT IT 'CAUSE... 'CAUSE THAT RAT DOOM STOLE IT...
IT'S...
...HE...
...THEY MAY STILL BE ALIVE.

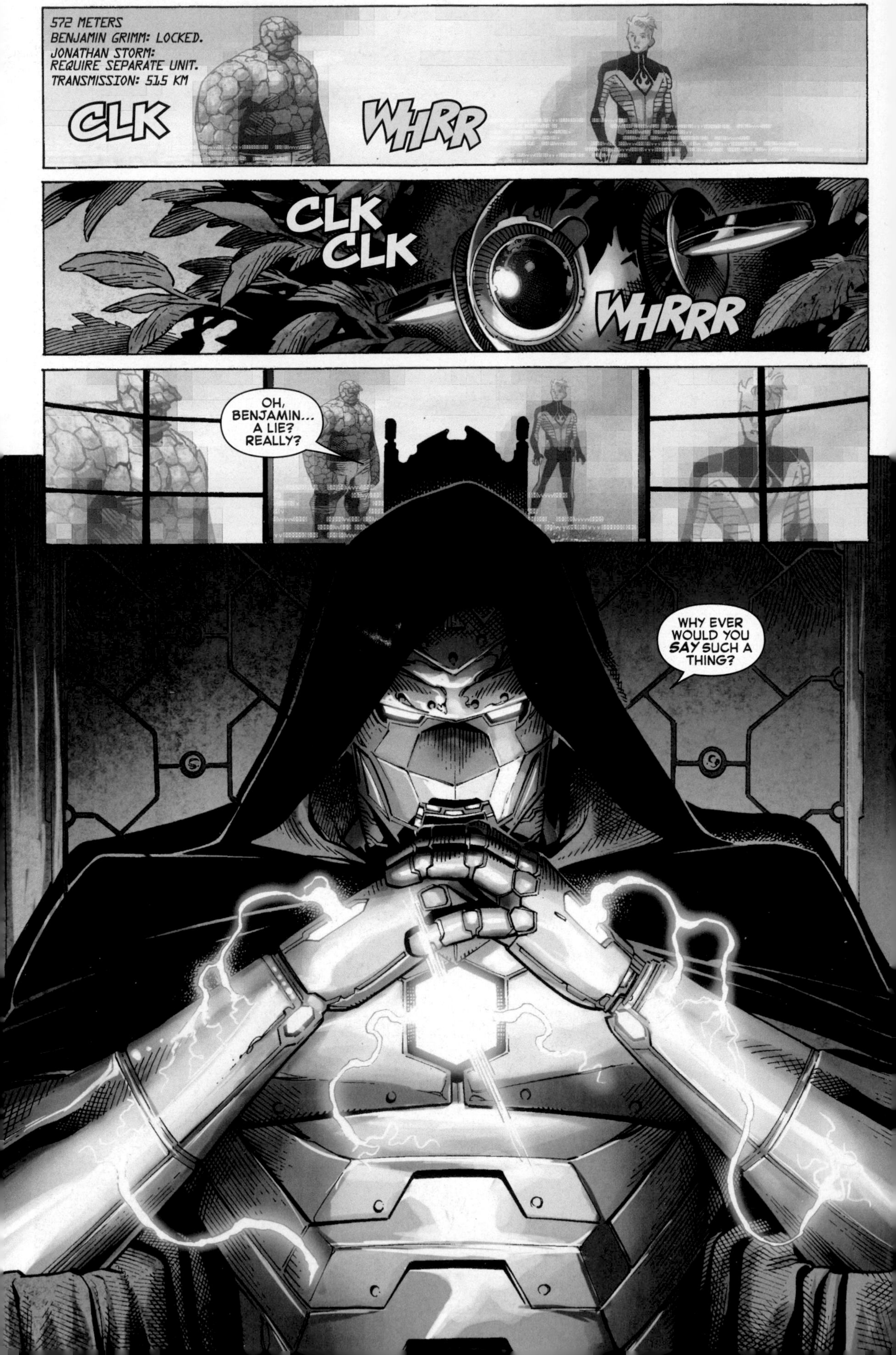

572 METERS
BENJAMIN GRIMM: LOCKED.
JONATHAN STORM: REQUIRE SEPARATE UNIT.
TRANSMISSION: 515 KM
CLK
WHRR
CLK CLK
WHRRR
OH, BENJAMIN... A LIE? REALLY?
WHY EVER WOULD YOU SAY SUCH A THING?

2

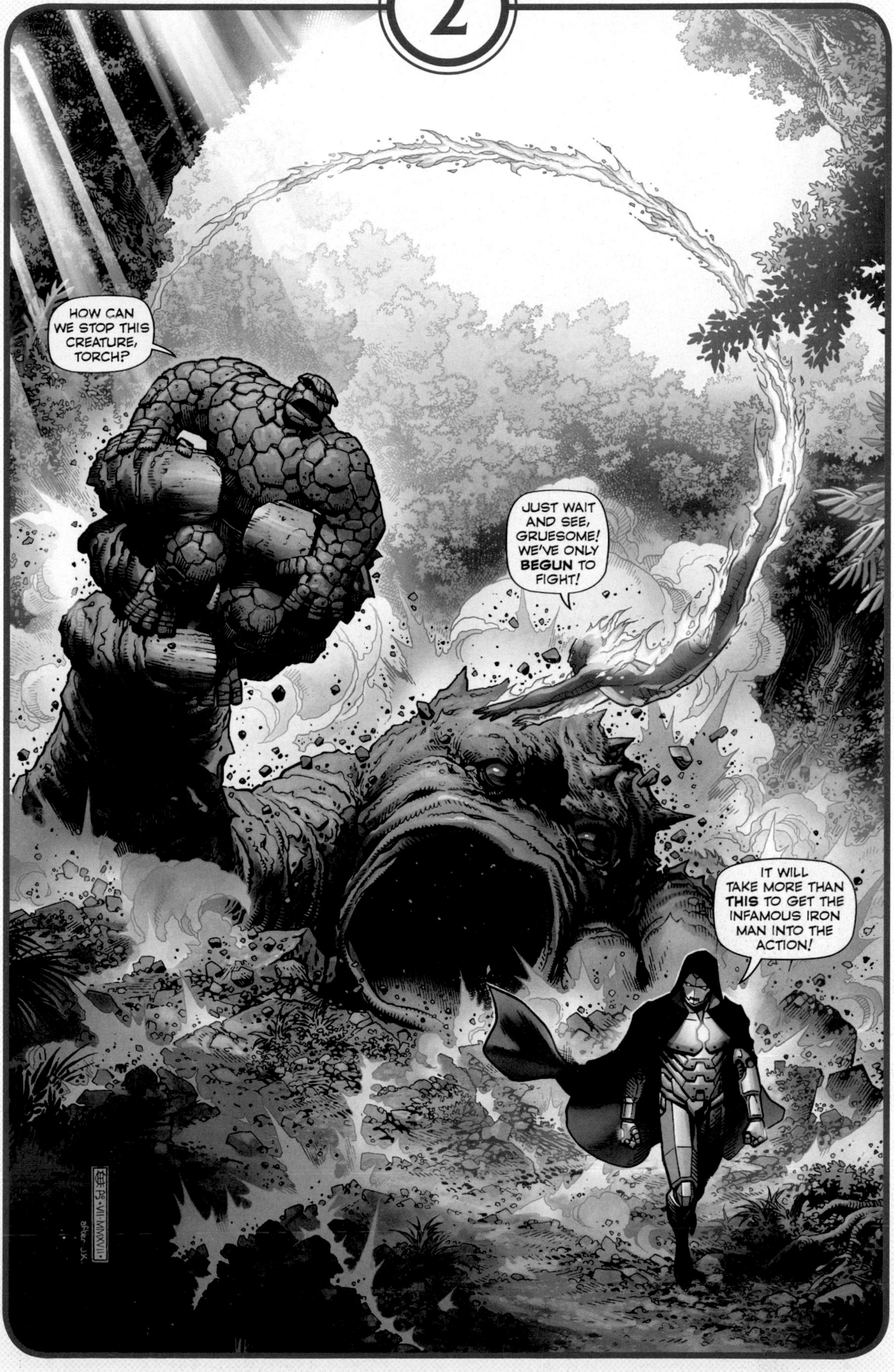
HOW CAN WE STOP THIS CREATURE, TORCH?
JUST WAIT AND SEE, GRUESOME! WE'VE ONLY BEGUN TO FIGHT!
IT WILL TAKE MORE THAN THIS TO GET THE INFAMOUS IRON MAN INTO THE ACTION!

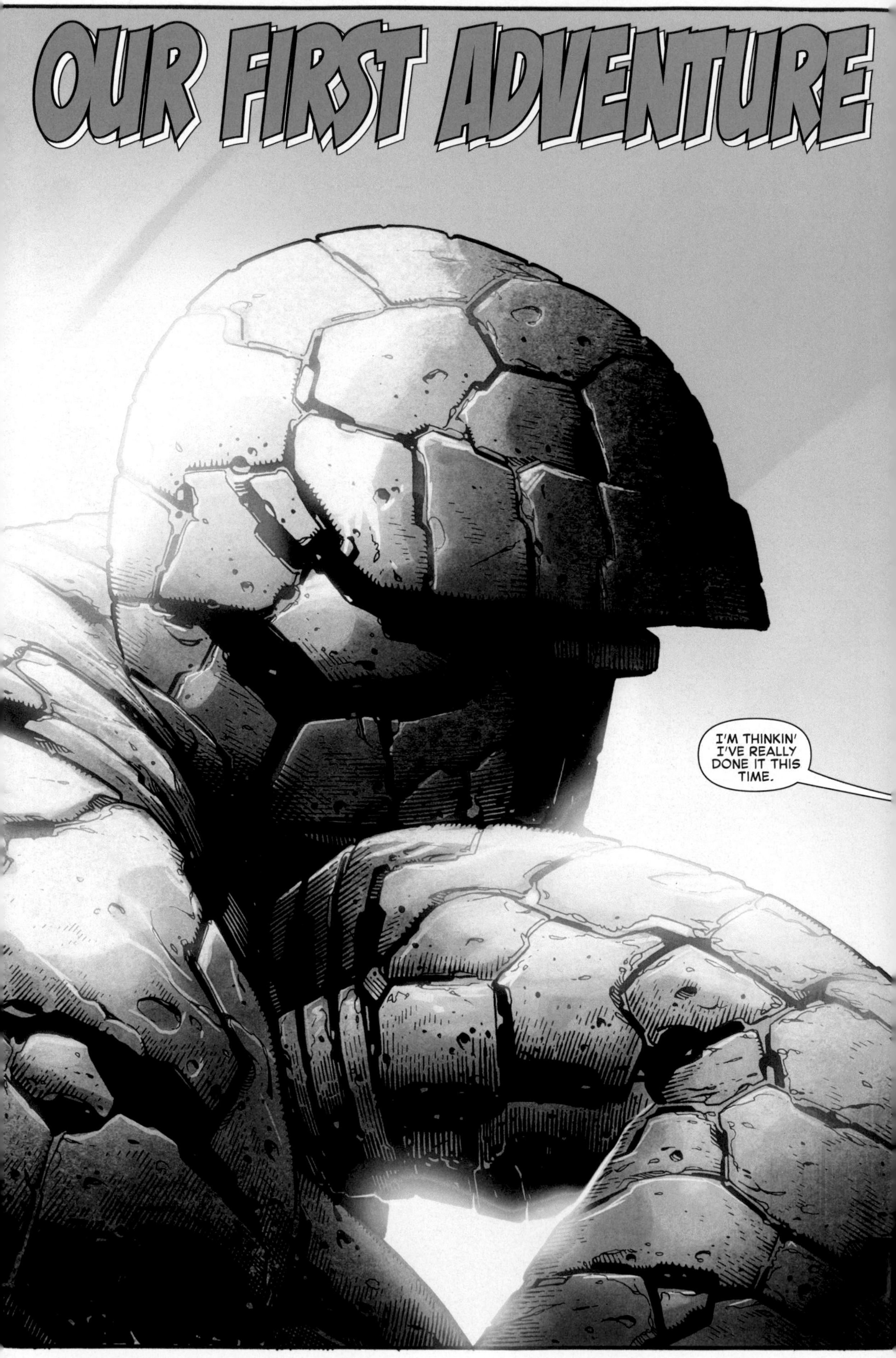
OUR FIRST ADVENTURE
I'M THINKIN' I'VE REALLY DONE IT THIS TIME.

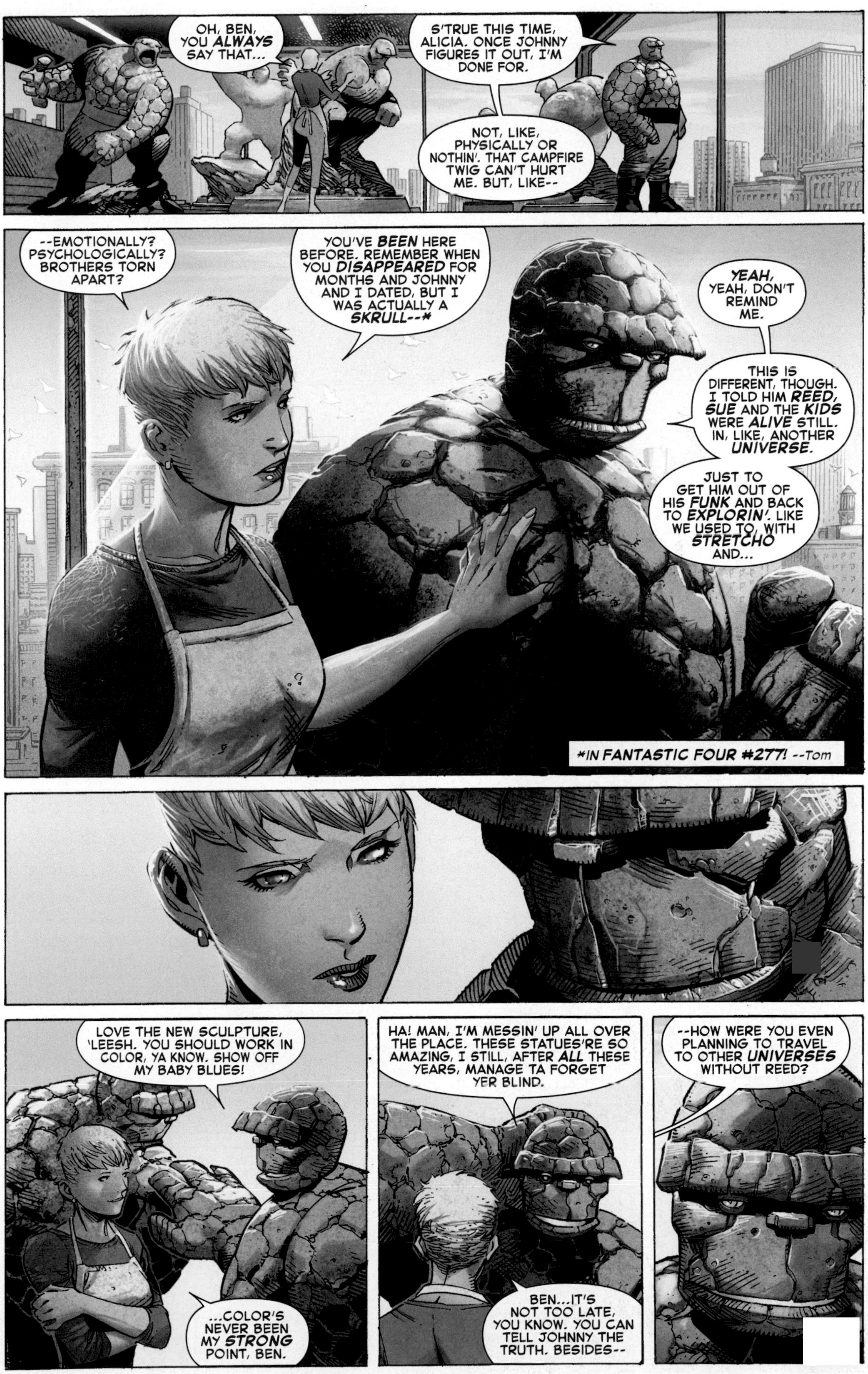

OH, BEN, YOU ALWAYS SAY THAT...
S'TRUE THIS TIME, ALICIA. ONCE JOHNNY FIGURES IT OUT, I'M DONE FOR.
NOT, LIKE, PHYSICALLY OR NOTHIN'. THAT CAMPFIRE TWIG CAN'T HURT ME. BUT, LIKE--
--EMOTIONALLY? PSYCHOLOGICALLY? BROTHERS TORN APART?
YOU'VE BEEN HERE BEFORE. REMEMBER WHEN YOU DISAPPEARED FOR MONTHS AND JOHNNY AND I DATED, BUT I WAS ACTUALLY A SKRULL--*
YEAH, YEAH, DON'T REMIND ME.
THIS IS DIFFERENT, THOUGH. I TOLD HIM REED, SUE AND THE KIDS WERE ALIVE STILL. IN, LIKE, ANOTHER UNIVERSE.
JUST TO GET HIM OUT OF HIS FUNK AND BACK TO EXPLORIN'. LIKE WE USED TO, WITH STRETCHO AND...
*IN FANTASTIC FOUR #277! --Tom
LOVE THE NEW SCULPTURE, 'LEESH. YOU SHOULD WORK IN COLOR, YA KNOW. SHOW OFF MY BABY BLUES!
...COLOR'S NEVER BEEN MY STRONG POINT, BEN.
HA! MAN, I'M MESSIN' UP ALL OVER THE PLACE. THESE STATUES'RE SO AMAZING, I STILL, AFTER ALL THESE YEARS, MANAGE TA FORGET YER BLIND.
BEN...IT'S NOT TOO LATE, YOU KNOW. YOU CAN TELL JOHNNY THE TRUTH. BESIDES--
--HOW WERE YOU EVEN PLANNING TO TRAVEL TO OTHER UNIVERSES WITHOUT REED?

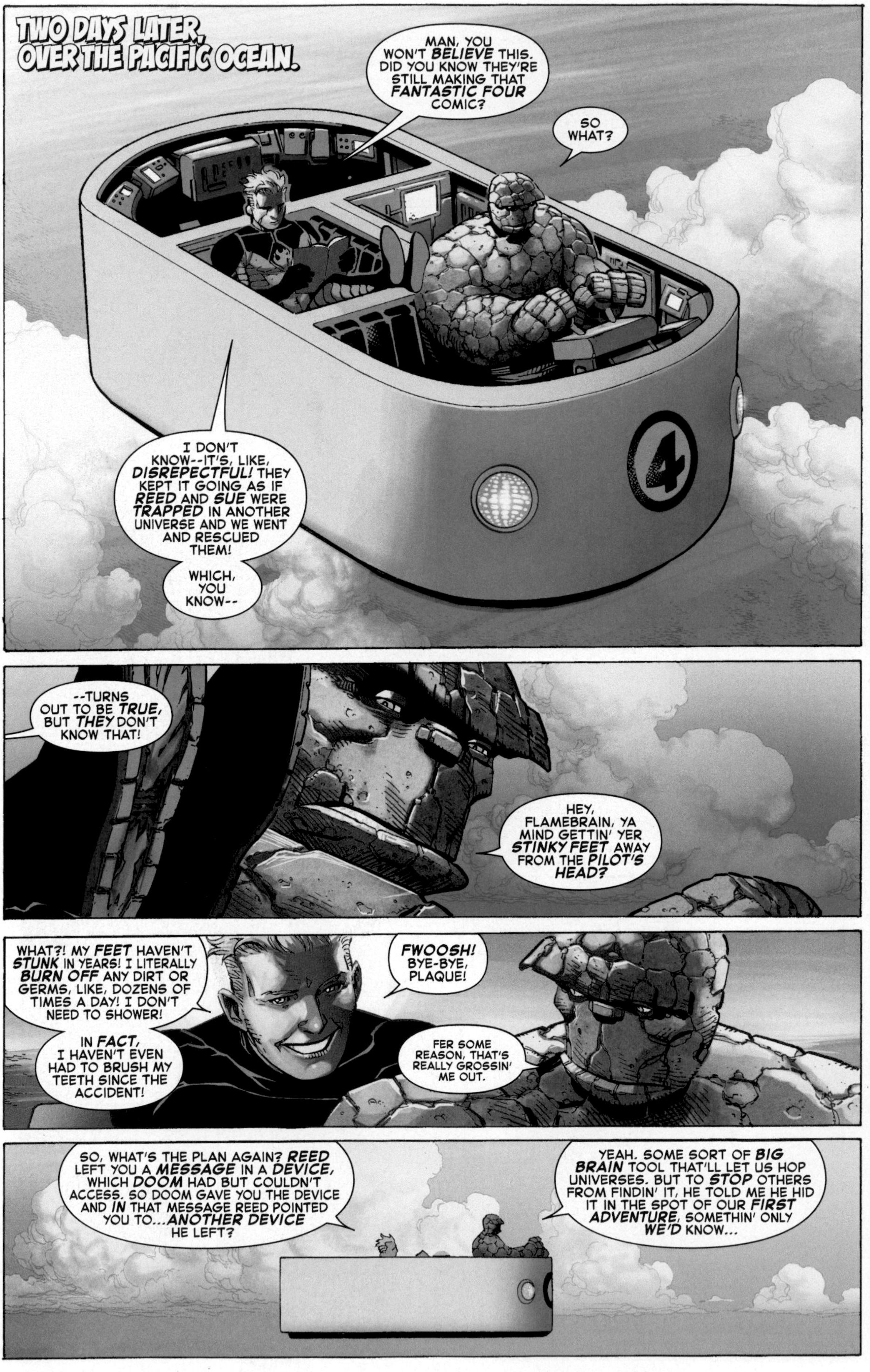
TWO DAYS LATER, OVER THE PACIFIC OCEAN.
MAN, YOU WON'T BELIEVE THIS. DID YOU KNOW THEY'RE STILL MAKING THAT FANTASTIC FOUR COMIC?
SO WHAT?
I DON'T KNOW--IT'S, LIKE, DISREPECTFUL! THEY KEPT IT GOING AS IF REED AND SUE WERE TRAPPED IN ANOTHER UNIVERSE AND WE WENT AND RESCUED THEM!
WHICH, YOU KNOW--
--TURNS OUT TO BE TRUE, BUT THEY DON'T KNOW THAT!
HEY, FLAMEBRAIN, YA MIND GETTIN' YER STINKY FEET AWAY FROM THE PILOT'S HEAD?
WHAT?! MY FEET HAVEN'T STUNK IN YEARS! I LITERALLY BURN OFF ANY DIRT OR GERMS, LIKE, DOZENS OF TIMES A DAY! I DON'T NEED TO SHOWER!
IN FACT, I HAVEN'T EVEN HAD TO BRUSH MY TEETH SINCE THE ACCIDENT!
FWOOSH! BYE-BYE, PLAQUE!
FER SOME REASON, THAT'S REALLY GROSSIN' ME OUT.
SO, WHAT'S THE PLAN AGAIN? REED LEFT YOU A MESSAGE IN A DEVICE, WHICH DOOM HAD BUT COULDN'T ACCESS. SO DOOM GAVE YOU THE DEVICE AND IN THAT MESSAGE REED POINTED YOU TO...ANOTHER DEVICE HE LEFT?
YEAH. SOME SORT OF BIG BRAIN TOOL THAT'LL LET US HOP UNIVERSES. BUT TO STOP OTHERS FROM FINDIN' IT, HE TOLD ME HE HID IT IN THE SPOT OF OUR FIRST ADVENTURE, SOMETHIN' ONLY WE'D KNOW...

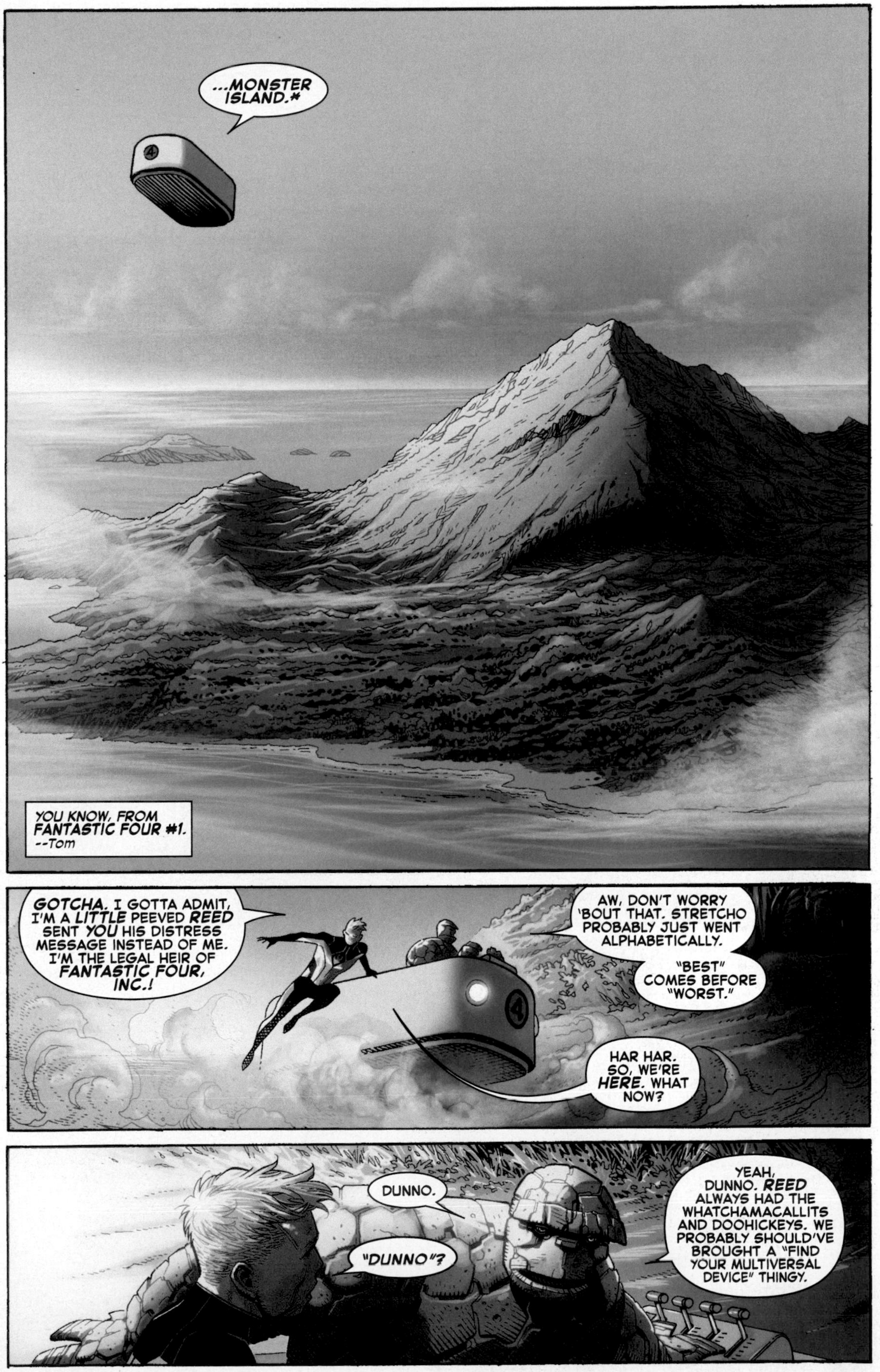
...MONSTER ISLAND.*
YOU KNOW, FROM FANTASTIC FOUR #1. --Tom
GOTCHA. I GOTTA ADMIT, I'M A LITTLE PEEVED REED SENT YOU HIS DISTRESS MESSAGE INSTEAD OF ME. I'M THE LEGAL HEIR OF FANTASTIC FOUR, INC.!
AW, DON'T WORRY 'BOUT THAT. STRETCHO PROBABLY JUST WENT ALPHABETICALLY.
"BEST" COMES BEFORE "WORST."
HAR HAR. SO, WE'RE HERE. WHAT NOW?
DUNNO.
"DUNNO"?
YEAH, DUNNO. REED ALWAYS HAD THE WHATCHAMACALLITS AND DOOHICKEYS. WE PROBABLY SHOULD'VE BROUGHT A "FIND YOUR MULTIVERSAL DEVICE" THINGY.

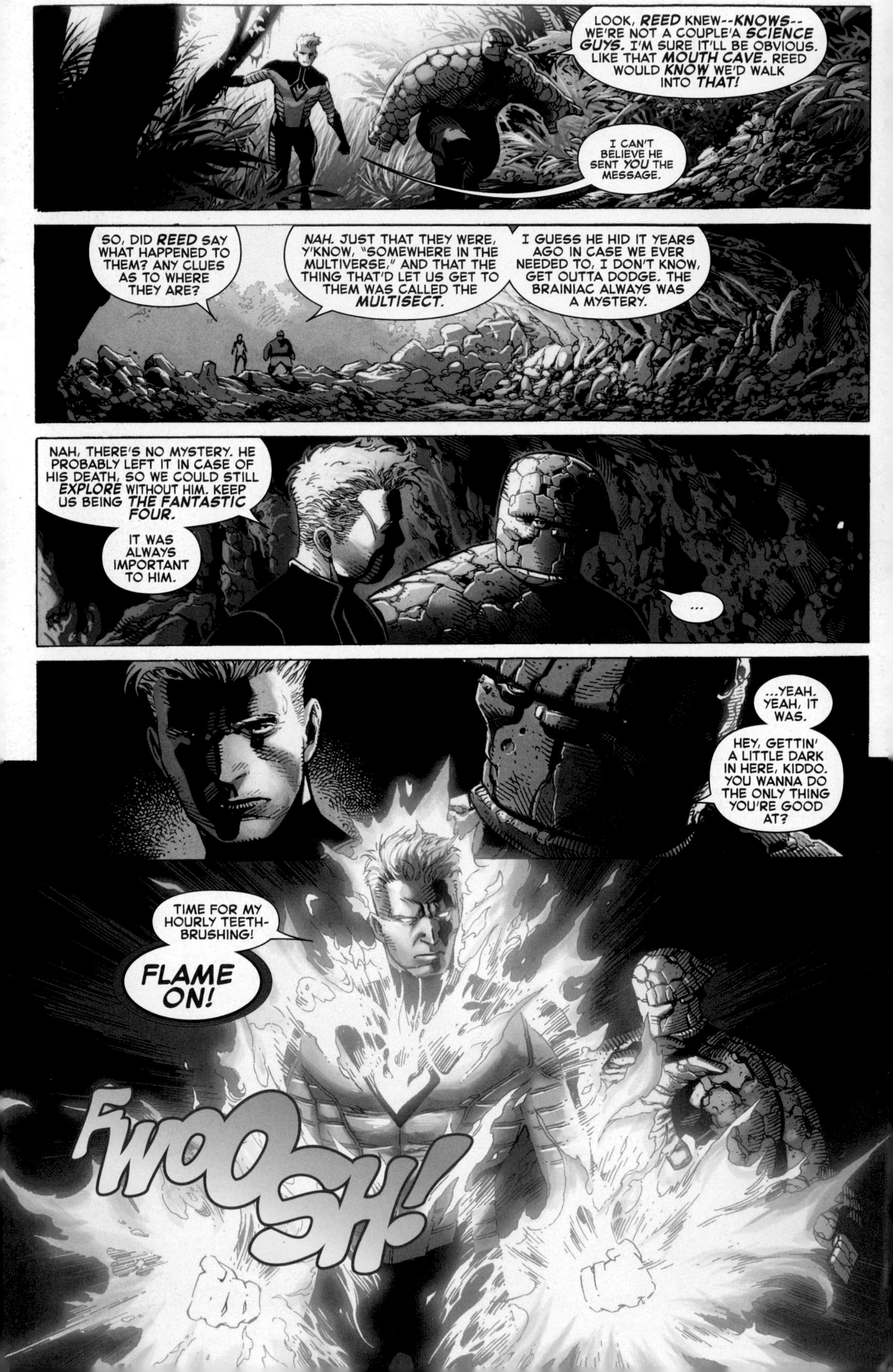
LOOK, REED KNEW--KNOWS--WE'RE NOT A COUPLE'A SCIENCE GUYS. I'M SURE IT'LL BE OBVIOUS. LIKE THAT MOUTH CAVE. REED WOULD KNOW WE'D WALK INTO THAT!
I CAN'T BELIEVE HE SENT YOU THE MESSAGE.
SO, DID REED SAY WHAT HAPPENED TO THEM? ANY CLUES AS TO WHERE THEY ARE?
NAH. JUST THAT THEY WERE, Y'KNOW, "SOMEWHERE IN THE MULTIVERSE," AND THAT THE THING THAT'D LET US GET TO THEM WAS CALLED THE MULTISECT.
I GUESS HE HID IT YEARS AGO IN CASE WE EVER NEEDED TO, I DON'T KNOW, GET OUTTA DODGE. THE BRAINIAC ALWAYS WAS A MYSTERY.
NAH, THERE'S NO MYSTERY. HE PROBABLY LEFT IT IN CASE OF HIS DEATH, SO WE COULD STILL EXPLORE WITHOUT HIM. KEEP US BEING THE FANTASTIC FOUR.
IT WAS ALWAYS IMPORTANT TO HIM.
...
...YEAH. YEAH, IT WAS.
HEY, GETTIN' A LITTLE DARK IN HERE, KIDDO. YOU WANNA DO THE ONLY THING YOU'RE GOOD AT?
TIME FOR MY HOURLY TEETH-BRUSHING!
FLAME ON!
FWOOSH!

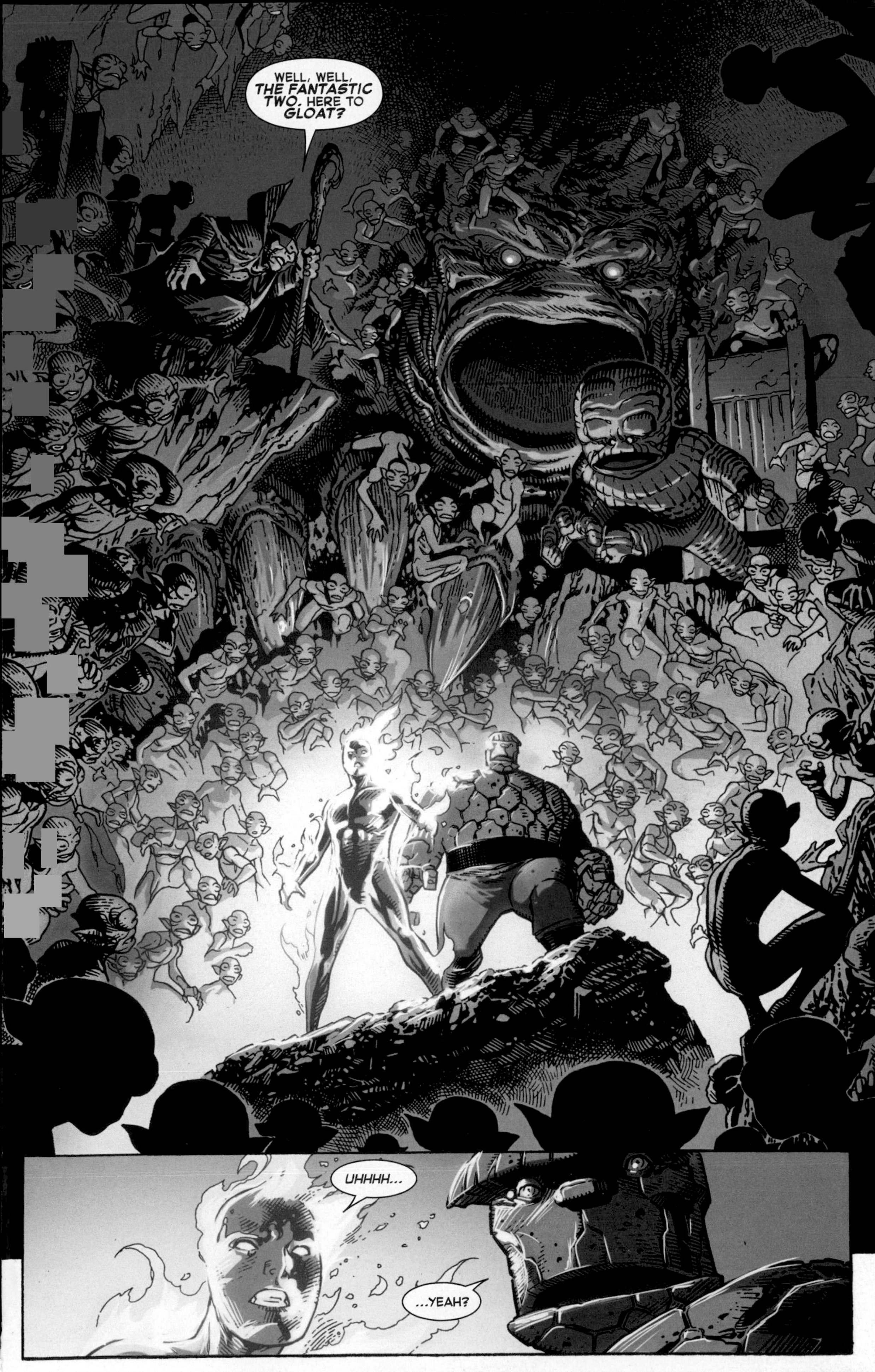
WELL, WELL, THE FANTASTIC TWO. HERE TO GLOAT?
UHHHH...
...YEAH?

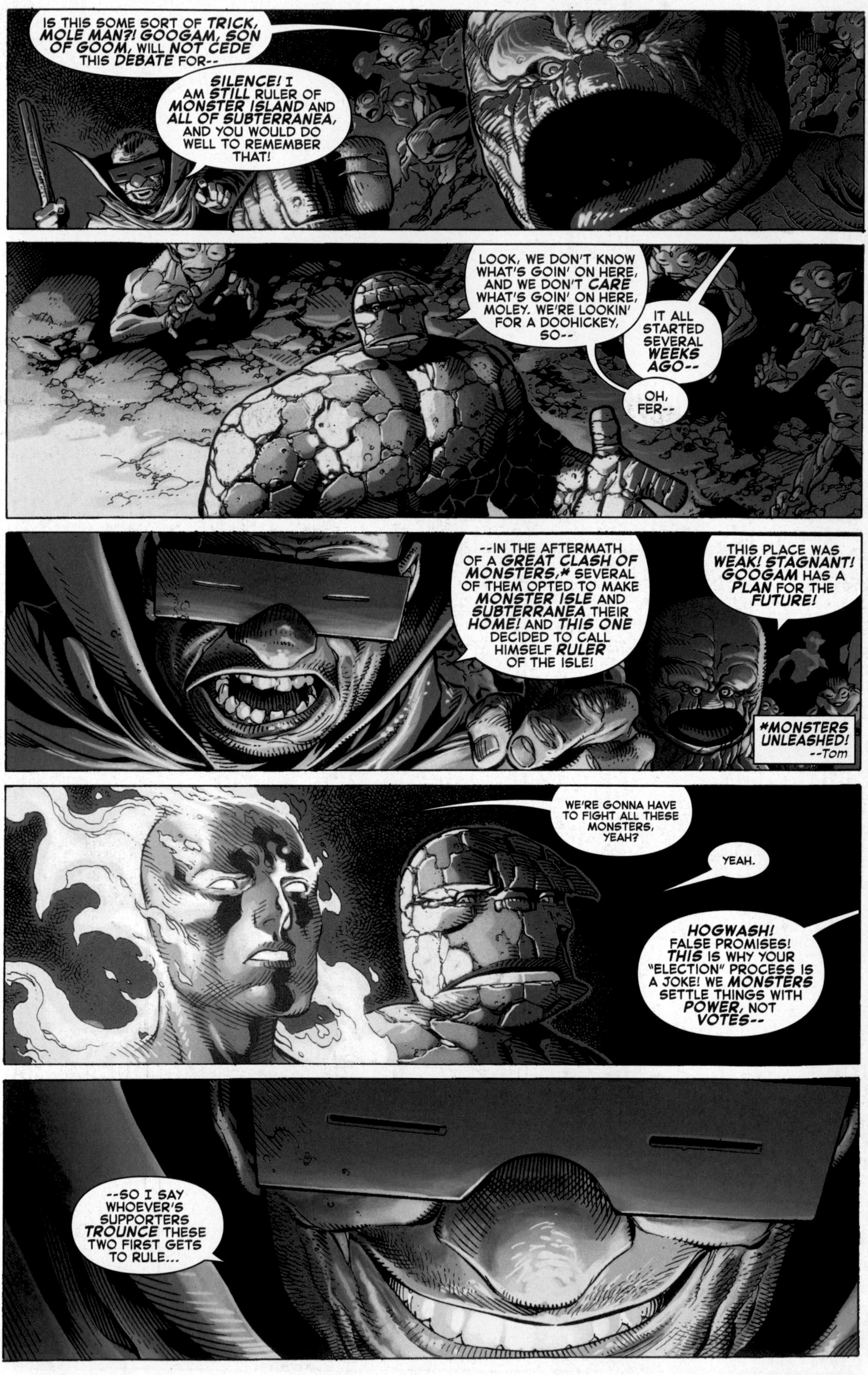
IS THIS SOME SORT OF TRICK, MOLE MAN?! GOOGAM, SON OF GOOM, WILL NOT CEDE THIS DEBATE FOR--
SILENCE! I AM STILL RULER OF MONSTER ISLAND AND ALL OF SUBTERRANEA, AND YOU WOULD DO WELL TO REMEMBER THAT!
LOOK, WE DON'T KNOW WHAT'S GOIN' ON HERE, AND WE DON'T CARE WHAT'S GOIN' ON HERE, MOLEY. WE'RE LOOKIN' FOR A DOOHICKEY, SO--
IT ALL STARTED SEVERAL WEEKS AGO--
OH, FER--
--IN THE AFTERMATH OF A GREAT CLASH OF MONSTERS,* SEVERAL OF THEM OPTED TO MAKE MONSTER ISLE AND SUBTERRANEA THEIR HOME! AND THIS ONE DECIDED TO CALL HIMSELF RULER OF THE ISLE!
THIS PLACE WAS WEAK! STAGNANT! GOOGAM HAS A PLAN FOR THE FUTURE!
*MONSTERS UNLEASHED! --Tom
WE'RE GONNA HAVE TO FIGHT ALL THESE MONSTERS, YEAH?
YEAH.
HOGWASH! FALSE PROMISES! THIS IS WHY YOUR "ELECTION" PROCESS IS A JOKE! WE MONSTERS SETTLE THINGS WITH POWER, NOT VOTES--
--SO I SAY WHOEVER'S SUPPORTERS TROUNCE THESE TWO FIRST GETS TO RULE...

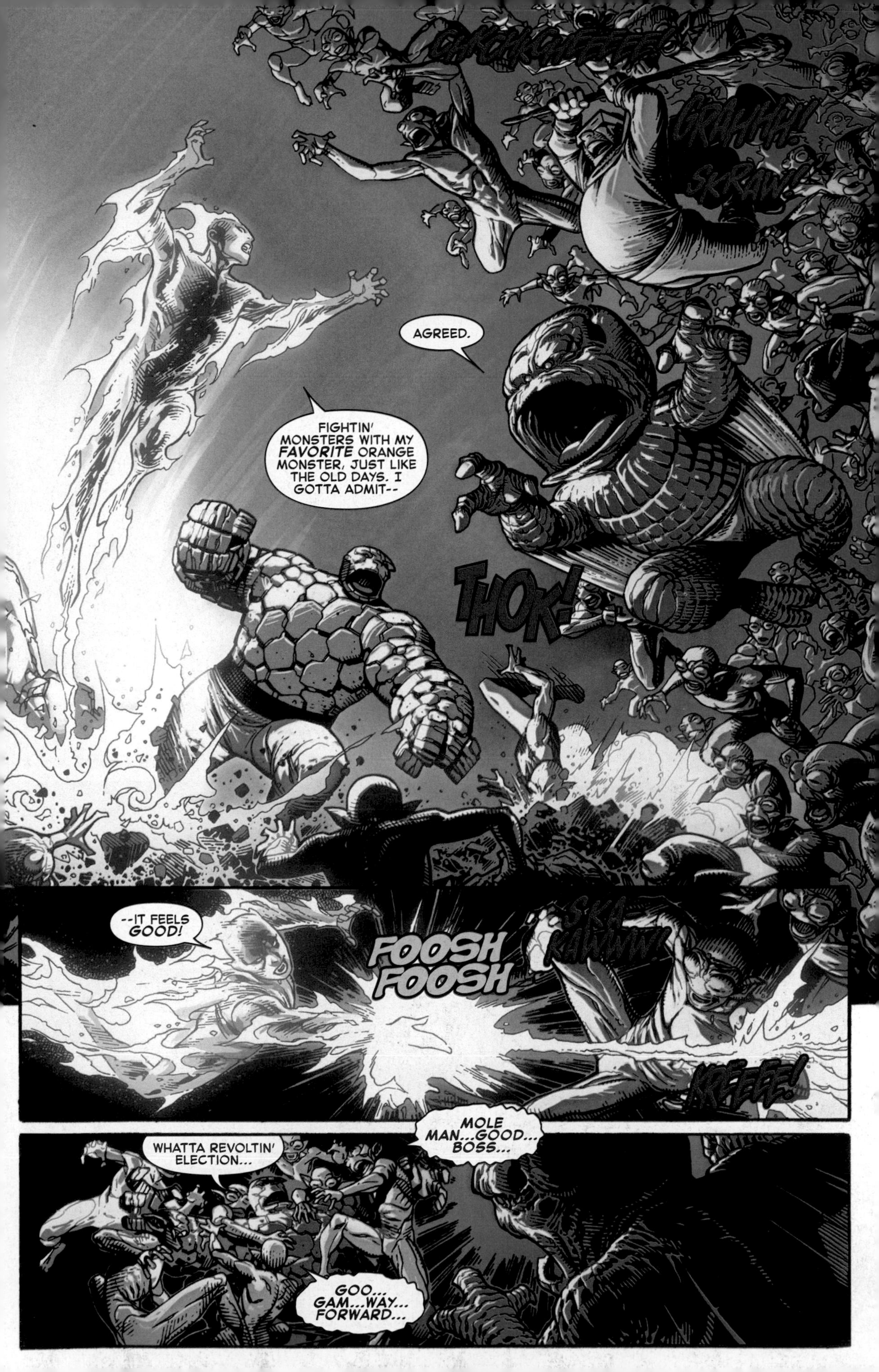
GRAHHH!
SKRAW!
AGREED.
FIGHTIN' MONSTERS WITH MY FAVORITE ORANGE MONSTER, JUST LIKE THE OLD DAYS. I GOTTA ADMIT--
THOK!
--IT FEELS GOOD!
FOOSH FOOSH
SKA KAWWW!
KREEE!
WHATTA REVOLTIN' ELECTION...
MOLE MAN...GOOD... BOSS...
GOO... GAM...WAY... FORWARD...

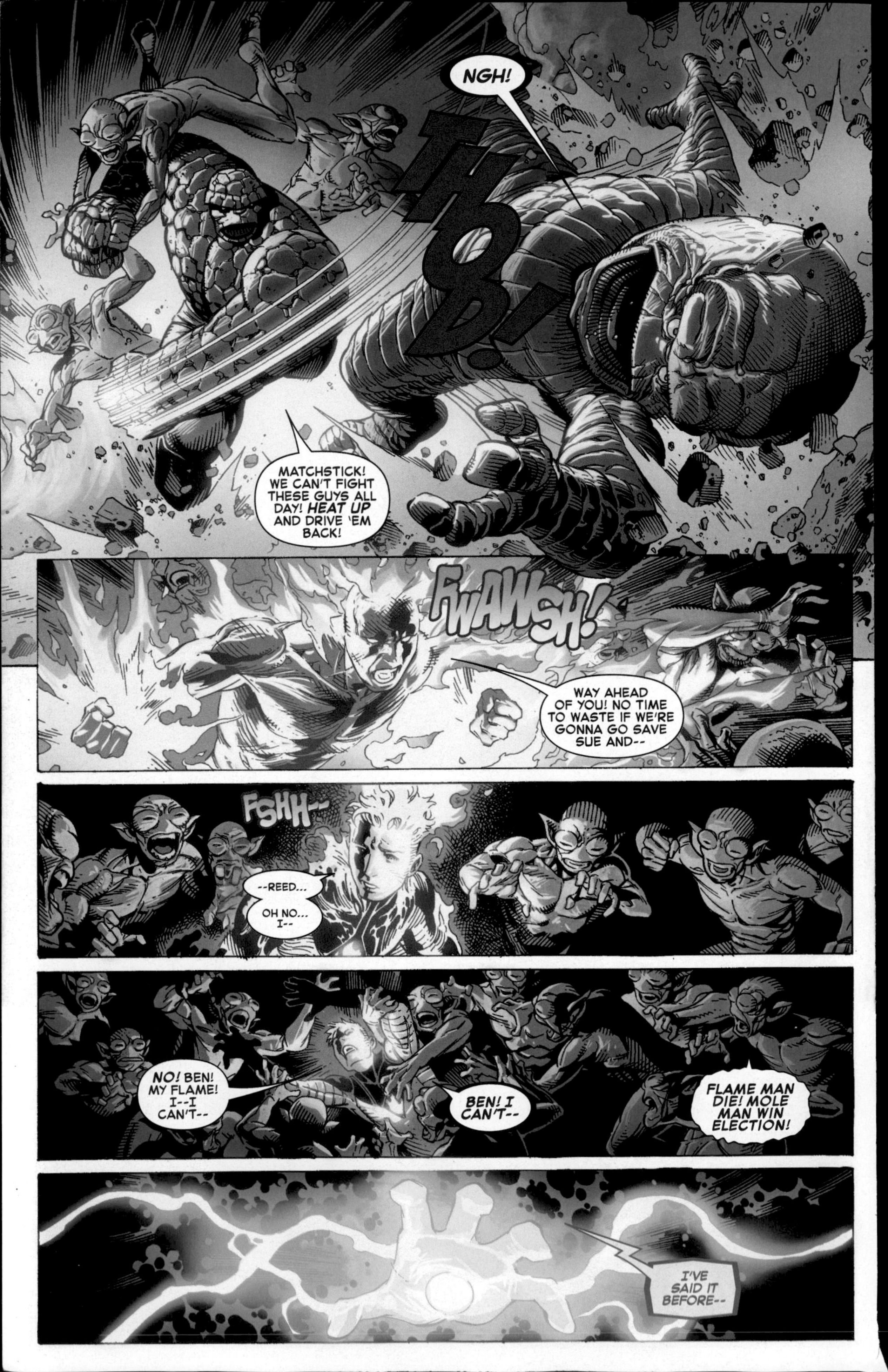
NGH!
THOOD!
MATCHSTICK! WE CAN'T FIGHT THESE GUYS ALL DAY! HEAT UP AND DRIVE 'EM BACK!
FWAWSH!
WAY AHEAD OF YOU! NO TIME TO WASTE IF WE'RE GONNA GO SAVE SUE AND--
FSHH--
--REED...
OH NO... I--
NO! BEN! MY FLAME! I--I CAN'T--
BEN! I CAN'T--
FLAME MAN DIE! MOLE MAN WIN ELECTION!
I'VE SAID IT BEFORE--

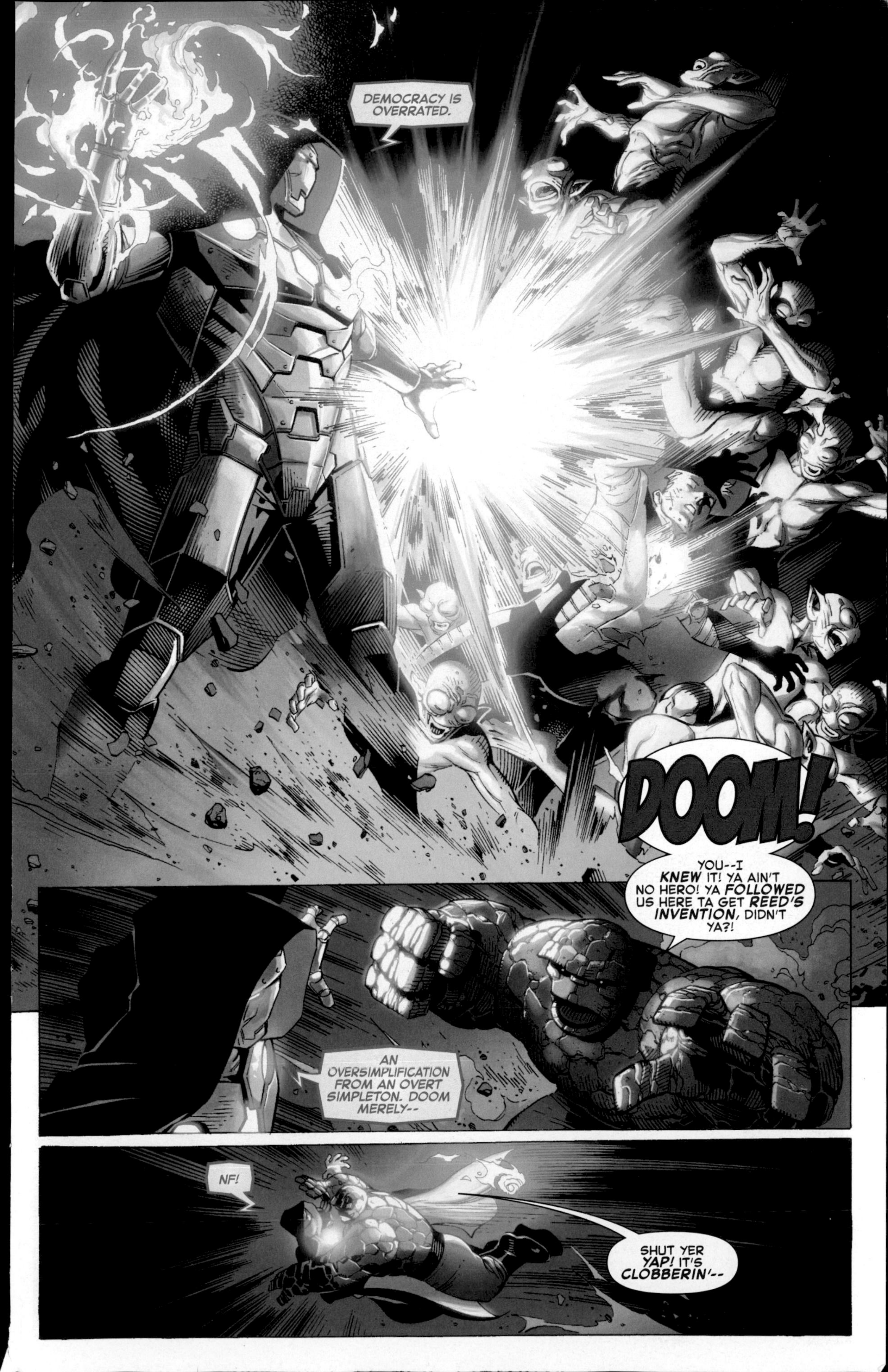
DEMOCRACY IS OVERRATED.
DOOM!
YOU--I KNEW IT! YA AIN'T NO HERO! YA FOLLOWED US HERE TA GET REED'S INVENTION, DIDN'T YA?!
AN OVERSIMPLIFICATION FROM AN OVERT SIMPLETON. DOOM MERELY--
NF!
SHUT YER YAP! IT'S CLOBBERIN'--

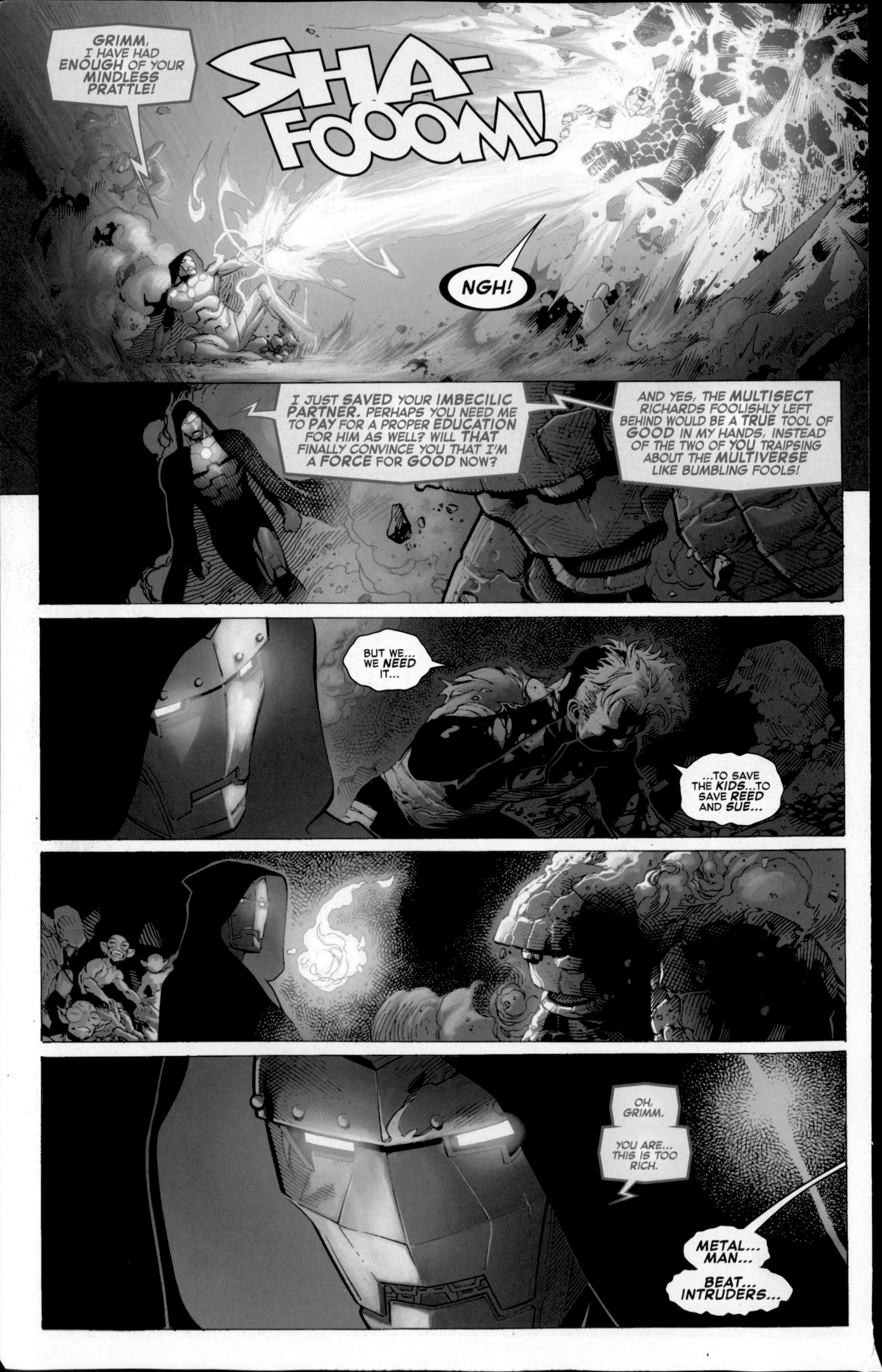
GRIMM, I HAVE HAD ENOUGH OF YOUR MINDLESS PRATTLE!
SHA-FOOOM!
NGH!
I JUST SAVED YOUR IMBECILIC PARTNER. PERHAPS YOU NEED ME TO PAY FOR A PROPER EDUCATION FOR HIM AS WELL? WILL THAT FINALLY CONVINCE YOU THAT I'M A FORCE FOR GOOD NOW?
AND YES, THE MULTISECT RICHARDS FOOLISHLY LEFT BEHIND WOULD BE A TRUE TOOL OF GOOD IN MY HANDS, INSTEAD OF THE TWO OF YOU TRAIPSING ABOUT THE MULTIVERSE LIKE BUMBLING FOOLS!
BUT WE... WE NEED IT...
...TO SAVE THE KIDS...TO SAVE REED AND SUE...
OH, GRIMM.
YOU ARE... THIS IS TOO RICH.
METAL... MAN...
BEAT... INTRUDERS...

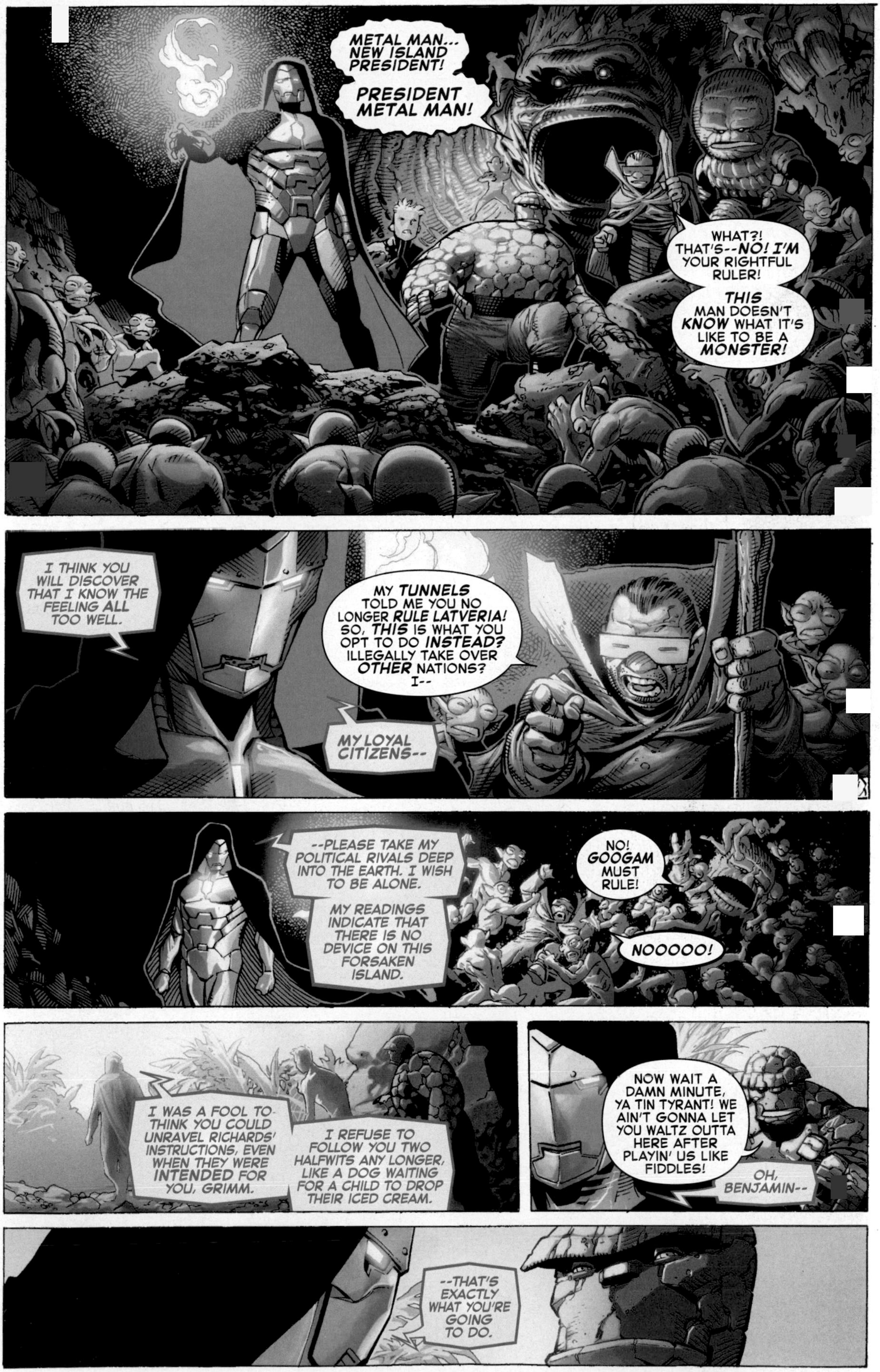

METAL MAN... NEW ISLAND PRESIDENT!
PRESIDENT METAL MAN!
WHAT?! THAT'S--NO! I'M YOUR RIGHTFUL RULER!
THIS MAN DOESN'T KNOW WHAT IT'S LIKE TO BE A MONSTER!
I THINK YOU WILL DISCOVER THAT I KNOW THE FEELING ALL TOO WELL.
MY TUNNELS TOLD ME YOU NO LONGER RULE LATVERIA! SO, THIS IS WHAT YOU OPT TO DO INSTEAD? ILLEGALLY TAKE OVER OTHER NATIONS? I--
MY LOYAL CITIZENS--
--PLEASE TAKE MY POLITICAL RIVALS DEEP INTO THE EARTH. I WISH TO BE ALONE.
MY READINGS INDICATE THAT THERE IS NO DEVICE ON THIS FORSAKEN ISLAND.
NO! GOOGAM MUST RULE!
NOOOOO!
I WAS A FOOL TO THINK YOU COULD UNRAVEL RICHARDS' INSTRUCTIONS, EVEN WHEN THEY WERE INTENDED FOR YOU, GRIMM.
I REFUSE TO FOLLOW YOU TWO HALFWITS ANY LONGER, LIKE A DOG WAITING FOR A CHILD TO DROP THEIR ICED CREAM.
NOW WAIT A DAMN MINUTE, YA TIN TYRANT! WE AIN'T GONNA LET YOU WALTZ OUTTA HERE AFTER PLAYIN' US LIKE FIDDLES!
OH, BENJAMIN--
--THAT'S EXACTLY WHAT YOU'RE GOING TO DO.

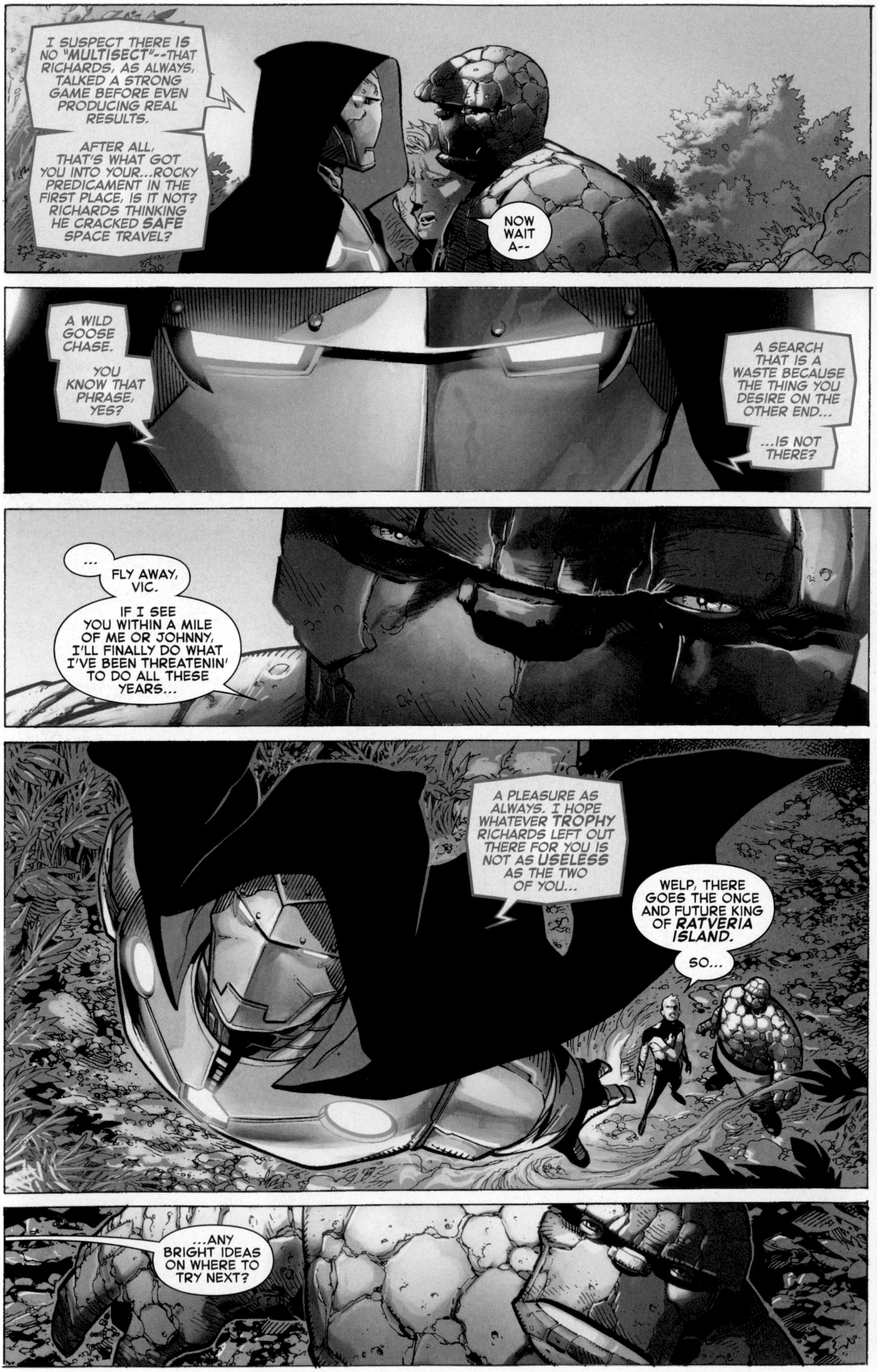

I SUSPECT THERE IS NO "MULTISECT"--THAT RICHARDS, AS ALWAYS, TALKED A STRONG GAME BEFORE EVEN PRODUCING REAL RESULTS.
AFTER ALL, THAT'S WHAT GOT YOU INTO YOUR...ROCKY PREDICAMENT IN THE FIRST PLACE, IS IT NOT? RICHARDS THINKING HE CRACKED SAFE SPACE TRAVEL?
NOW WAIT A--
A WILD GOOSE CHASE.
YOU KNOW THAT PHRASE, YES?
A SEARCH THAT IS A WASTE BECAUSE THE THING YOU DESIRE ON THE OTHER END...
...IS NOT THERE?
...
FLY AWAY, VIC.
IF I SEE YOU WITHIN A MILE OF ME OR JOHNNY, I'LL FINALLY DO WHAT I'VE BEEN THREATENIN' TO DO ALL THESE YEARS...
A PLEASURE AS ALWAYS. I HOPE WHATEVER TROPHY RICHARDS LEFT OUT THERE FOR YOU IS NOT AS USELESS AS THE TWO OF YOU...
WELP, THERE GOES THE ONCE AND FUTURE KING OF RATVERIA ISLAND.
SO...
...ANY BRIGHT IDEAS ON WHERE TO TRY NEXT?

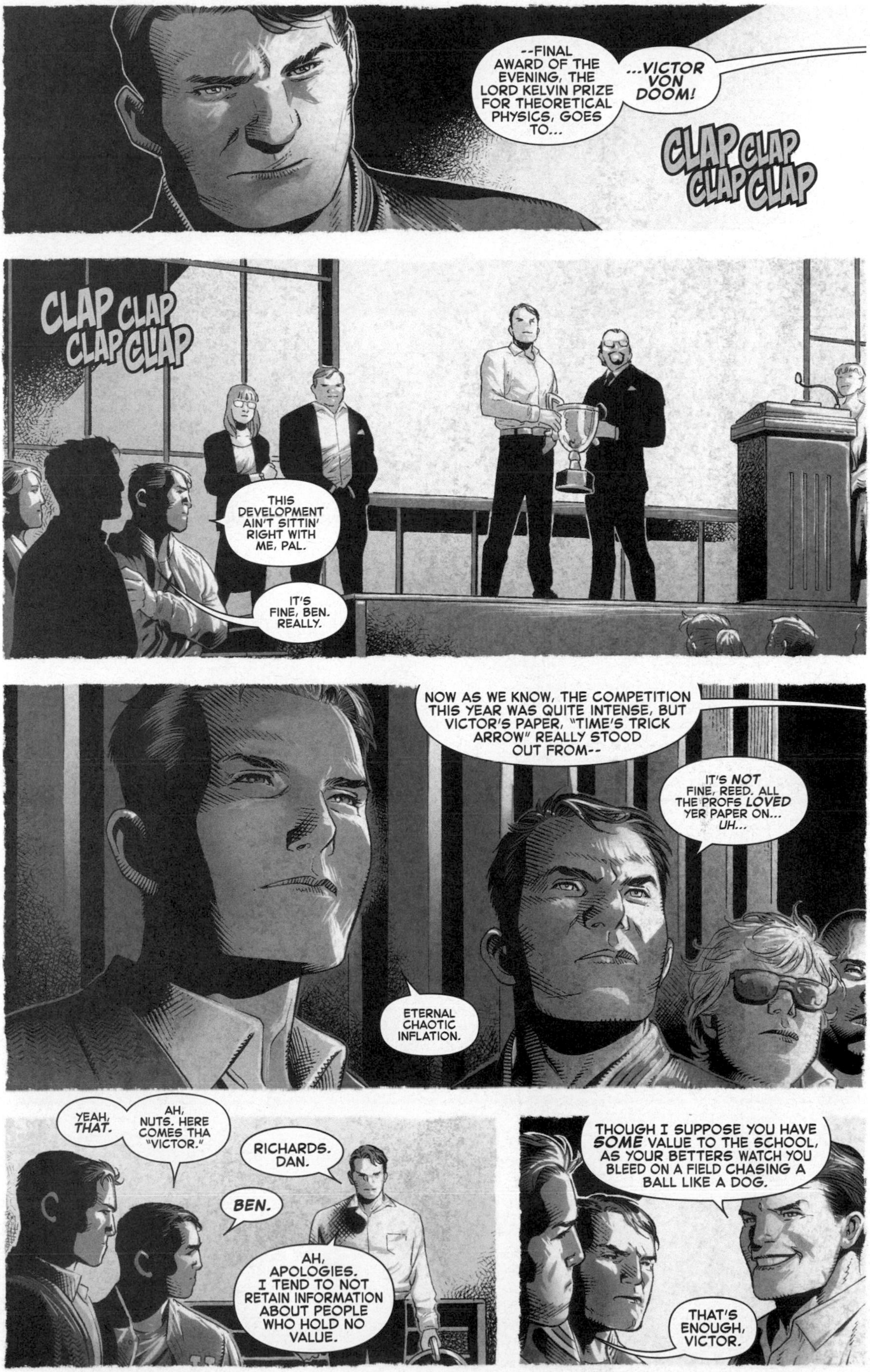
--FINAL AWARD OF THE EVENING, THE LORD KELVIN PRIZE FOR THEORETICAL PHYSICS, GOES TO...
...VICTOR VON DOOM!
CLAP CLAP CLAP CLAP
CLAP CLAP CLAP CLAP
THIS DEVELOPMENT AIN'T SITTIN' RIGHT WITH ME, PAL.
IT'S FINE, BEN. REALLY.
NOW AS WE KNOW, THE COMPETITION THIS YEAR WAS QUITE INTENSE, BUT VICTOR'S PAPER, "TIME'S TRICK ARROW" REALLY STOOD OUT FROM--
IT'S NOT FINE, REED. ALL THE PROFS LOVED YER PAPER ON... UH...
ETERNAL CHAOTIC INFLATION.
YEAH, THAT.
AH, NUTS. HERE COMES THA "VICTOR."
RICHARDS. DAN.
BEN.
AH, APOLOGIES. I TEND TO NOT RETAIN INFORMATION ABOUT PEOPLE WHO HOLD NO VALUE.
THOUGH I SUPPOSE YOU HAVE SOME VALUE TO THE SCHOOL, AS YOUR BETTERS WATCH YOU BLEED ON A FIELD CHASING A BALL LIKE A DOG.
THAT'S ENOUGH, VICTOR.

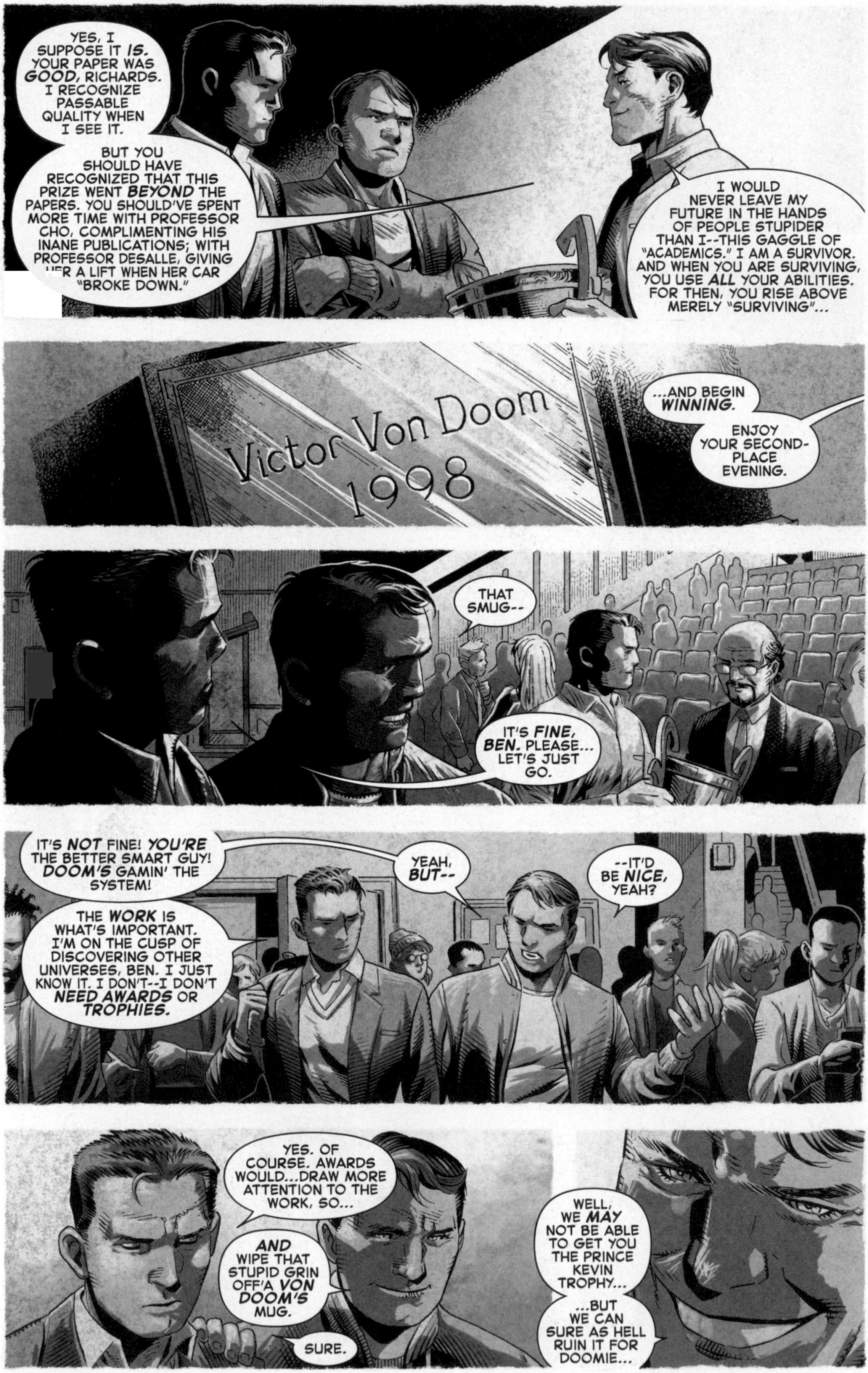

YES, I SUPPOSE IT IS. YOUR PAPER WAS GOOD, RICHARDS. I RECOGNIZE PASSABLE QUALITY WHEN I SEE IT.
BUT YOU SHOULD HAVE RECOGNIZED THAT THIS PRIZE WENT BEYOND THE PAPERS. YOU SHOULD'VE SPENT MORE TIME WITH PROFESSOR CHO, COMPLIMENTING HIS INANE PUBLICATIONS; WITH PROFESSOR DESALLE, GIVING HER A LIFT WHEN HER CAR "BROKE DOWN."
I WOULD NEVER LEAVE MY FUTURE IN THE HANDS OF PEOPLE STUPIDER THAN I--THIS GAGGLE OF "ACADEMICS." I AM A SURVIVOR. AND WHEN YOU ARE SURVIVING, YOU USE ALL YOUR ABILITIES. FOR THEN, YOU RISE ABOVE MERELY "SURVIVING"...
Victor Von Doom
1998
...AND BEGIN WINNING.
ENJOY YOUR SECOND-PLACE EVENING.
THAT SMUG--
IT'S FINE, BEN. PLEASE... LET'S JUST GO.
IT'S NOT FINE! YOU'RE THE BETTER SMART GUY! DOOM'S GAMIN' THE SYSTEM!
THE WORK IS WHAT'S IMPORTANT. I'M ON THE CUSP OF DISCOVERING OTHER UNIVERSES, BEN. I JUST KNOW IT. I DON'T--I DON'T NEED AWARDS OR TROPHIES.
YEAH, BUT--
--IT'D BE NICE, YEAH?
YES. OF COURSE. AWARDS WOULD...DRAW MORE ATTENTION TO THE WORK, SO...
AND WIPE THAT STUPID GRIN OFF'A VON DOOM'S MUG.
SURE.
WELL, WE MAY NOT BE ABLE TO GET YOU THE PRINCE KEVIN TROPHY...
...BUT WE CAN SURE AS HELL RUIN IT FOR DOOMIE...

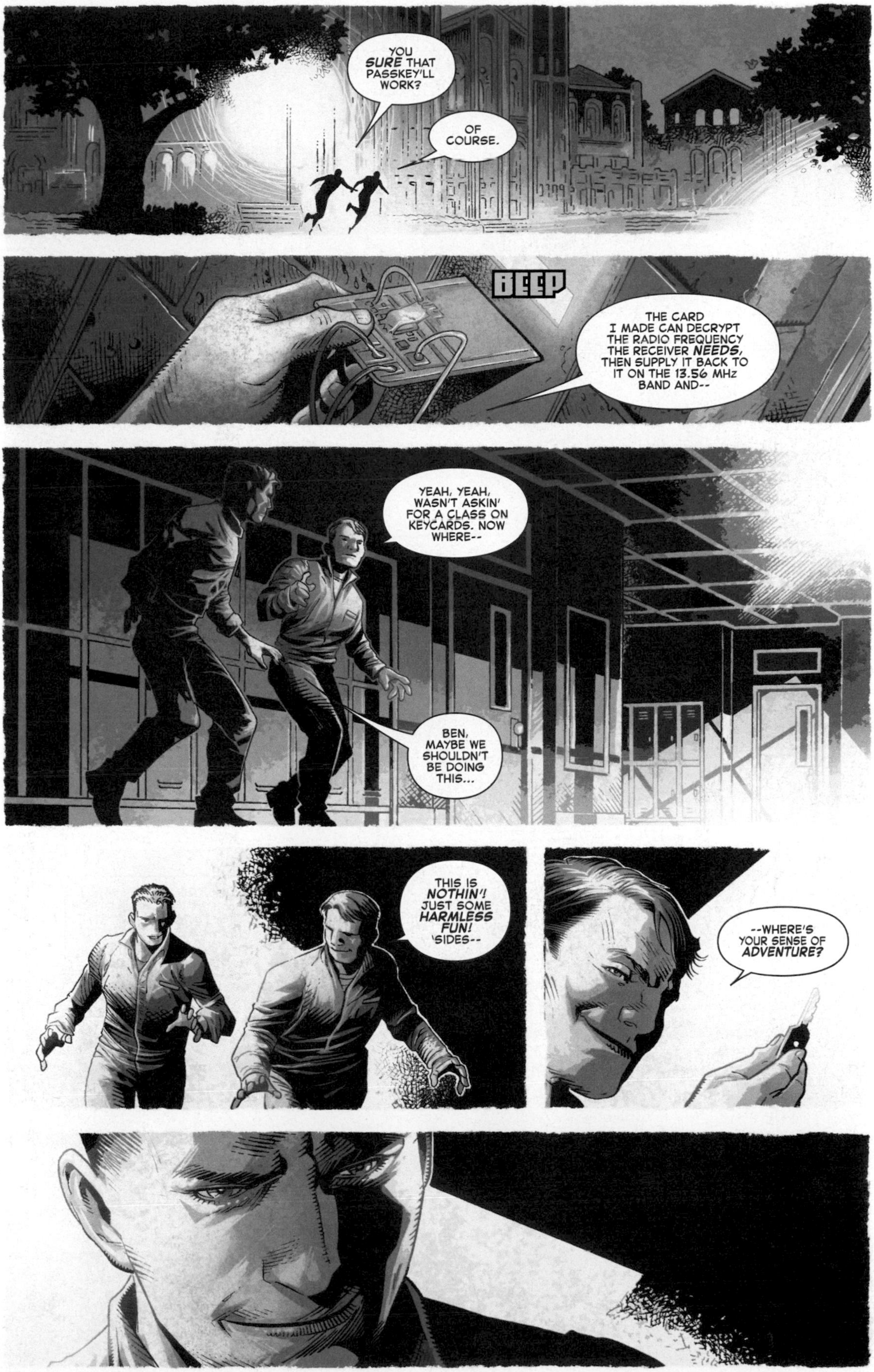
YOU SURE THAT PASSKEY'LL WORK?
OF COURSE.
BEEP
THE CARD I MADE CAN DECRYPT THE RADIO FREQUENCY THE RECEIVER NEEDS, THEN SUPPLY IT BACK TO IT ON THE 13.56 MHz BAND AND--
YEAH, YEAH, WASN'T ASKIN' FOR A CLASS ON KEYCARDS. NOW WHERE--
BEN, MAYBE WE SHOULDN'T BE DOING THIS...
THIS IS NOTHIN'! JUST SOME HARMLESS FUN! 'SIDES--
--WHERE'S YOUR SENSE OF ADVENTURE?

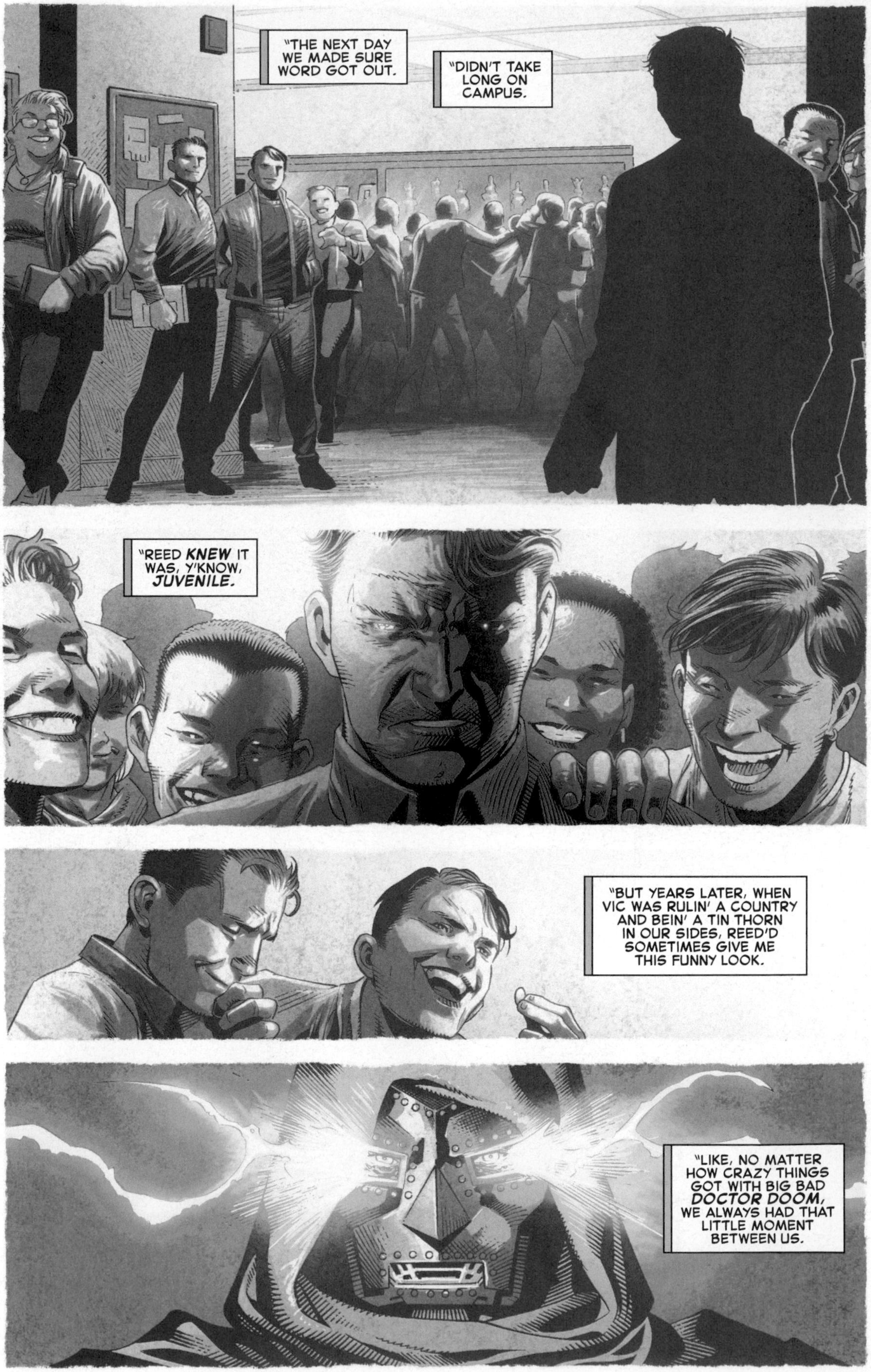
"THE NEXT DAY WE MADE SURE WORD GOT OUT.
"DIDN'T TAKE LONG ON CAMPUS.
"REED KNEW IT WAS, Y'KNOW, JUVENILE.
"BUT YEARS LATER, WHEN VIC WAS RULIN' A COUNTRY AND BEIN' A TIN THORN IN OUR SIDES, REED'D SOMETIMES GIVE ME THIS FUNNY LOOK.
"LIKE, NO MATTER HOW CRAZY THINGS GOT WITH BIG BAD DOCTOR DOOM, WE ALWAYS HAD THAT LITTLE MOMENT BETWEEN US.

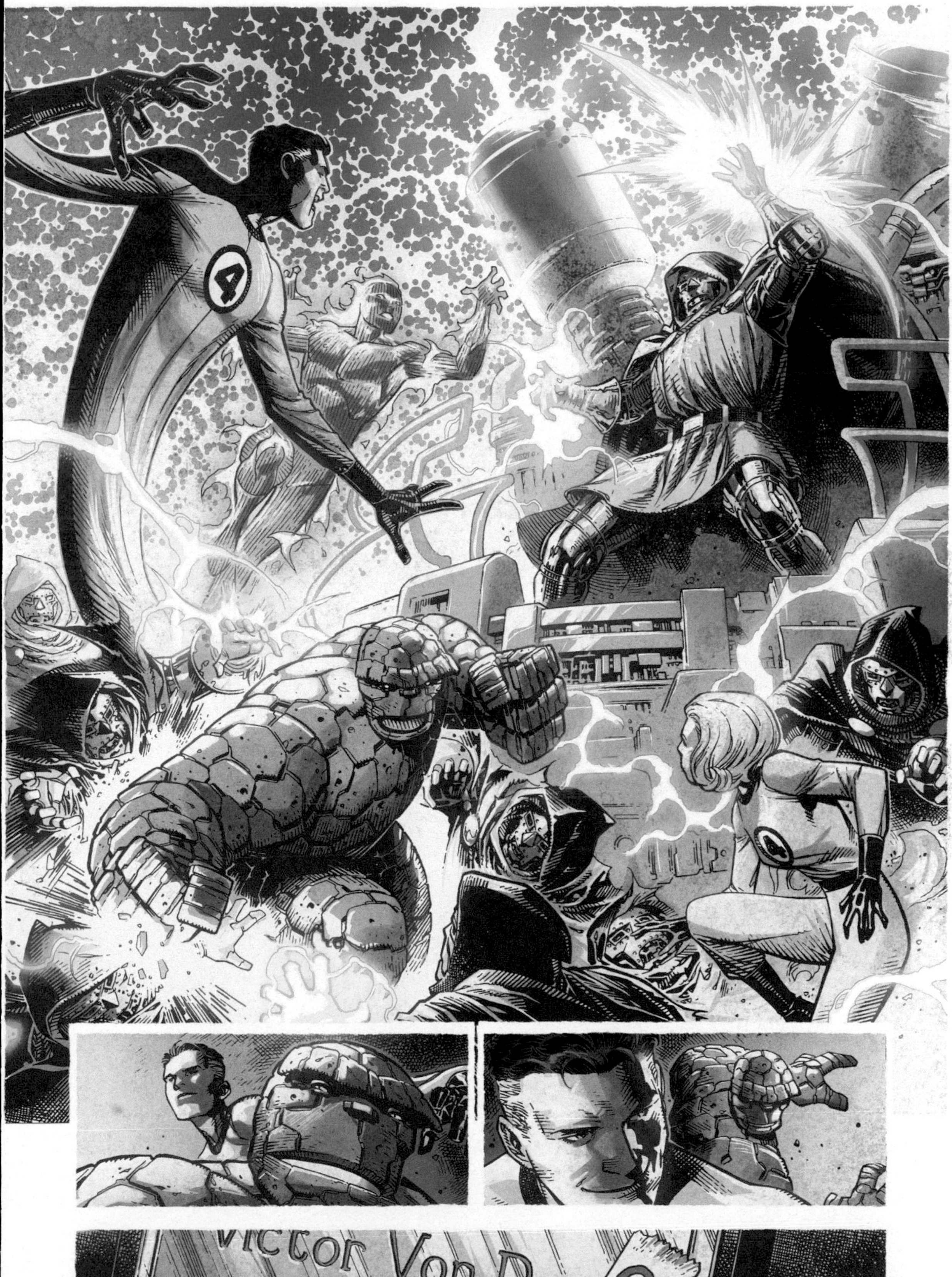
Victor Von Doo
1998
"THE THING REED CALLED 'OUR FIRST ADVENTURE TOGETHER.'"

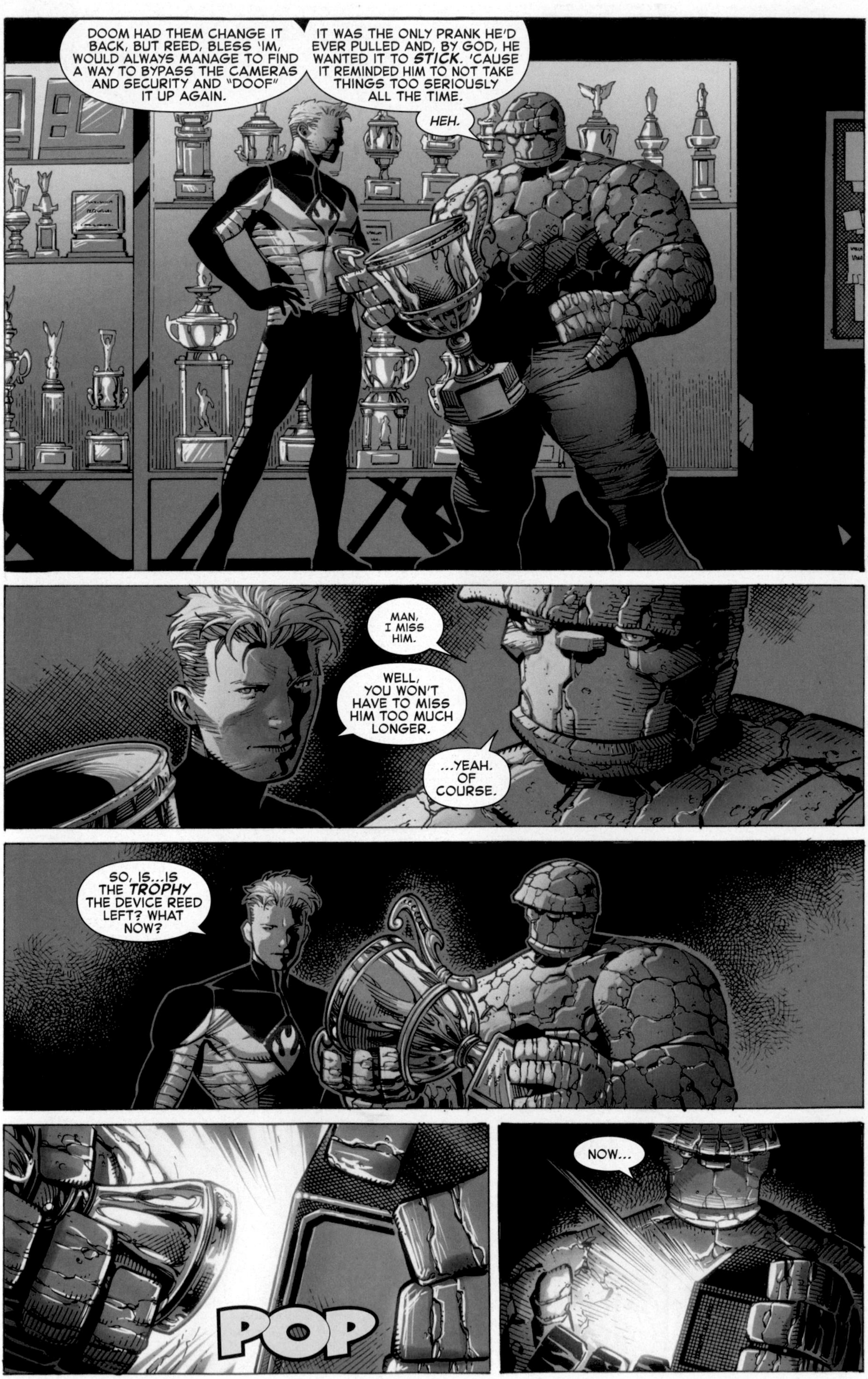
DOOM HAD THEM CHANGE IT BACK, BUT REED, BLESS 'IM, WOULD ALWAYS MANAGE TO FIND A WAY TO BYPASS THE CAMERAS AND SECURITY AND "DOOF" IT UP AGAIN.
IT WAS THE ONLY PRANK HE'D EVER PULLED AND, BY GOD, HE WANTED IT TO STICK. 'CAUSE IT REMINDED HIM TO NOT TAKE THINGS TOO SERIOUSLY ALL THE TIME.
HEH.
MAN, I MISS HIM.
WELL, YOU WON'T HAVE TO MISS HIM TOO MUCH LONGER.
...YEAH. OF COURSE.
SO, IS...IS THE TROPHY THE DEVICE REED LEFT? WHAT NOW?
POP
NOW...

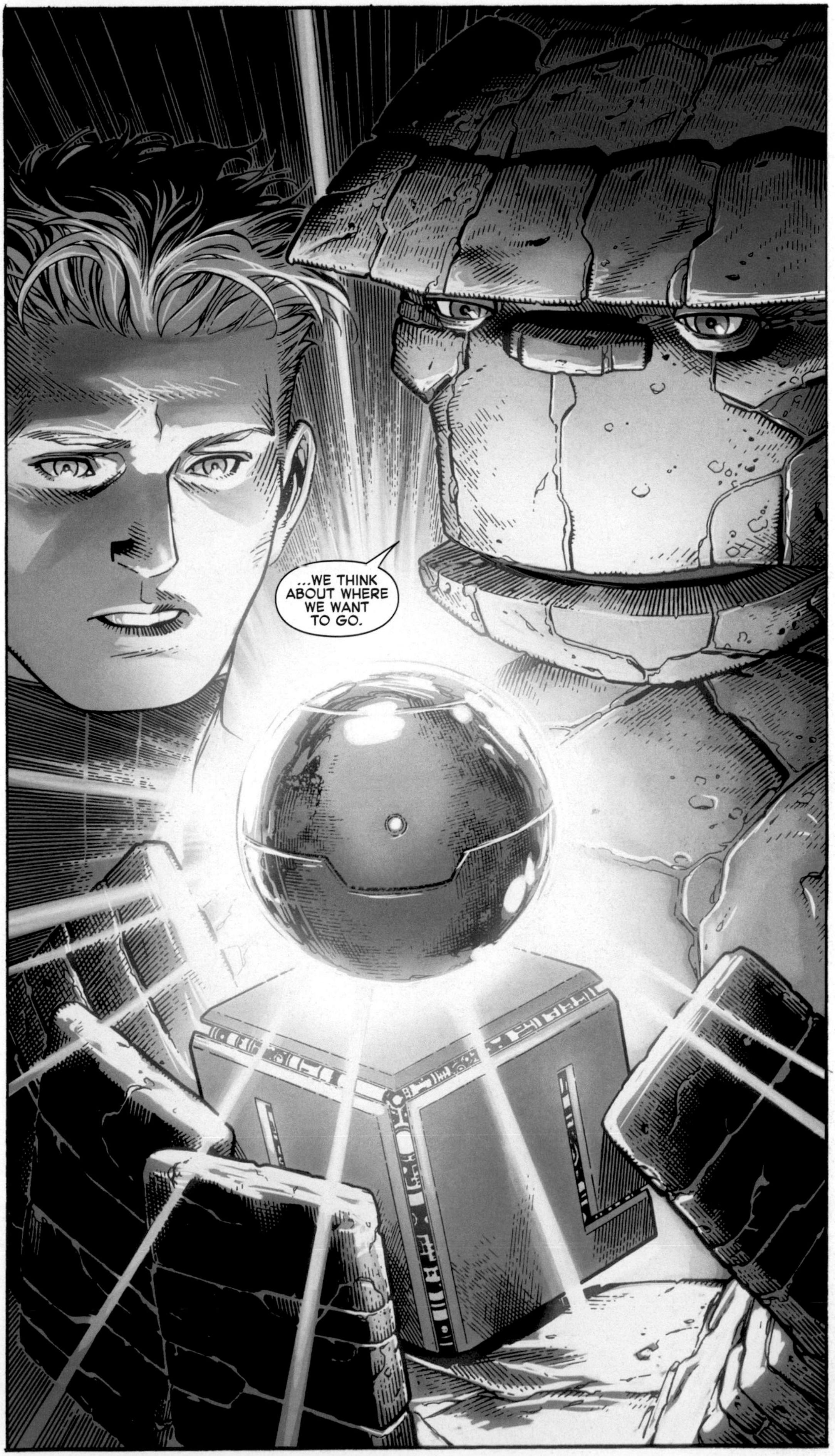
...WE THINK ABOUT WHERE WE WANT TO GO.

3

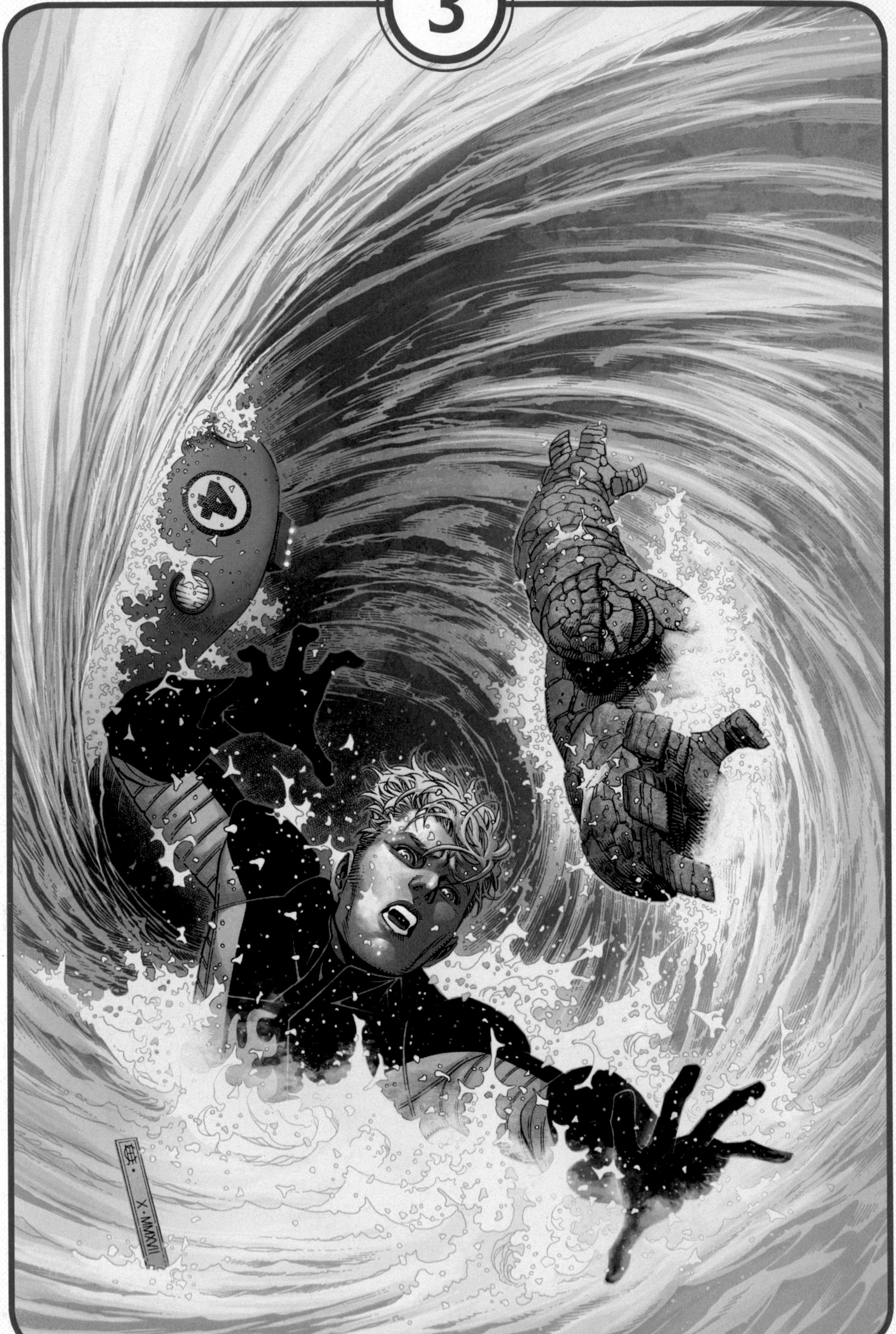
X · MMXVII

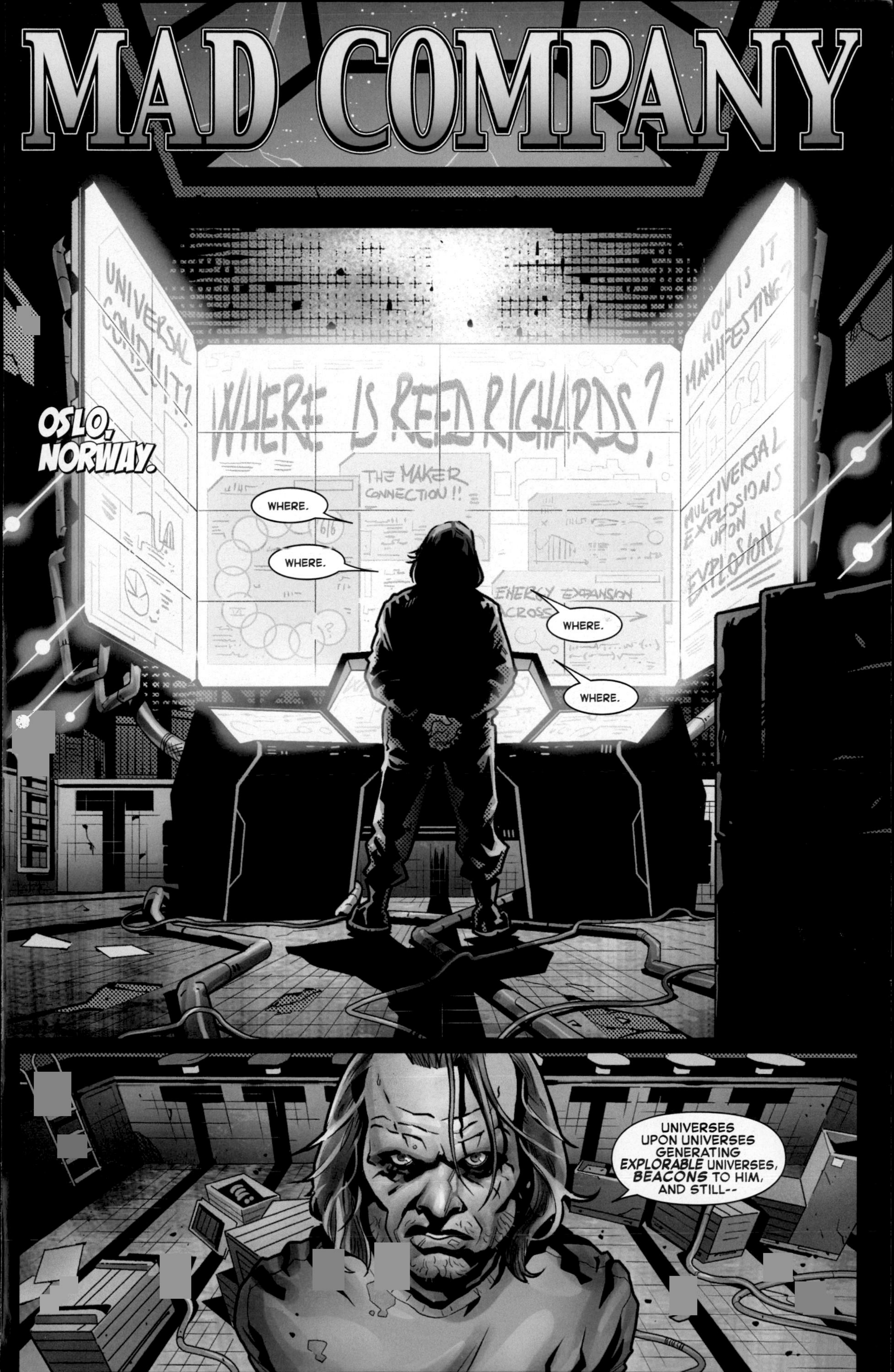
MAD COMPANY
OSLO, NORWAY.
UNIVERSAL CONDUIT!
WHERE IS REED RICHARDS?
HOW IS IT MANIFESTING?
THE MAKER CONNECTION!!
MULTIVERSAL EXPLOSIONS UPON EXPLOSIONS
WHERE.
WHERE.
WHERE.
WHERE.
UNIVERSES UPON UNIVERSES GENERATING *EXPLORABLE* UNIVERSES, *BEACONS* TO HIM, AND STILL--

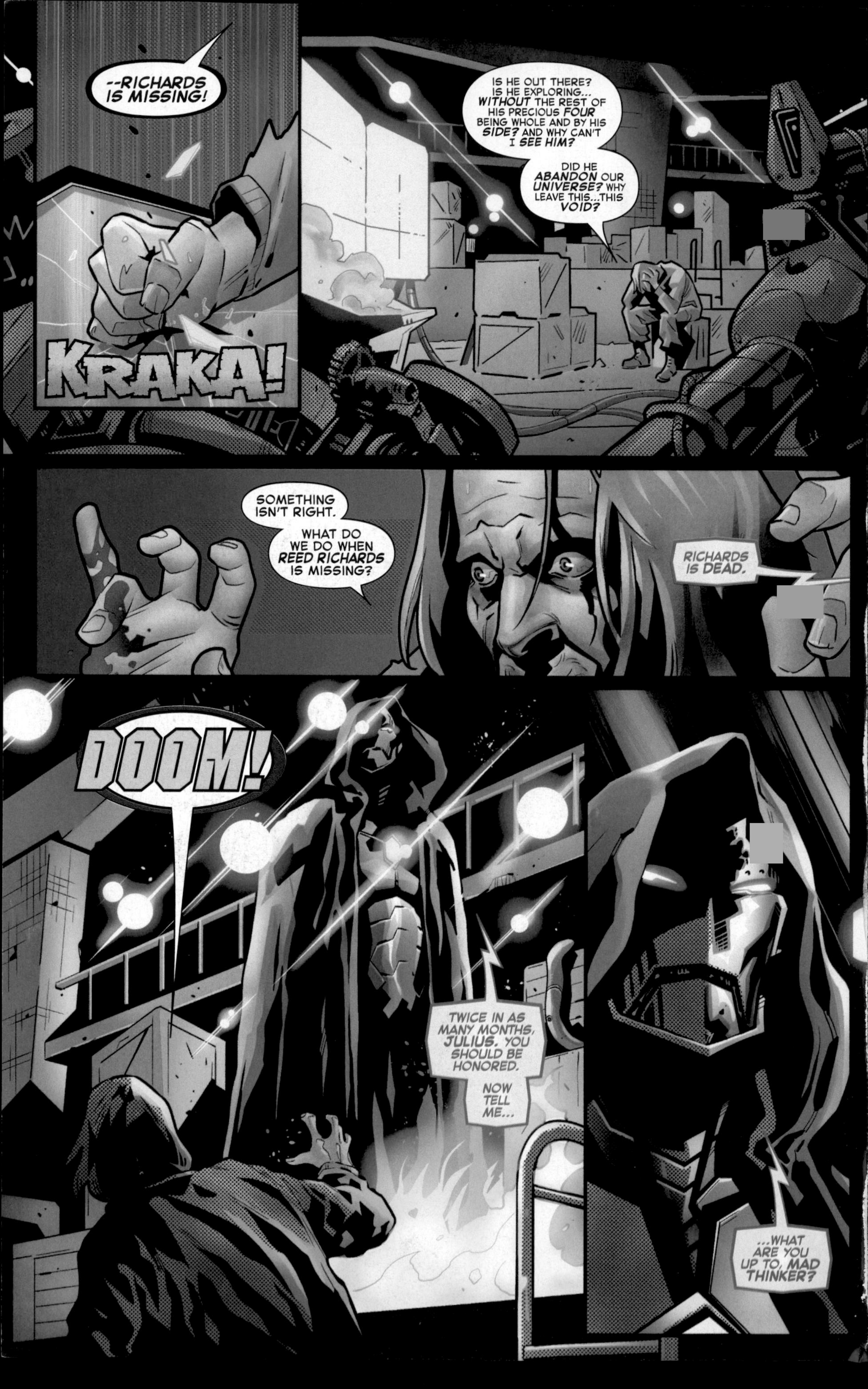
--RICHARDS IS MISSING!
KRAKA!
IS HE OUT THERE? IS HE EXPLORING... WITHOUT THE REST OF HIS PRECIOUS FOUR BEING WHOLE AND BY HIS SIDE? AND WHY CAN'T I SEE HIM?
DID HE ABANDON OUR UNIVERSE? WHY LEAVE THIS...THIS VOID?
SOMETHING ISN'T RIGHT.
WHAT DO WE DO WHEN REED RICHARDS IS MISSING?
RICHARDS IS DEAD.
DOOM!
TWICE IN AS MANY MONTHS, JULIUS. YOU SHOULD BE HONORED.
NOW TELL ME...
...WHAT ARE YOU UP TO, MAD THINKER?

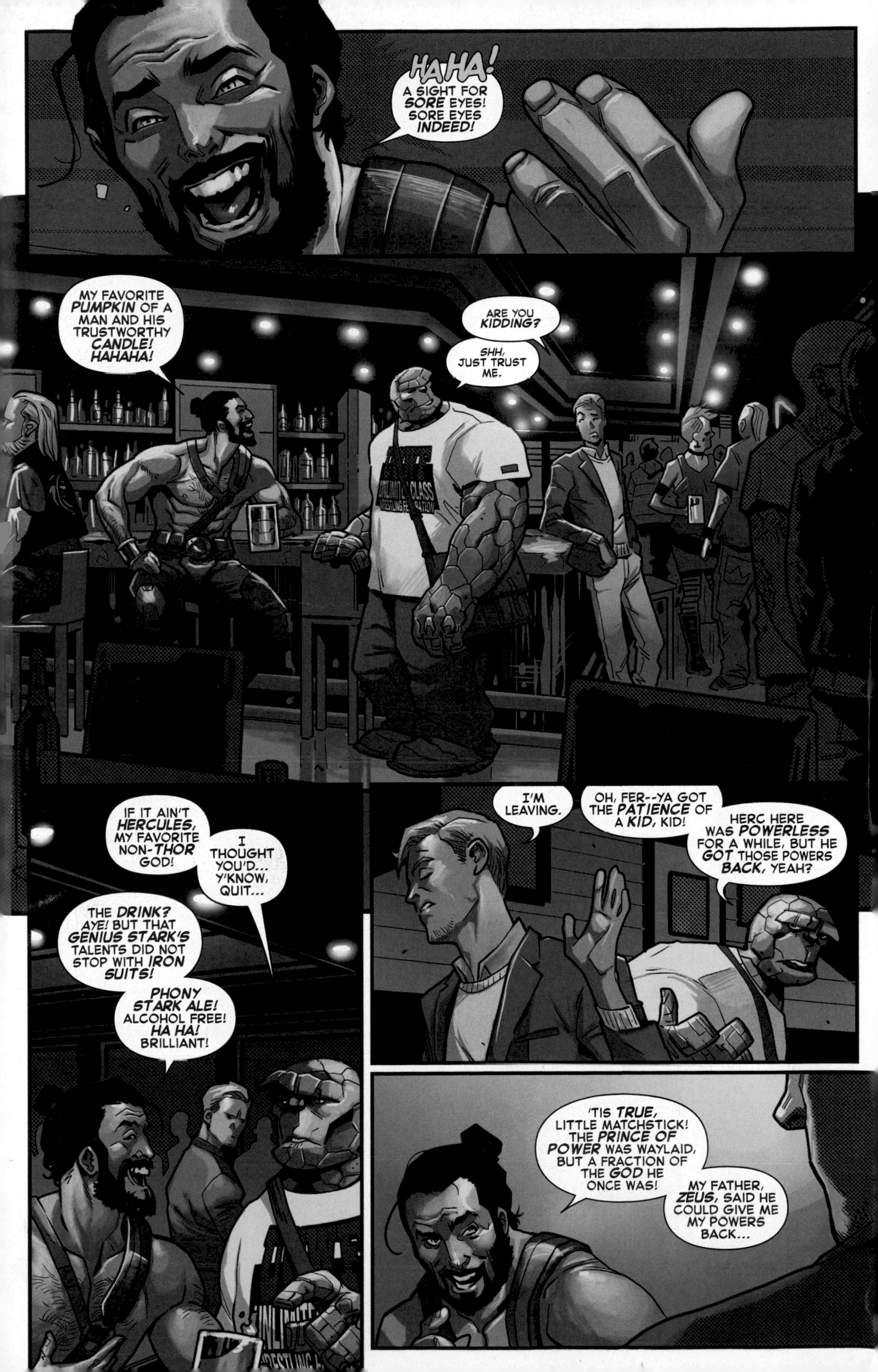
HAHA!
A SIGHT FOR SORE EYES! SORE EYES INDEED!
MY FAVORITE PUMPKIN OF A MAN AND HIS TRUSTWORTHY CANDLE! HAHAHA!
ARE YOU KIDDING?
SHH, JUST TRUST ME.
IF IT AIN'T HERCULES, MY FAVORITE NON-THOR GOD!
I THOUGHT YOU'D... Y'KNOW, QUIT...
THE DRINK? AYE! BUT THAT GENIUS STARK'S TALENTS DID NOT STOP WITH IRON SUITS!
PHONY STARK ALE! ALCOHOL FREE! HA HA! BRILLIANT!
I'M LEAVING.
OH, FER--YA GOT THE PATIENCE OF A KID, KID!
HERC HERE WAS POWERLESS FOR A WHILE, BUT HE GOT THOSE POWERS BACK, YEAH?
'TIS TRUE, LITTLE MATCHSTICK! THE PRINCE OF POWER WAS WAYLAID, BUT A FRACTION OF THE GOD HE ONCE WAS!
MY FATHER, ZEUS, SAID HE COULD GIVE ME MY POWERS BACK...

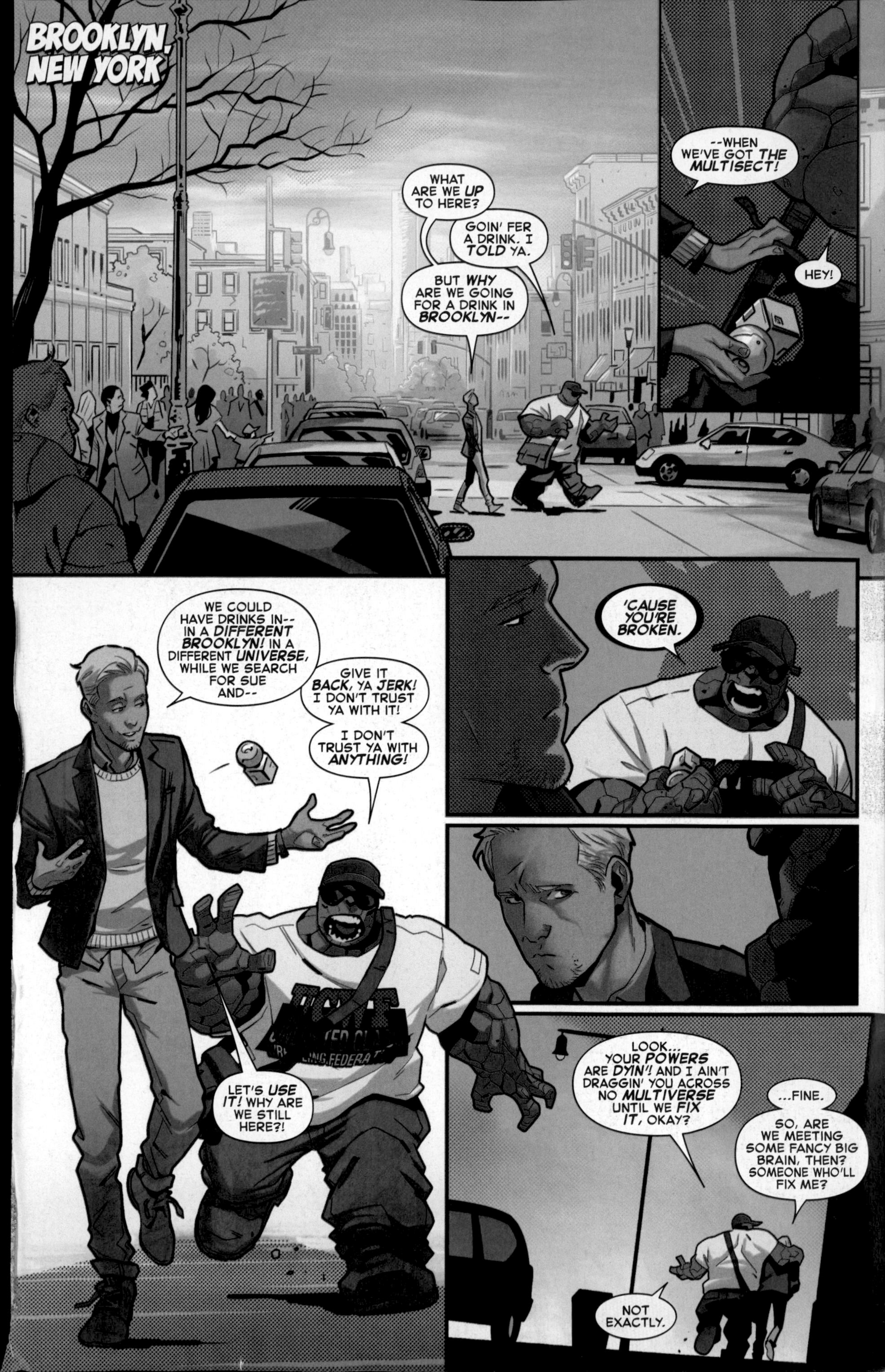
BROOKLYN, NEW YORK
WHAT ARE WE UP TO HERE?
GOIN' FER A DRINK. I TOLD YA.
BUT WHY ARE WE GOING FOR A DRINK IN BROOKLYN--
--WHEN WE'VE GOT THE MULTISECT!
HEY!
WE COULD HAVE DRINKS IN-- IN A DIFFERENT BROOKLYN! IN A DIFFERENT UNIVERSE, WHILE WE SEARCH FOR SUE AND--
GIVE IT BACK, YA JERK! I DON'T TRUST YA WITH IT!
I DON'T TRUST YA WITH ANYTHING!
LET'S USE IT! WHY ARE WE STILL HERE?!
'CAUSE YOU'RE BROKEN.
LOOK... YOUR POWERS ARE DYIN'! AND I AIN'T DRAGGIN' YOU ACROSS NO MULTIVERSE UNTIL WE FIX IT, OKAY?
...FINE.
SO, ARE WE MEETING SOME FANCY BIG BRAIN, THEN? SOMEONE WHO'LL FIX ME?
NOT EXACTLY.

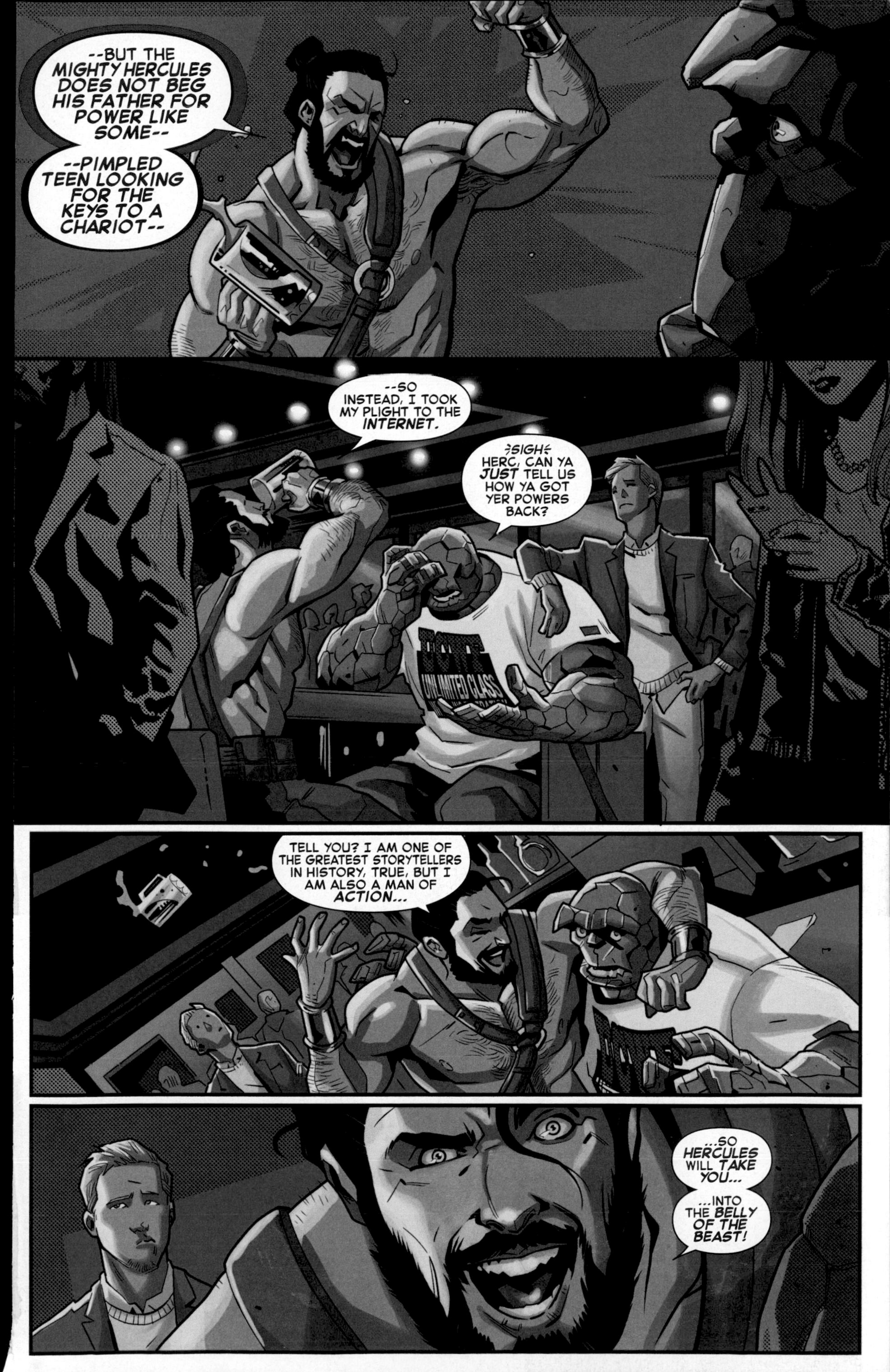
--BUT THE MIGHTY HERCULES DOES NOT BEG HIS FATHER FOR POWER LIKE SOME--
--PIMPLED TEEN LOOKING FOR THE KEYS TO A CHARIOT--
--SO INSTEAD, I TOOK MY PLIGHT TO THE INTERNET.
SIGH HERC, CAN YA JUST TELL US HOW YA GOT YER POWERS BACK?
UNLIMITED CLASS
TELL YOU? I AM ONE OF THE GREATEST STORYTELLERS IN HISTORY, TRUE, BUT I AM ALSO A MAN OF ACTION...
...SO HERCULES WILL TAKE YOU...
...INTO THE BELLY OF THE BEAST!

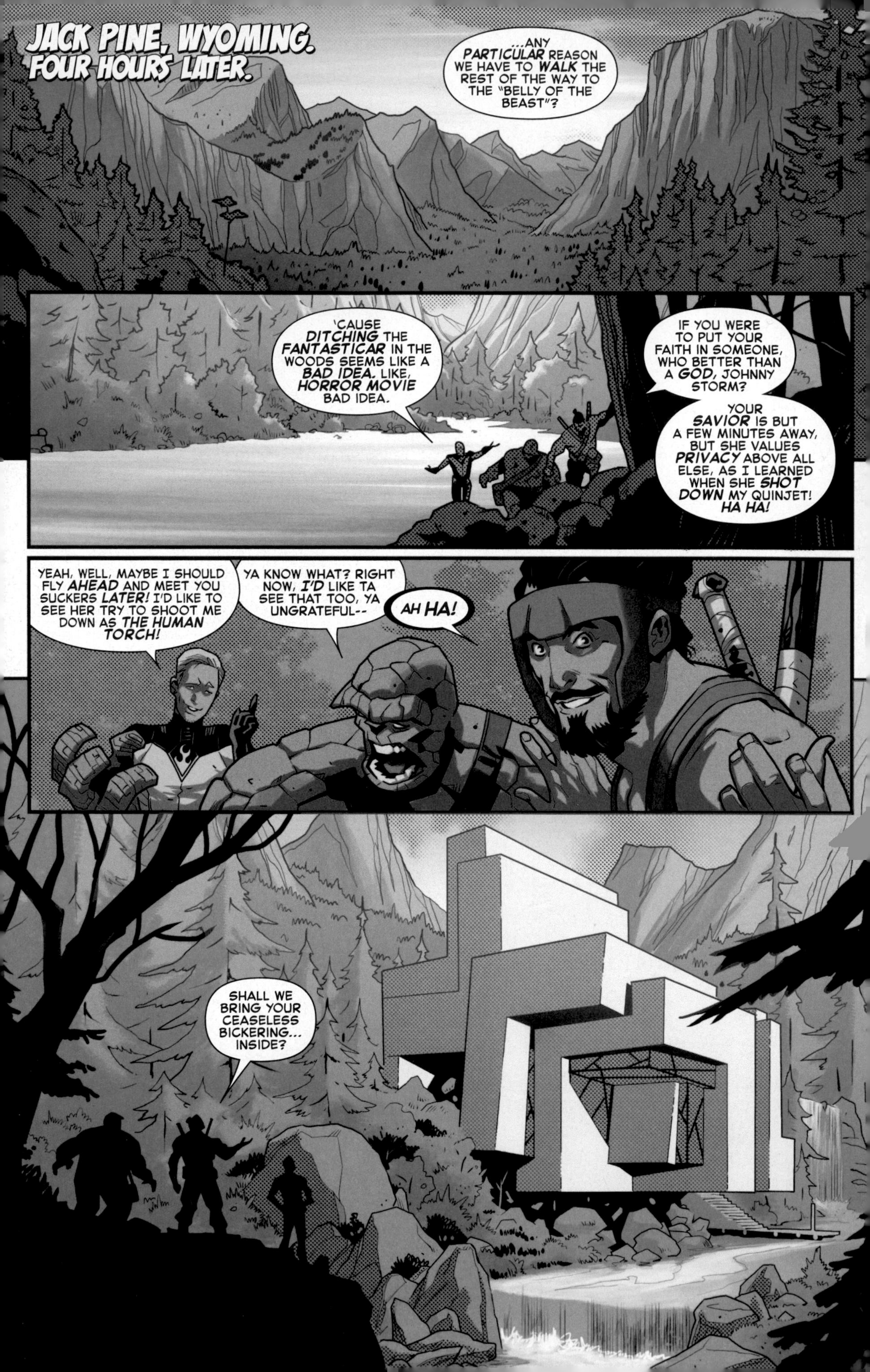

JACK PINE, WYOMING. FOUR HOURS LATER.
...ANY PARTICULAR REASON WE HAVE TO WALK THE REST OF THE WAY TO THE "BELLY OF THE BEAST"?
'CAUSE DITCHING THE FANTASTICAR IN THE WOODS SEEMS LIKE A BAD IDEA. LIKE, HORROR MOVIE BAD IDEA.
IF YOU WERE TO PUT YOUR FAITH IN SOMEONE, WHO BETTER THAN A GOD, JOHNNY STORM?
YOUR SAVIOR IS BUT A FEW MINUTES AWAY, BUT SHE VALUES PRIVACY ABOVE ALL ELSE, AS I LEARNED WHEN SHE SHOT DOWN MY QUINJET! HA HA!
YEAH, WELL, MAYBE I SHOULD FLY AHEAD AND MEET YOU SUCKERS LATER! I'D LIKE TO SEE HER TRY TO SHOOT ME DOWN AS THE HUMAN TORCH!
YA KNOW WHAT? RIGHT NOW, I'D LIKE TA SEE THAT TOO, YA UNGRATEFUL--
AH HA!
SHALL WE BRING YOUR CEASELESS BICKERING... INSIDE?

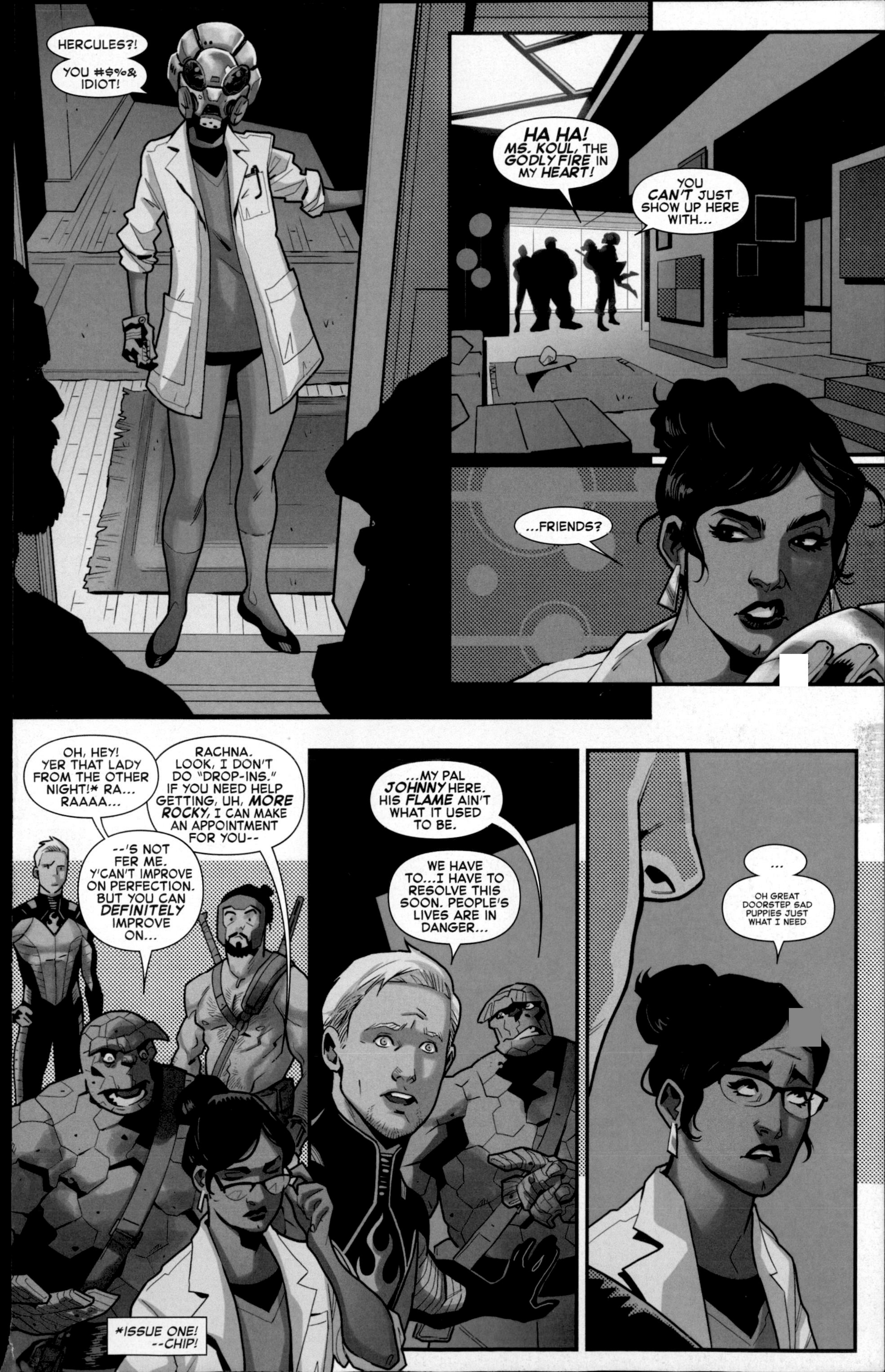
HERCULES?!
YOU #$%& IDIOT!
HA HA! MS. KOUL, THE GODLY FIRE IN MY HEART!
YOU CAN'T JUST SHOW UP HERE WITH...
...FRIENDS?
OH, HEY! YER THAT LADY FROM THE OTHER NIGHT!* RA... RAAAA...
RACHNA. LOOK, I DON'T DO "DROP-INS." IF YOU NEED HELP GETTING, UH, MORE ROCKY, I CAN MAKE AN APPOINTMENT FOR YOU--
--'S NOT FER ME. Y'CAN'T IMPROVE ON PERFECTION. BUT YOU CAN DEFINITELY IMPROVE ON...
*ISSUE ONE! --CHIP!
...MY PAL JOHNNY HERE. HIS FLAME AIN'T WHAT IT USED TO BE.
WE HAVE TO...I HAVE TO RESOLVE THIS SOON. PEOPLE'S LIVES ARE IN DANGER...
...
OH GREAT DOORSTEP SAD PUPPIES JUST WHAT I NEED

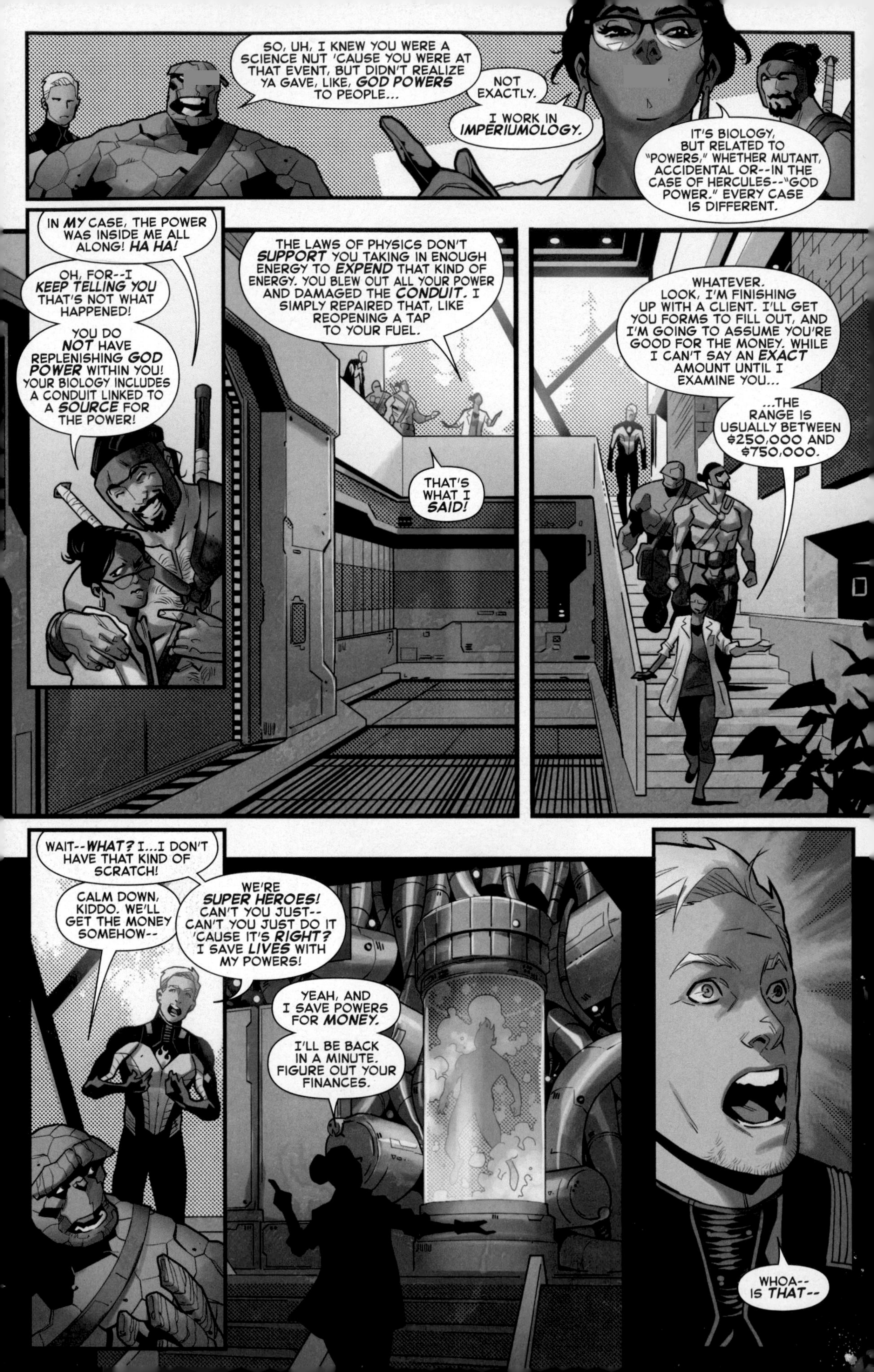
SO, UH, I KNEW YOU WERE A SCIENCE NUT 'CAUSE YOU WERE AT THAT EVENT, BUT DIDN'T REALIZE YA GAVE, LIKE, GOD POWERS TO PEOPLE...
NOT EXACTLY.
I WORK IN IMPERIUMOLOGY.
IT'S BIOLOGY, BUT RELATED TO "POWERS," WHETHER MUTANT, ACCIDENTAL OR--IN THE CASE OF HERCULES--"GOD POWER." EVERY CASE IS DIFFERENT.
IN MY CASE, THE POWER WAS INSIDE ME ALL ALONG! HA HA!
OH, FOR--I KEEP TELLING YOU THAT'S NOT WHAT HAPPENED!
YOU DO NOT HAVE REPLENISHING GOD POWER WITHIN YOU! YOUR BIOLOGY INCLUDES A CONDUIT LINKED TO A SOURCE FOR THE POWER!
THE LAWS OF PHYSICS DON'T SUPPORT YOU TAKING IN ENOUGH ENERGY TO EXPEND THAT KIND OF ENERGY. YOU BLEW OUT ALL YOUR POWER AND DAMAGED THE CONDUIT. I SIMPLY REPAIRED THAT, LIKE REOPENING A TAP TO YOUR FUEL.
THAT'S WHAT I SAID!
WHATEVER. LOOK, I'M FINISHING UP WITH A CLIENT. I'LL GET YOU FORMS TO FILL OUT, AND I'M GOING TO ASSUME YOU'RE GOOD FOR THE MONEY. WHILE I CAN'T SAY AN EXACT AMOUNT UNTIL I EXAMINE YOU...
...THE RANGE IS USUALLY BETWEEN $250,000 AND $750,000.
WAIT--WHAT? I...I DON'T HAVE THAT KIND OF SCRATCH!
CALM DOWN, KIDDO. WE'LL GET THE MONEY SOMEHOW--
WE'RE SUPER HEROES! CAN'T YOU JUST--CAN'T YOU JUST DO IT 'CAUSE IT'S RIGHT? I SAVE LIVES WITH MY POWERS!
YEAH, AND I SAVE POWERS FOR MONEY.
I'LL BE BACK IN A MINUTE. FIGURE OUT YOUR FINANCES.
WHOA--IS THAT--

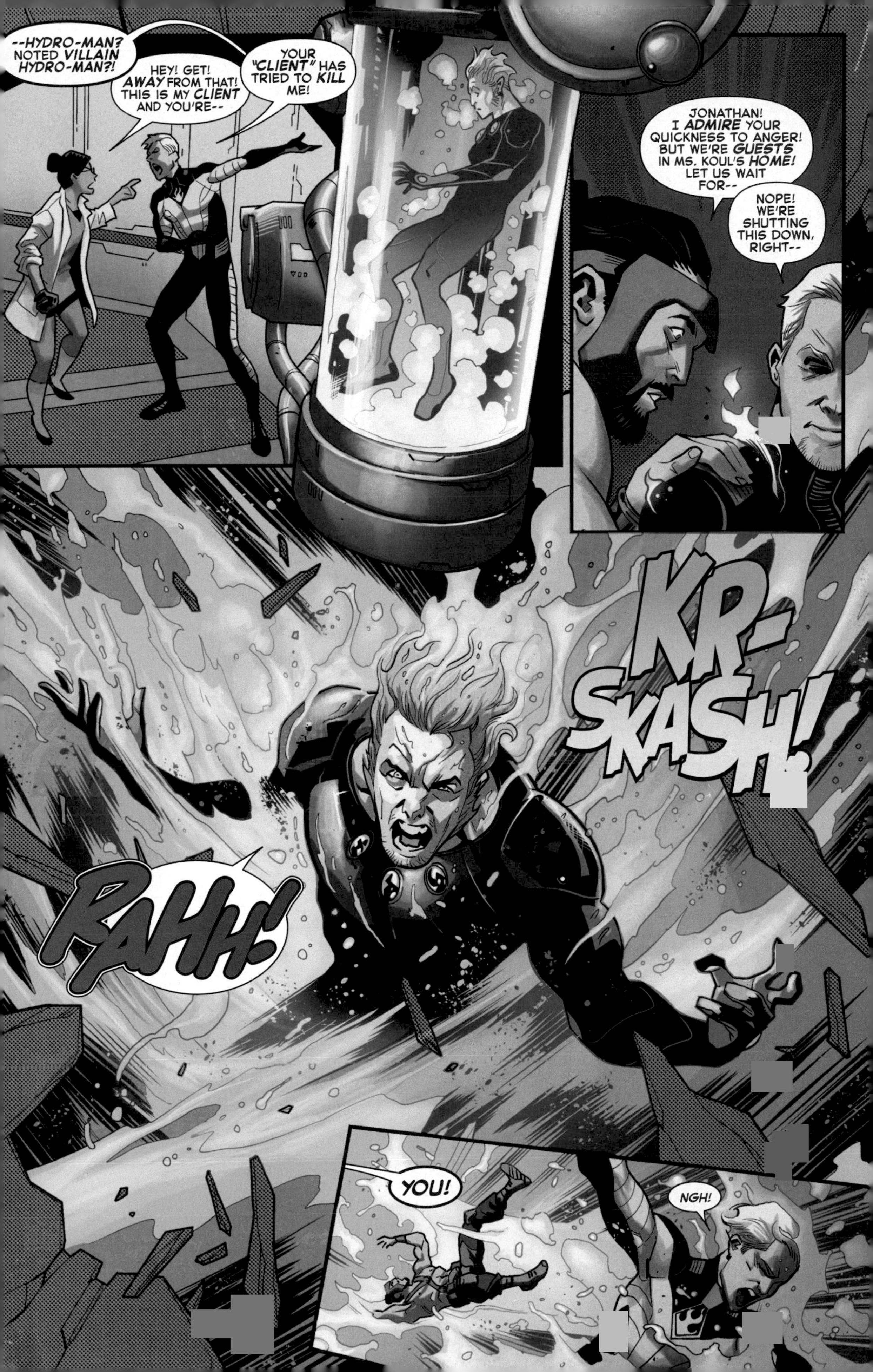
--HYDRO-MAN? NOTED VILLAIN HYDRO-MAN?!
HEY! GET! AWAY FROM THAT! THIS IS MY CLIENT AND YOU'RE--
YOUR "CLIENT" HAS TRIED TO KILL ME!
JONATHAN! I ADMIRE YOUR QUICKNESS TO ANGER! BUT WE'RE GUESTS IN MS. KOUL'S HOME! LET US WAIT FOR--
NOPE! WE'RE SHUTTING THIS DOWN, RIGHT--
KR-SKASH!
RAHH!
YOU!
NGH!

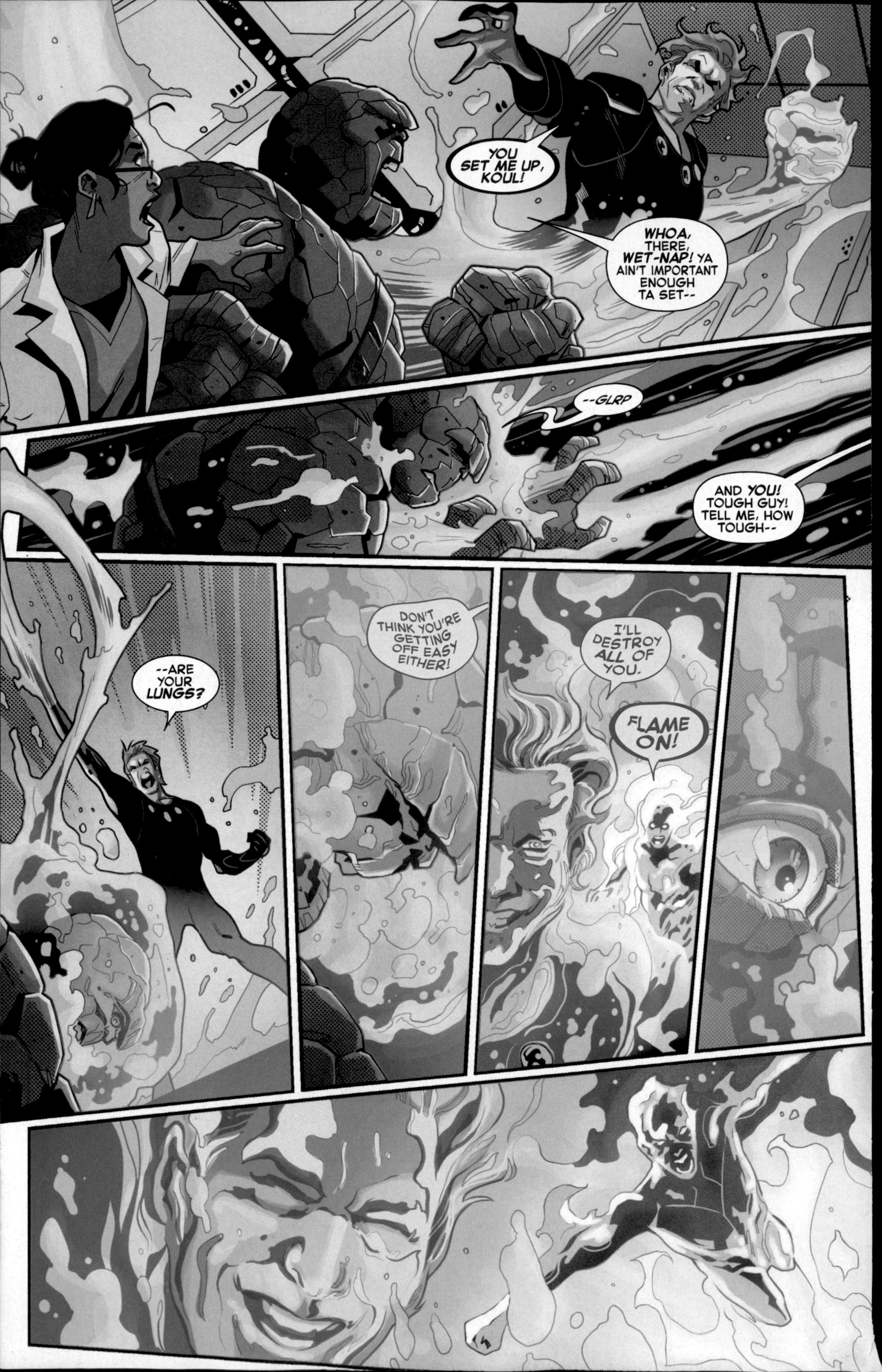
YOU SET ME UP, KOUL!
WHOA, THERE, WET-NAP! YA AIN'T IMPORTANT ENOUGH TA SET--
--GLRP
AND YOU! TOUGH GUY! TELL ME, HOW TOUGH--
--ARE YOUR LUNGS?
DON'T THINK YOU'RE GETTING OFF EASY EITHER!
I'LL DESTROY ALL OF YOU.
FLAME ON!

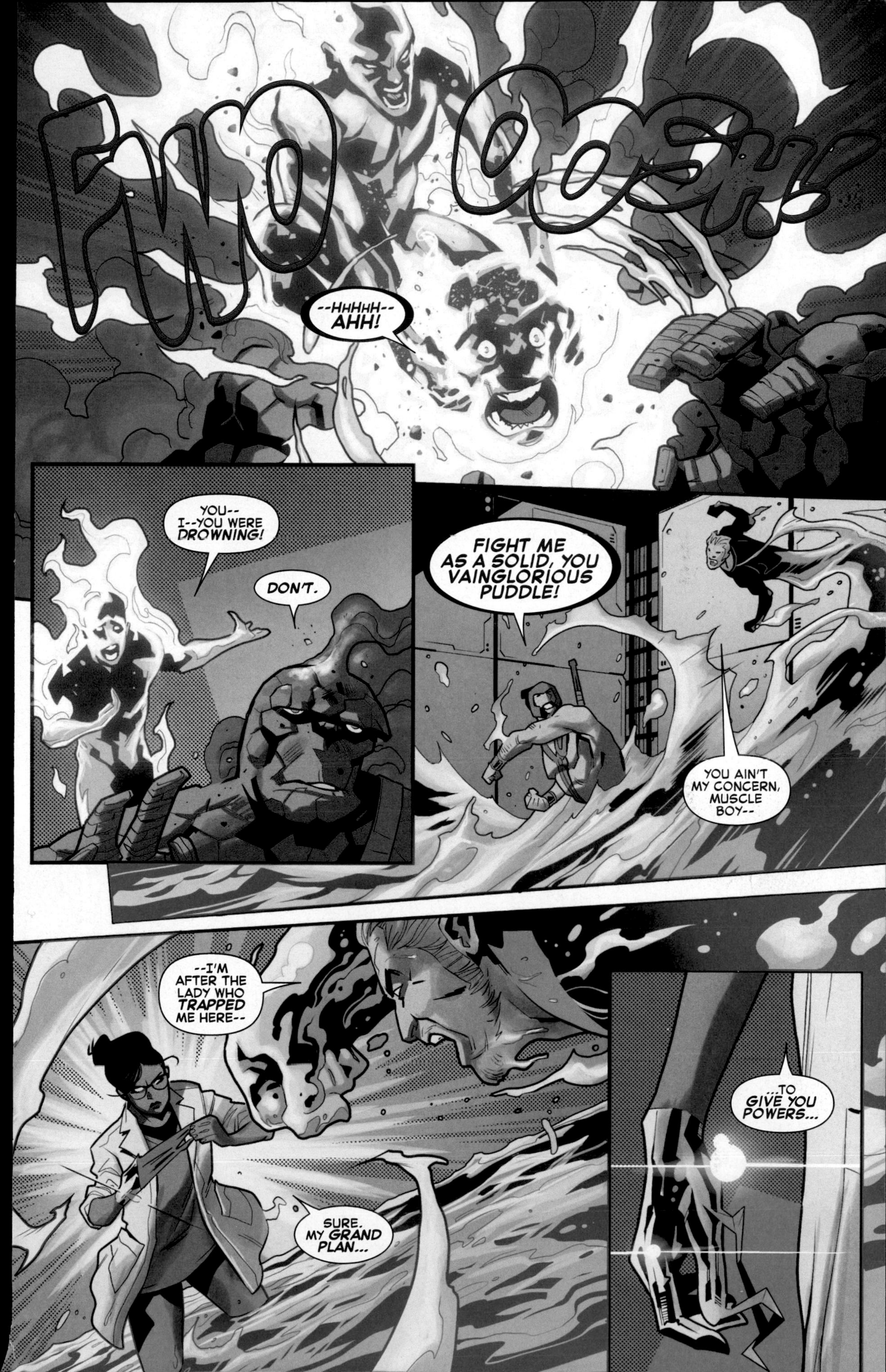
FWOOOOSH!
--HHHHH--
AHH!
YOU--
I--YOU WERE DROWNING!
DON'T.
FIGHT ME AS A SOLID, YOU VAINGLORIOUS PUDDLE!
YOU AIN'T MY CONCERN, MUSCLE BOY--
--I'M AFTER THE LADY WHO TRAPPED ME HERE--
SURE. MY GRAND PLAN...
...TO GIVE YOU POWERS...

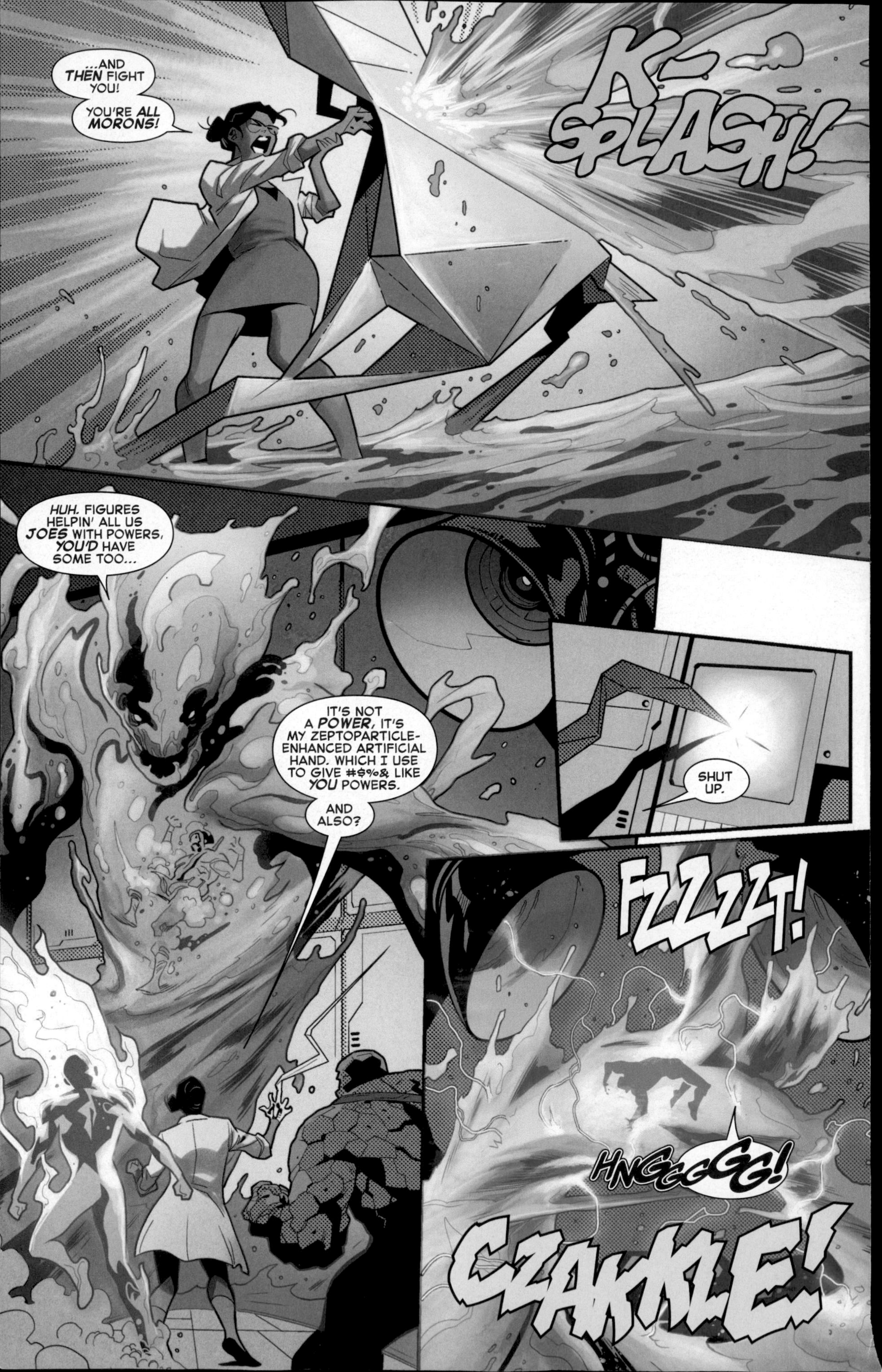
...AND THEN FIGHT YOU!
YOU'RE ALL MORONS!
K-SPLASH!
HUH. FIGURES HELPIN' ALL US JOES WITH POWERS, YOU'D HAVE SOME TOO...
IT'S NOT A POWER, IT'S MY ZEPTOPARTICLE-ENHANCED ARTIFICIAL HAND. WHICH I USE TO GIVE #$%& LIKE YOU POWERS.
AND ALSO?
SHUT UP.
FZZZZT!
HNGGGGG!
CZAKKLE!

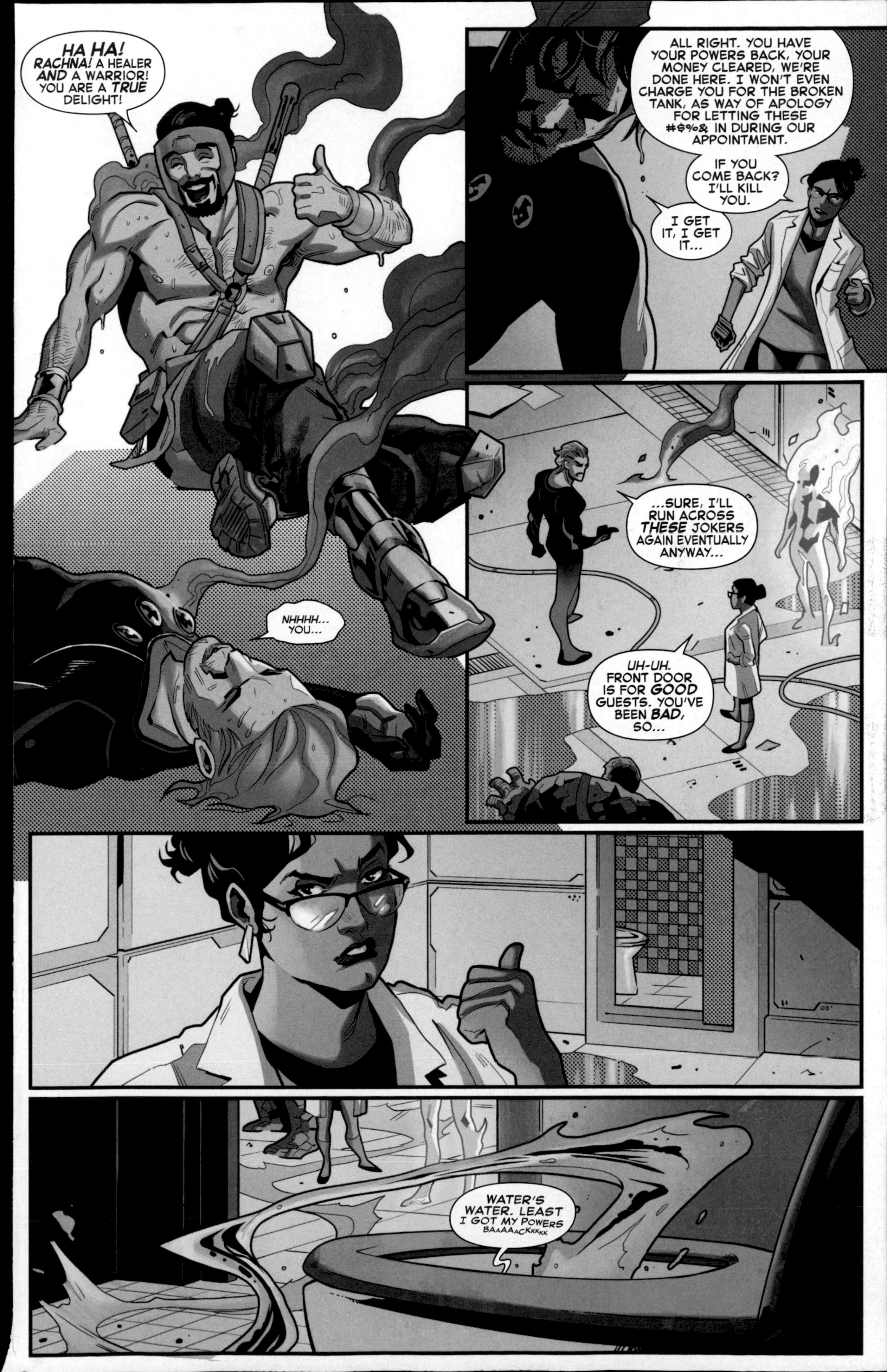

HA HA! RACHNA! A HEALER AND A WARRIOR! YOU ARE A TRUE DELIGHT!
NHHHH... YOU...
ALL RIGHT. YOU HAVE YOUR POWERS BACK, YOUR MONEY CLEARED, WE'RE DONE HERE. I WON'T EVEN CHARGE YOU FOR THE BROKEN TANK, AS WAY OF APOLOGY FOR LETTING THESE #$%& IN DURING OUR APPOINTMENT.
IF YOU COME BACK? I'LL KILL YOU.
I GET IT, I GET IT...
...SURE, I'LL RUN ACROSS THESE JOKERS AGAIN EVENTUALLY ANYWAY...
UH-UH. FRONT DOOR IS FOR GOOD GUESTS. YOU'VE BEEN BAD, SO...
WATER'S WATER. LEAST I GOT MY POWERS BAAAAACKKKKK

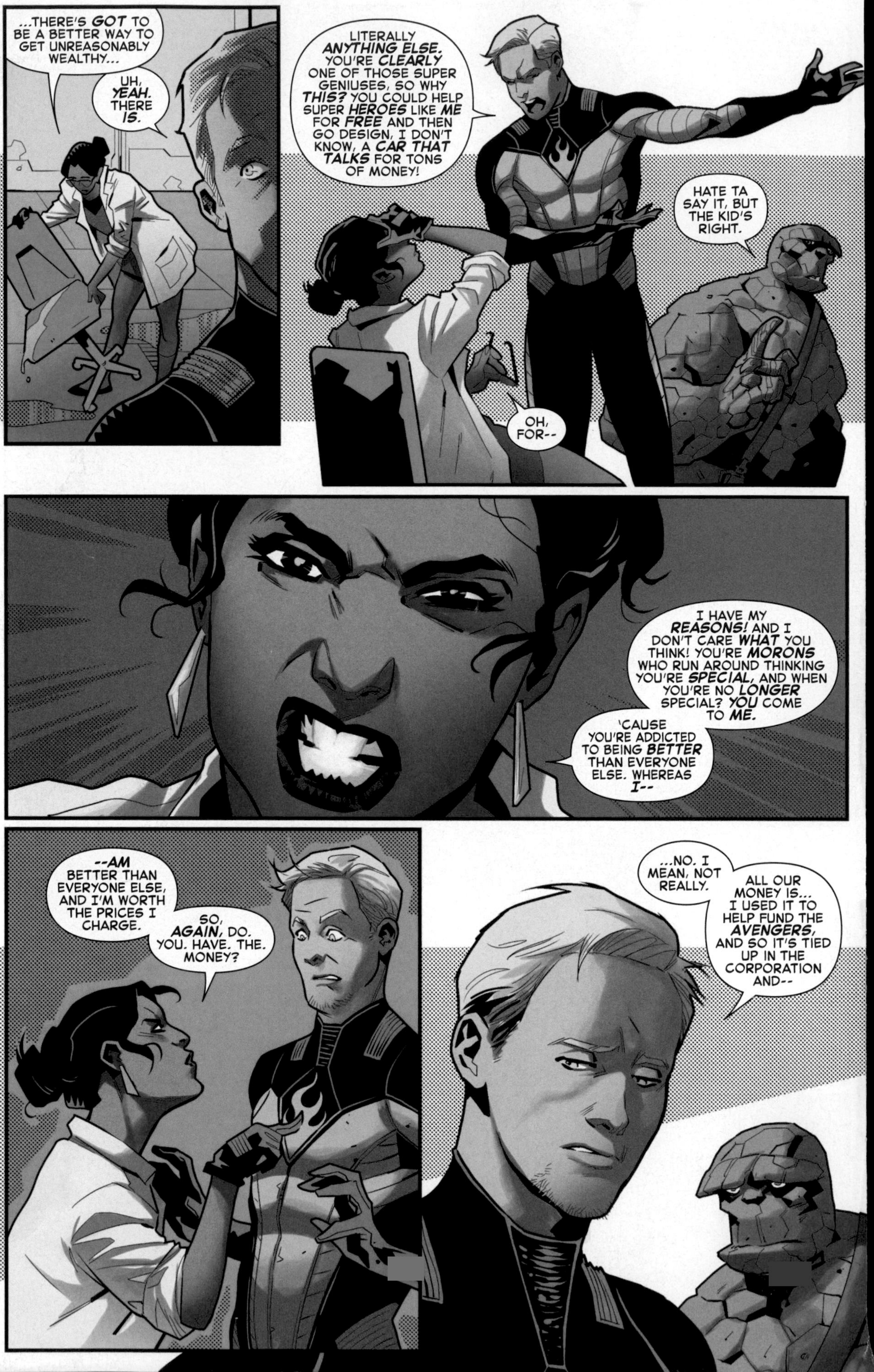
...THERE'S GOT TO BE A BETTER WAY TO GET UNREASONABLY WEALTHY...
UH, YEAH. THERE IS.
LITERALLY ANYTHING ELSE. YOU'RE CLEARLY ONE OF THOSE SUPER GENIUSES, SO WHY THIS? YOU COULD HELP SUPER HEROES LIKE ME FOR FREE AND THEN GO DESIGN, I DON'T KNOW, A CAR THAT TALKS FOR TONS OF MONEY!
HATE TA SAY IT, BUT THE KID'S RIGHT.
OH, FOR--
I HAVE MY REASONS! AND I DON'T CARE WHAT YOU THINK! YOU'RE MORONS WHO RUN AROUND THINKING YOU'RE SPECIAL, AND WHEN YOU'RE NO LONGER SPECIAL? YOU COME TO ME.
'CAUSE YOU'RE ADDICTED TO BEING BETTER THAN EVERYONE ELSE. WHEREAS I--
--AM BETTER THAN EVERYONE ELSE, AND I'M WORTH THE PRICES I CHARGE.
SO, AGAIN, DO. YOU. HAVE. THE. MONEY?
...NO. I MEAN, NOT REALLY.
ALL OUR MONEY IS... I USED IT TO HELP FUND THE AVENGERS, AND SO IT'S TIED UP IN THE CORPORATION AND--

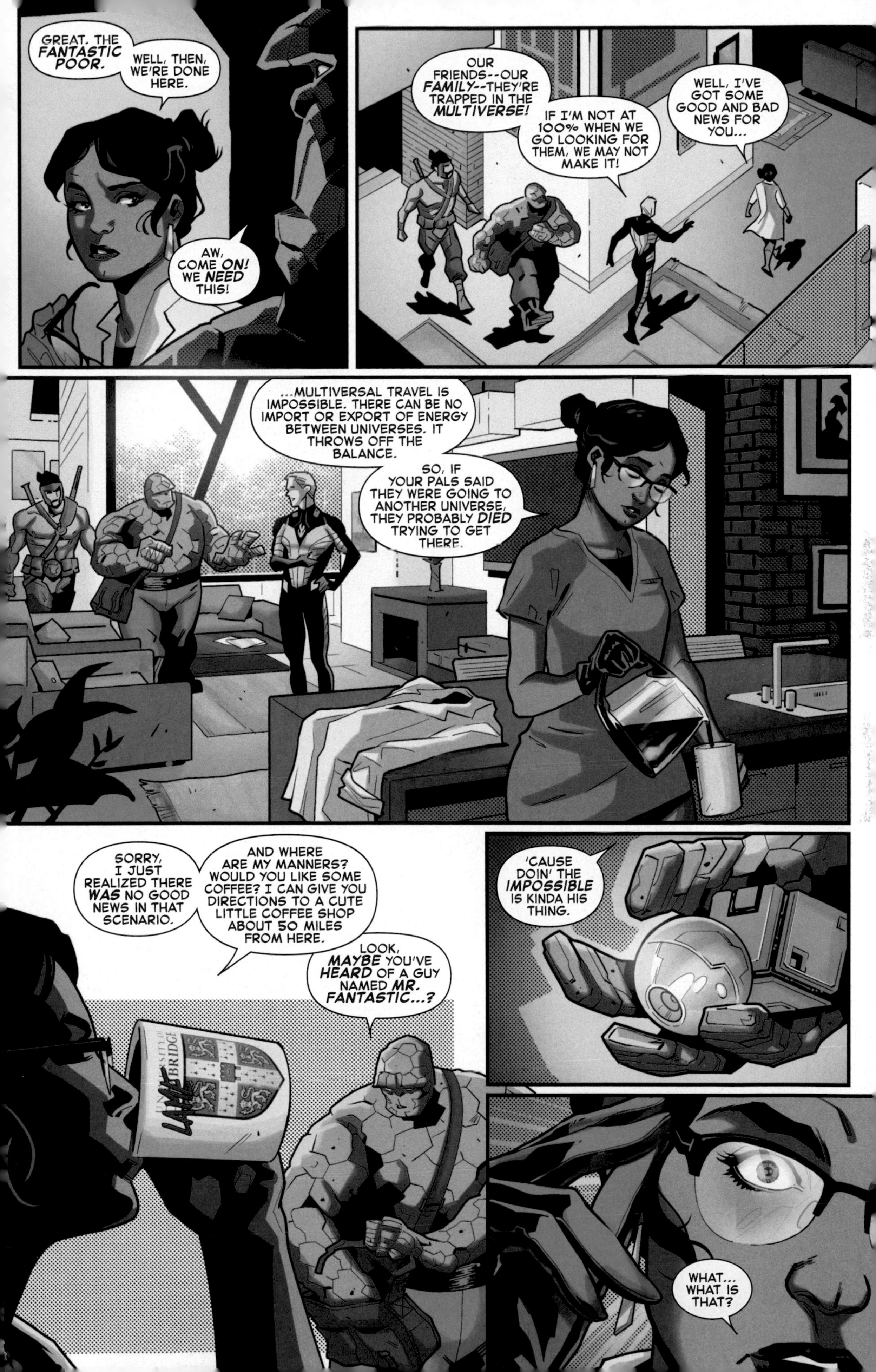
GREAT. THE FANTASTIC POOR.
WELL, THEN, WE'RE DONE HERE.
AW, COME ON! WE NEED THIS!
OUR FRIENDS--OUR FAMILY--THEY'RE TRAPPED IN THE MULTIVERSE!
IF I'M NOT AT 100% WHEN WE GO LOOKING FOR THEM, WE MAY NOT MAKE IT!
WELL, I'VE GOT SOME GOOD AND BAD NEWS FOR YOU...
...MULTIVERSAL TRAVEL IS IMPOSSIBLE. THERE CAN BE NO IMPORT OR EXPORT OF ENERGY BETWEEN UNIVERSES. IT THROWS OFF THE BALANCE.
SO, IF YOUR PALS SAID THEY WERE GOING TO ANOTHER UNIVERSE, THEY PROBABLY DIED TRYING TO GET THERE.
SORRY, I JUST REALIZED THERE WAS NO GOOD NEWS IN THAT SCENARIO.
AND WHERE ARE MY MANNERS? WOULD YOU LIKE SOME COFFEE? I CAN GIVE YOU DIRECTIONS TO A CUTE LITTLE COFFEE SHOP ABOUT 50 MILES FROM HERE.
LOOK, MAYBE YOU'VE HEARD OF A GUY NAMED MR. FANTASTIC...?
LAME
'CAUSE DOIN' THE IMPOSSIBLE IS KINDA HIS THING.
WHAT... WHAT IS THAT?

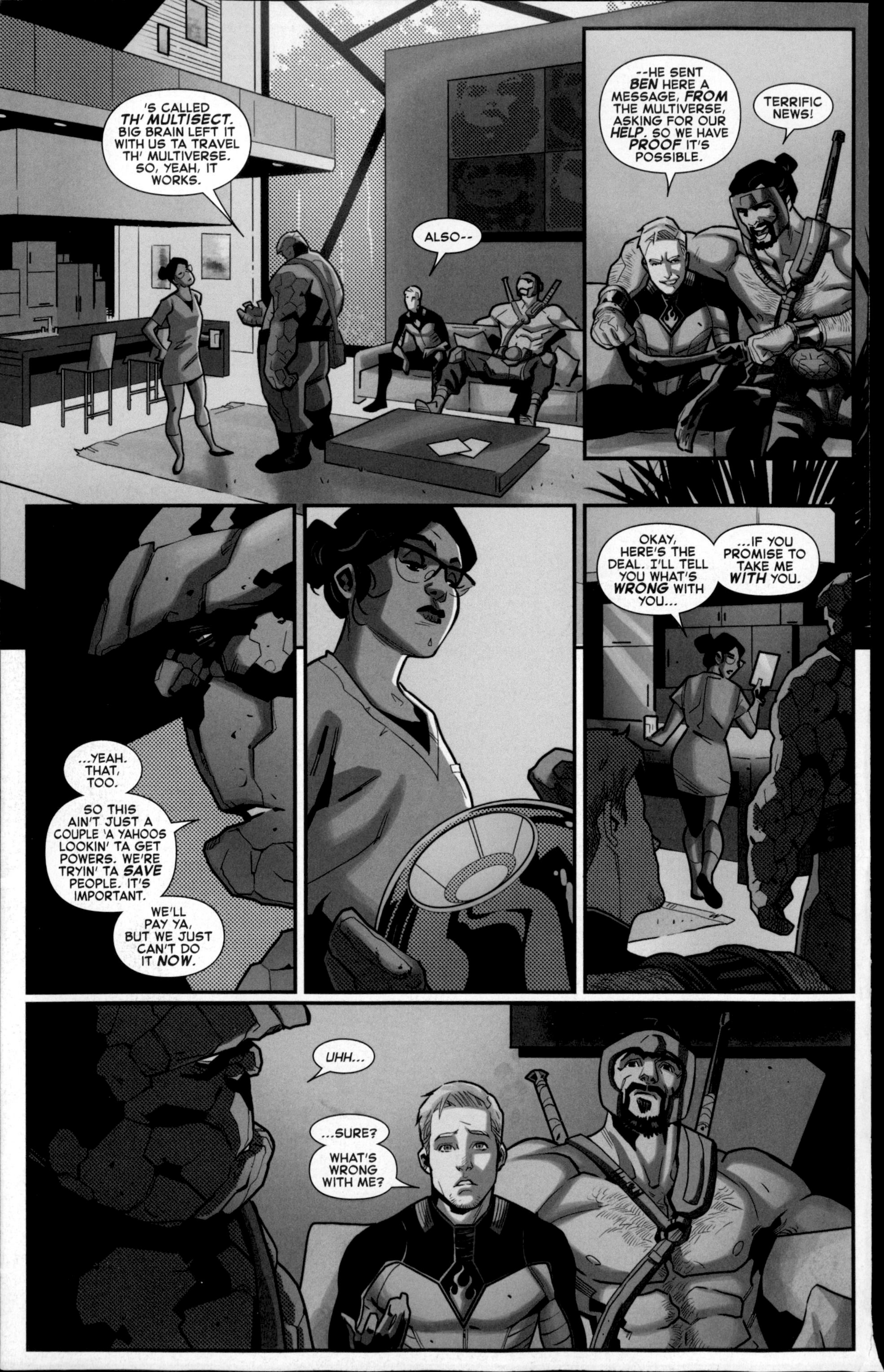

'S CALLED TH' MULTISECT. BIG BRAIN LEFT IT WITH US TA TRAVEL TH' MULTIVERSE. SO, YEAH, IT WORKS.
ALSO--
--HE SENT BEN HERE A MESSAGE, FROM THE MULTIVERSE, ASKING FOR OUR HELP. SO WE HAVE PROOF IT'S POSSIBLE.
TERRIFIC NEWS!
...YEAH. THAT, TOO.
SO THIS AIN'T JUST A COUPLE 'A YAHOOS LOOKIN' TA GET POWERS. WE'RE TRYIN' TA SAVE PEOPLE. IT'S IMPORTANT.
WE'LL PAY YA, BUT WE JUST CAN'T DO IT NOW.
OKAY, HERE'S THE DEAL. I'LL TELL YOU WHAT'S WRONG WITH YOU...
...IF YOU PROMISE TO TAKE ME WITH YOU.
UHH...
...SURE?
WHAT'S WRONG WITH ME?

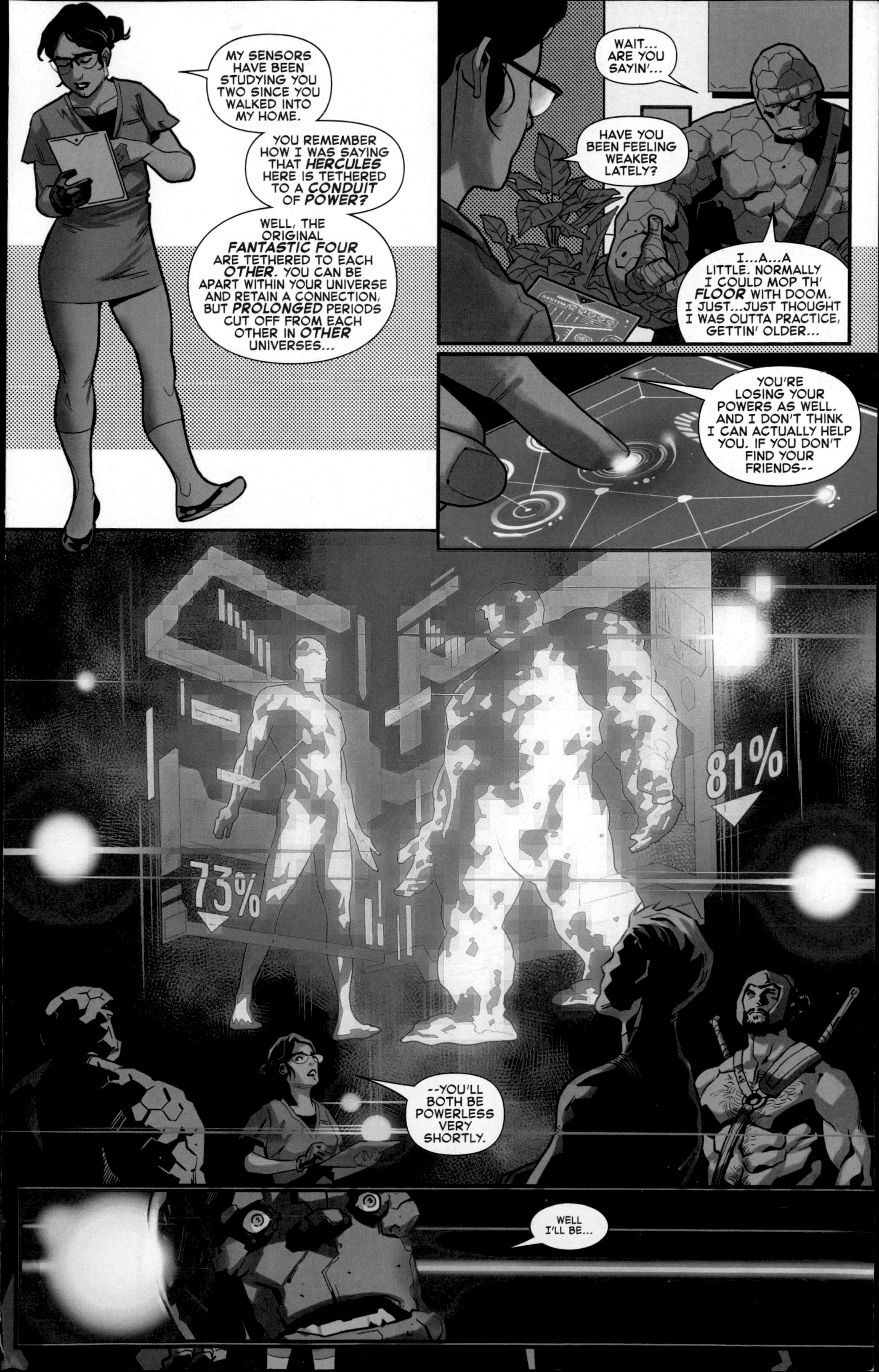
MY SENSORS HAVE BEEN STUDYING YOU TWO SINCE YOU WALKED INTO MY HOME.
YOU REMEMBER HOW I WAS SAYING THAT HERCULES HERE IS TETHERED TO A CONDUIT OF POWER?
WELL, THE ORIGINAL FANTASTIC FOUR ARE TETHERED TO EACH OTHER. YOU CAN BE APART WITHIN YOUR UNIVERSE AND RETAIN A CONNECTION, BUT PROLONGED PERIODS CUT OFF FROM EACH OTHER IN OTHER UNIVERSES...
WAIT... ARE YOU SAYIN'...
HAVE YOU BEEN FEELING WEAKER LATELY?
I...A...A LITTLE. NORMALLY I COULD MOP TH' FLOOR WITH DOOM. I JUST...JUST THOUGHT I WAS OUTTA PRACTICE, GETTIN' OLDER...
YOU'RE LOSING YOUR POWERS AS WELL. AND I DON'T THINK I CAN ACTUALLY HELP YOU. IF YOU DON'T FIND YOUR FRIENDS--
81%
73%
--YOU'LL BOTH BE POWERLESS VERY SHORTLY.
WELL I'LL BE...

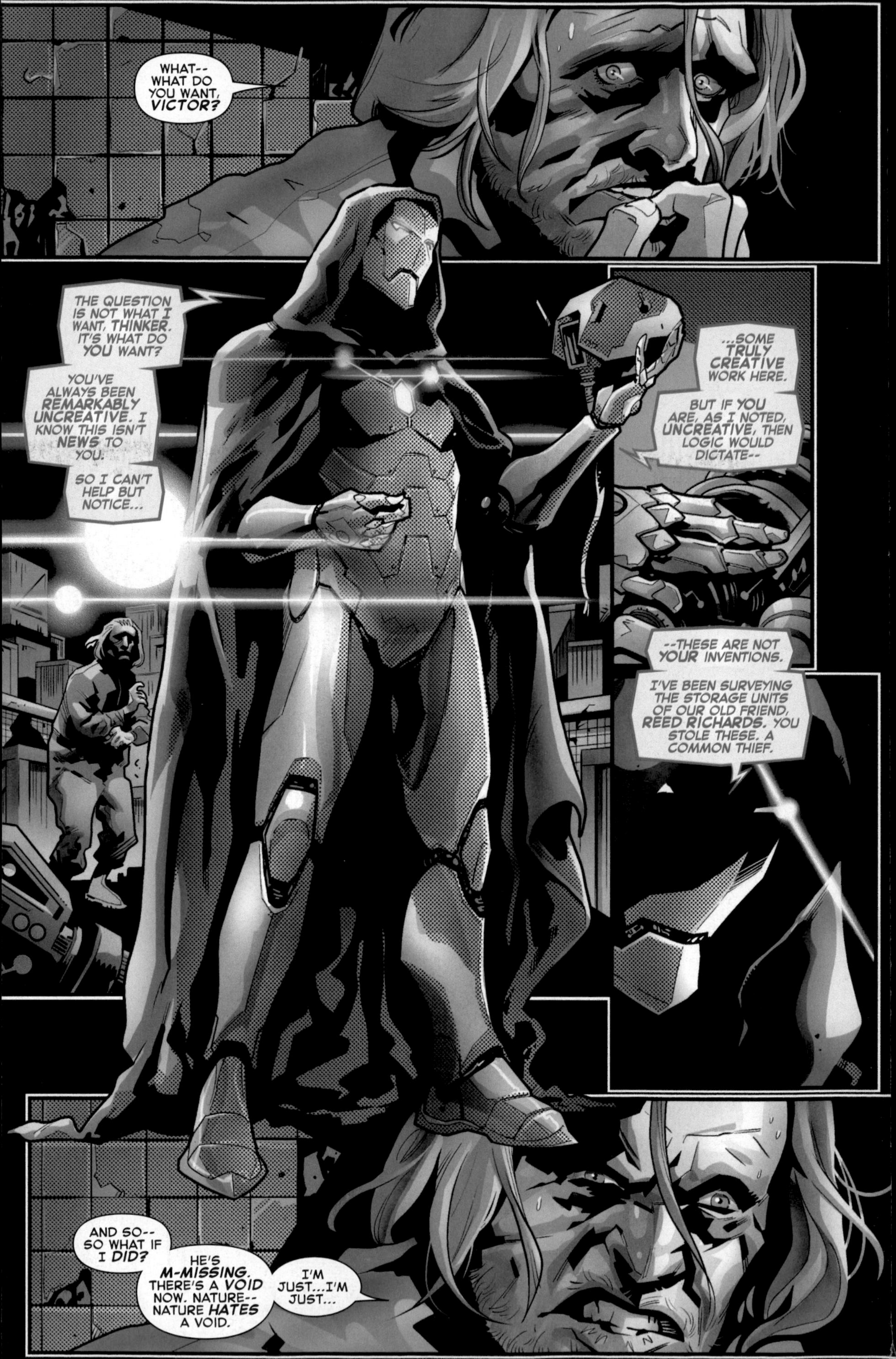

WHAT-- WHAT DO YOU WANT, VICTOR?
THE QUESTION IS NOT WHAT I WANT, THINKER. IT'S WHAT DO YOU WANT?
YOU'VE ALWAYS BEEN REMARKABLY UNCREATIVE. I KNOW THIS ISN'T NEWS TO YOU.
SO I CAN'T HELP BUT NOTICE...
...SOME TRULY CREATIVE WORK HERE.
BUT IF YOU ARE, AS I NOTED, UNCREATIVE, THEN LOGIC WOULD DICTATE--
--THESE ARE NOT YOUR INVENTIONS.
I'VE BEEN SURVEYING THE STORAGE UNITS OF OUR OLD FRIEND, REED RICHARDS. YOU STOLE THESE. A COMMON THIEF.
AND SO-- SO WHAT IF I DID?
HE'S M-MISSING. THERE'S A VOID NOW. NATURE-- NATURE HATES A VOID.
I'M JUST...I'M JUST...

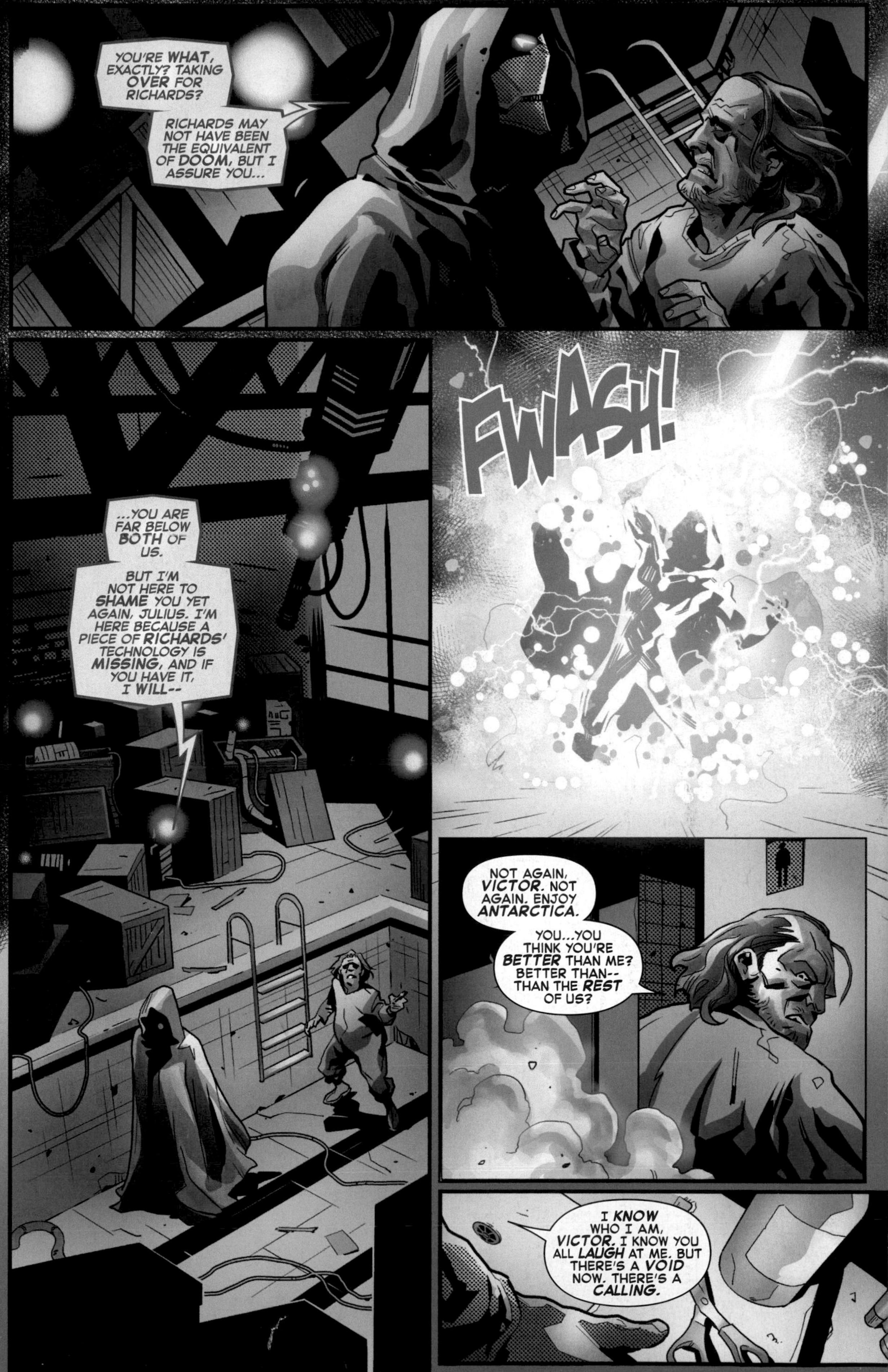
YOU'RE WHAT, EXACTLY? TAKING OVER FOR RICHARDS?
RICHARDS MAY NOT HAVE BEEN THE EQUIVALENT OF DOOM, BUT I ASSURE YOU...
...YOU ARE FAR BELOW BOTH OF US.
BUT I'M NOT HERE TO SHAME YOU YET AGAIN, JULIUS. I'M HERE BECAUSE A PIECE OF RICHARDS' TECHNOLOGY IS MISSING, AND IF YOU HAVE IT, I WILL--
FWASH!
NOT AGAIN, VICTOR. NOT AGAIN. ENJOY ANTARCTICA.
YOU...YOU THINK YOU'RE BETTER THAN ME? BETTER THAN-- THAN THE REST OF US?
I KNOW WHO I AM, VICTOR. I KNOW YOU ALL LAUGH AT ME. BUT THERE'S A VOID NOW. THERE'S A CALLING.

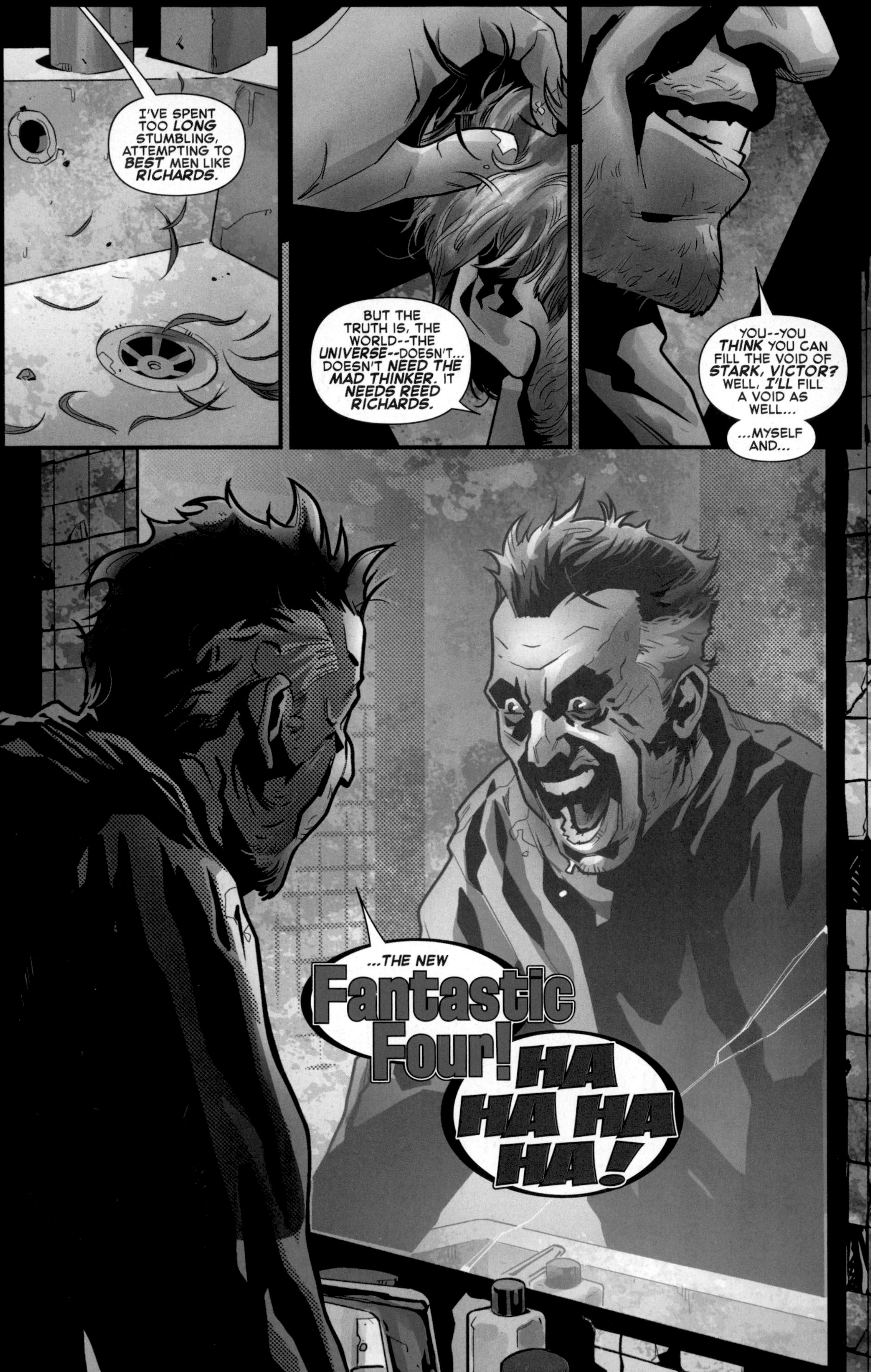
I'VE SPENT TOO LONG STUMBLING, ATTEMPTING TO BEST MEN LIKE RICHARDS.
BUT THE TRUTH IS, THE WORLD--THE UNIVERSE--DOESN'T... DOESN'T NEED THE MAD THINKER. IT NEEDS REED RICHARDS.
YOU--YOU THINK YOU CAN FILL THE VOID OF STARK, VICTOR? WELL, I'LL FILL A VOID AS WELL...
...MYSELF AND...
...THE NEW Fantastic Four!
HA HA HA HA HA!

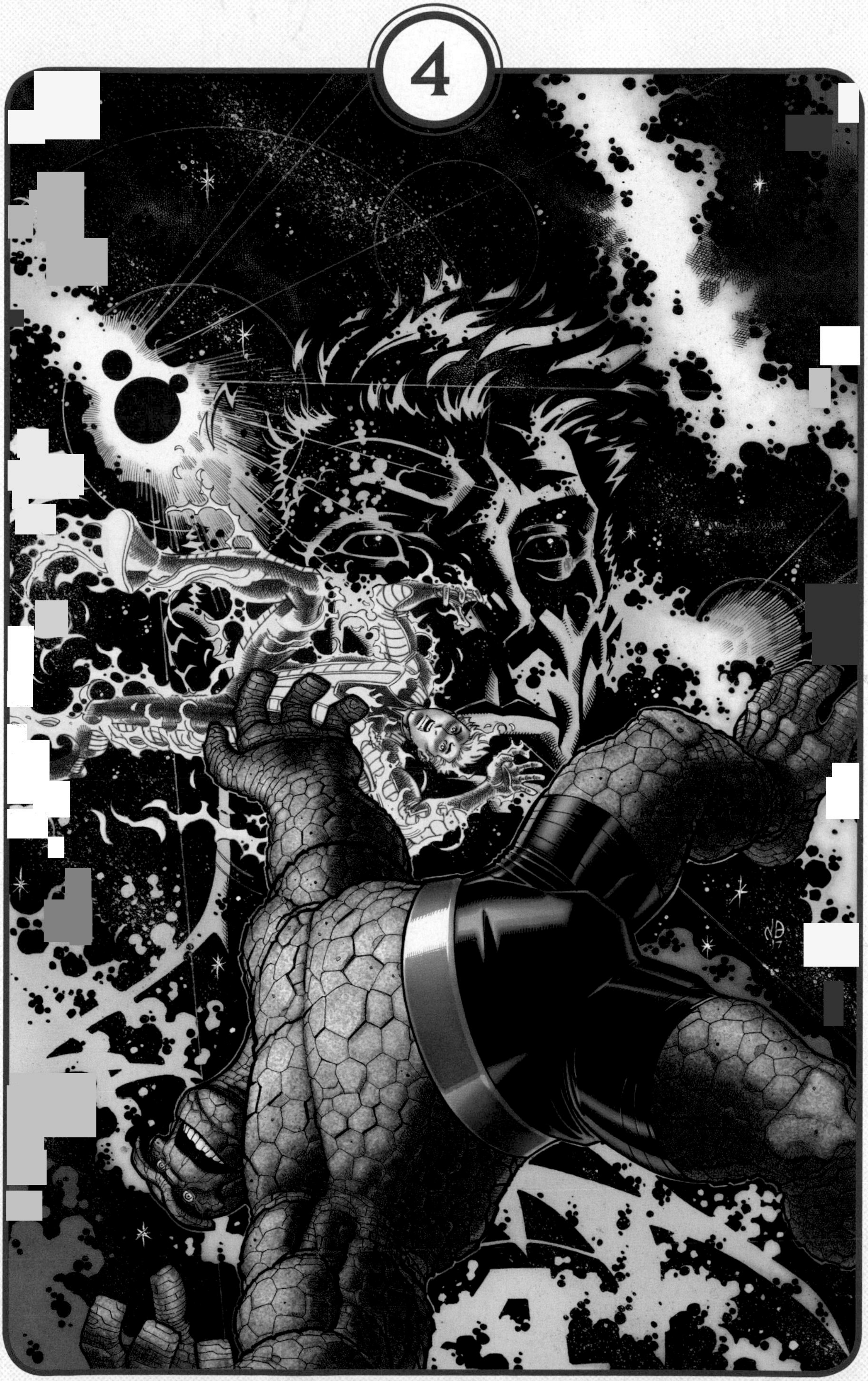
4

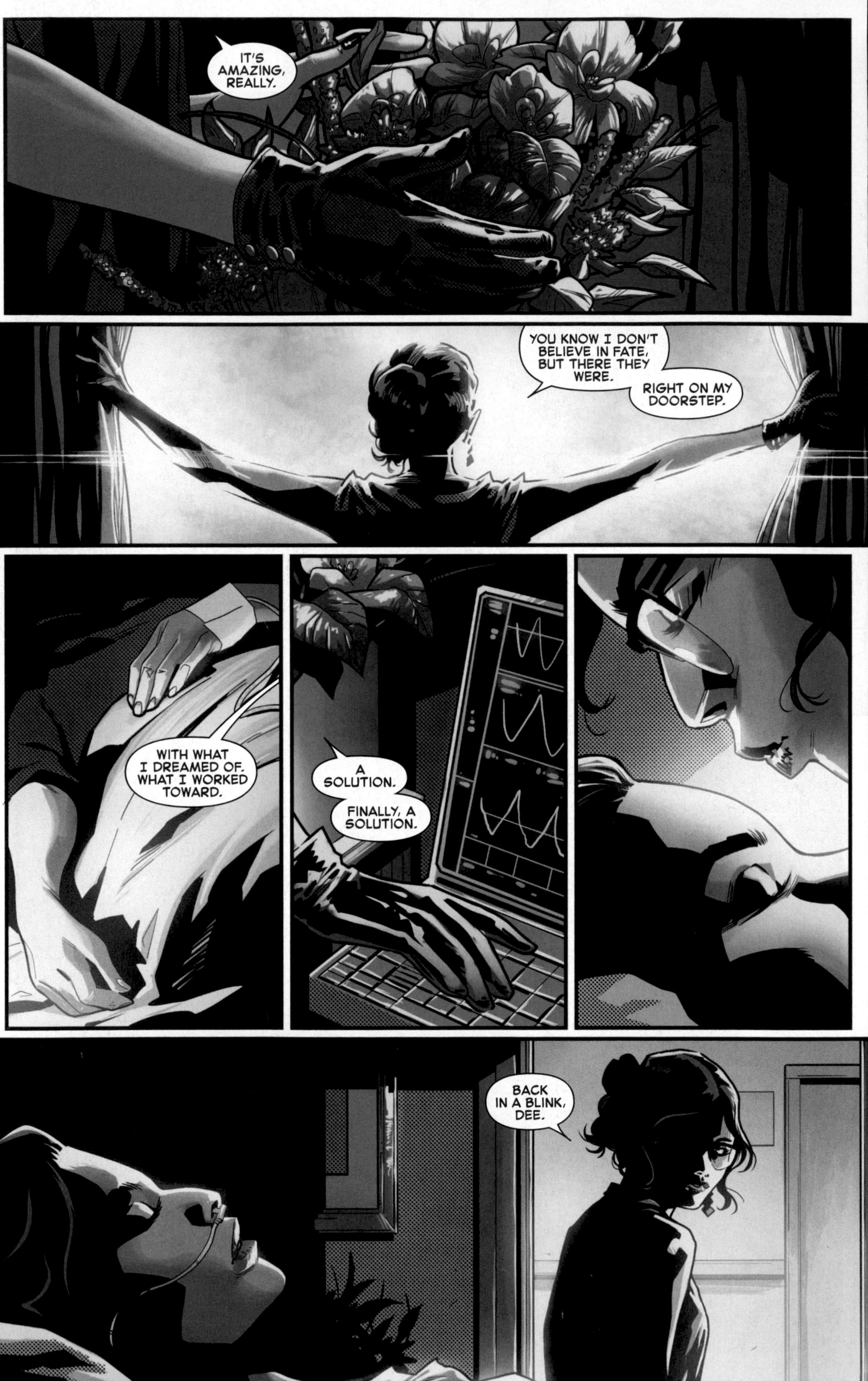
IT'S AMAZING, REALLY.
YOU KNOW I DON'T BELIEVE IN FATE, BUT THERE THEY WERE.
RIGHT ON MY DOORSTEP.
WITH WHAT I DREAMED OF. WHAT I WORKED TOWARD.
A SOLUTION.
FINALLY, A SOLUTION.
BACK IN A BLINK, DEE.

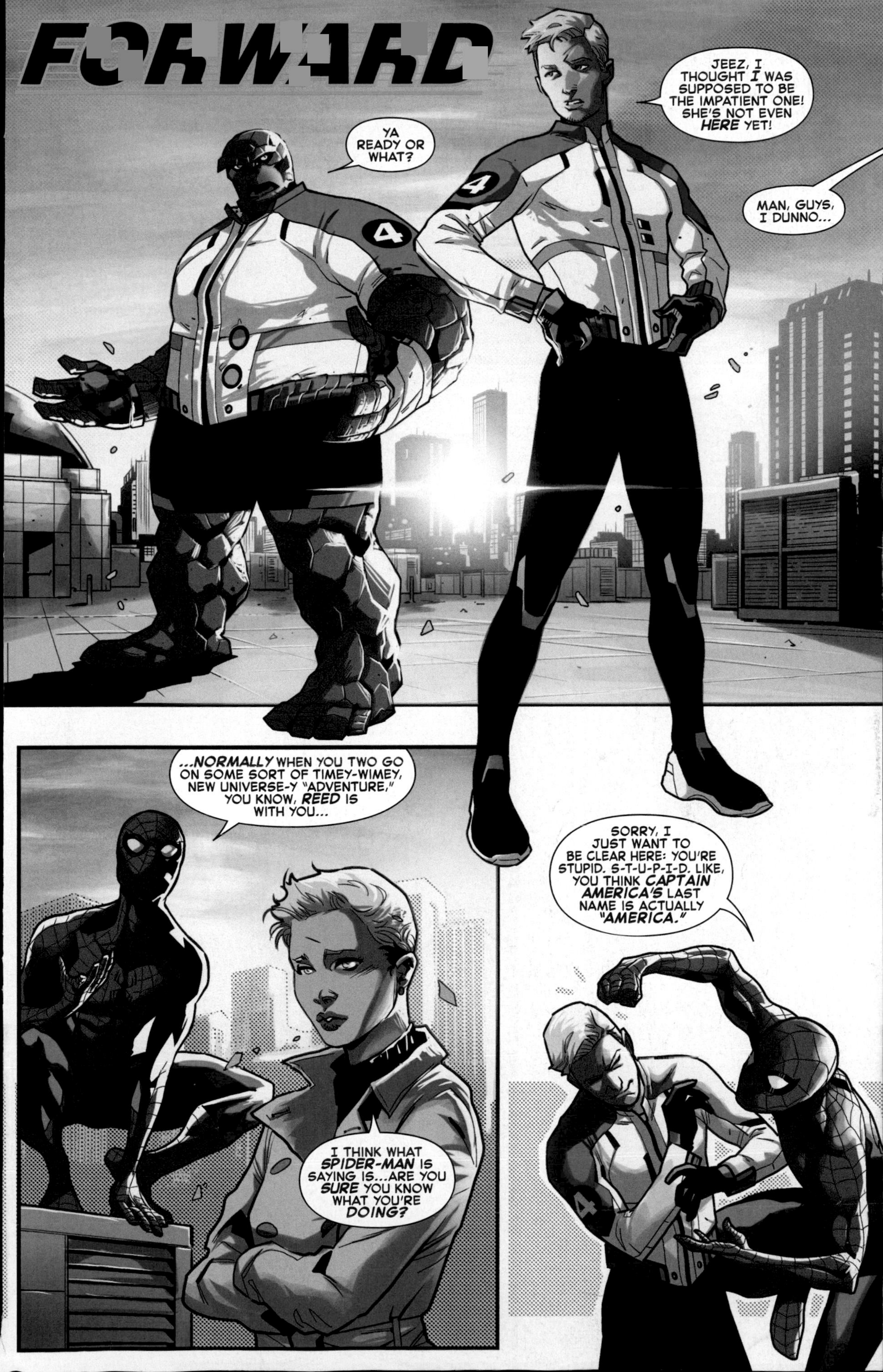
FORWARD
YA READY OR WHAT?
JEEZ, I THOUGHT I WAS SUPPOSED TO BE THE IMPATIENT ONE! SHE'S NOT EVEN HERE YET!
MAN, GUYS, I DUNNO...
...NORMALLY WHEN YOU TWO GO ON SOME SORT OF TIMEY-WIMEY, NEW UNIVERSE-Y "ADVENTURE," YOU KNOW, REED IS WITH YOU...
I THINK WHAT SPIDER-MAN IS SAYING IS...ARE YOU SURE YOU KNOW WHAT YOU'RE DOING?
SORRY, I JUST WANT TO BE CLEAR HERE: YOU'RE STUPID. S-T-U-P-I-D. LIKE, YOU THINK CAPTAIN AMERICA'S LAST NAME IS ACTUALLY "AMERICA."

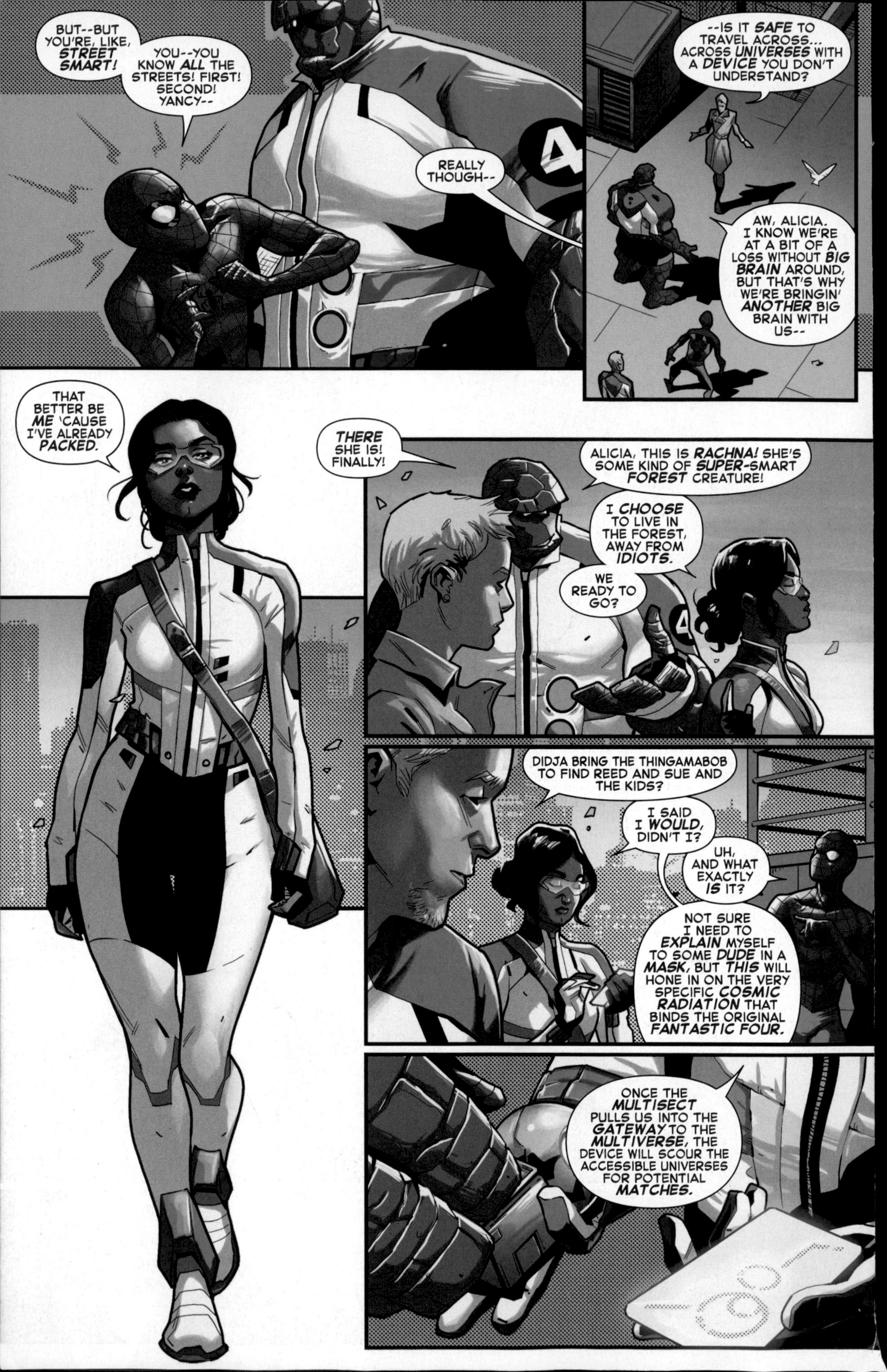

BUT--BUT YOU'RE, LIKE, STREET SMART!
YOU--YOU KNOW ALL THE STREETS! FIRST! SECOND! YANCY--
REALLY THOUGH--
--IS IT SAFE TO TRAVEL ACROSS... ACROSS UNIVERSES WITH A DEVICE YOU DON'T UNDERSTAND?
AW, ALICIA. I KNOW WE'RE AT A BIT OF A LOSS WITHOUT BIG BRAIN AROUND, BUT THAT'S WHY WE'RE BRINGIN' ANOTHER BIG BRAIN WITH US--
THAT BETTER BE ME 'CAUSE I'VE ALREADY PACKED.
THERE SHE IS! FINALLY!
ALICIA, THIS IS RACHNA! SHE'S SOME KIND OF SUPER-SMART FOREST CREATURE!
I CHOOSE TO LIVE IN THE FOREST, AWAY FROM IDIOTS.
WE READY TO GO?
DIDJA BRING THE THINGAMABOB TO FIND REED AND SUE AND THE KIDS?
I SAID I WOULD, DIDN'T I?
UH, AND WHAT EXACTLY IS IT?
NOT SURE I NEED TO EXPLAIN MYSELF TO SOME DUDE IN A MASK, BUT THIS WILL HONE IN ON THE VERY SPECIFIC COSMIC RADIATION THAT BINDS THE ORIGINAL FANTASTIC FOUR.
ONCE THE MULTISECT PULLS US INTO THE GATEWAY TO THE MULTIVERSE, THE DEVICE WILL SCOUR THE ACCESSIBLE UNIVERSES FOR POTENTIAL MATCHES.

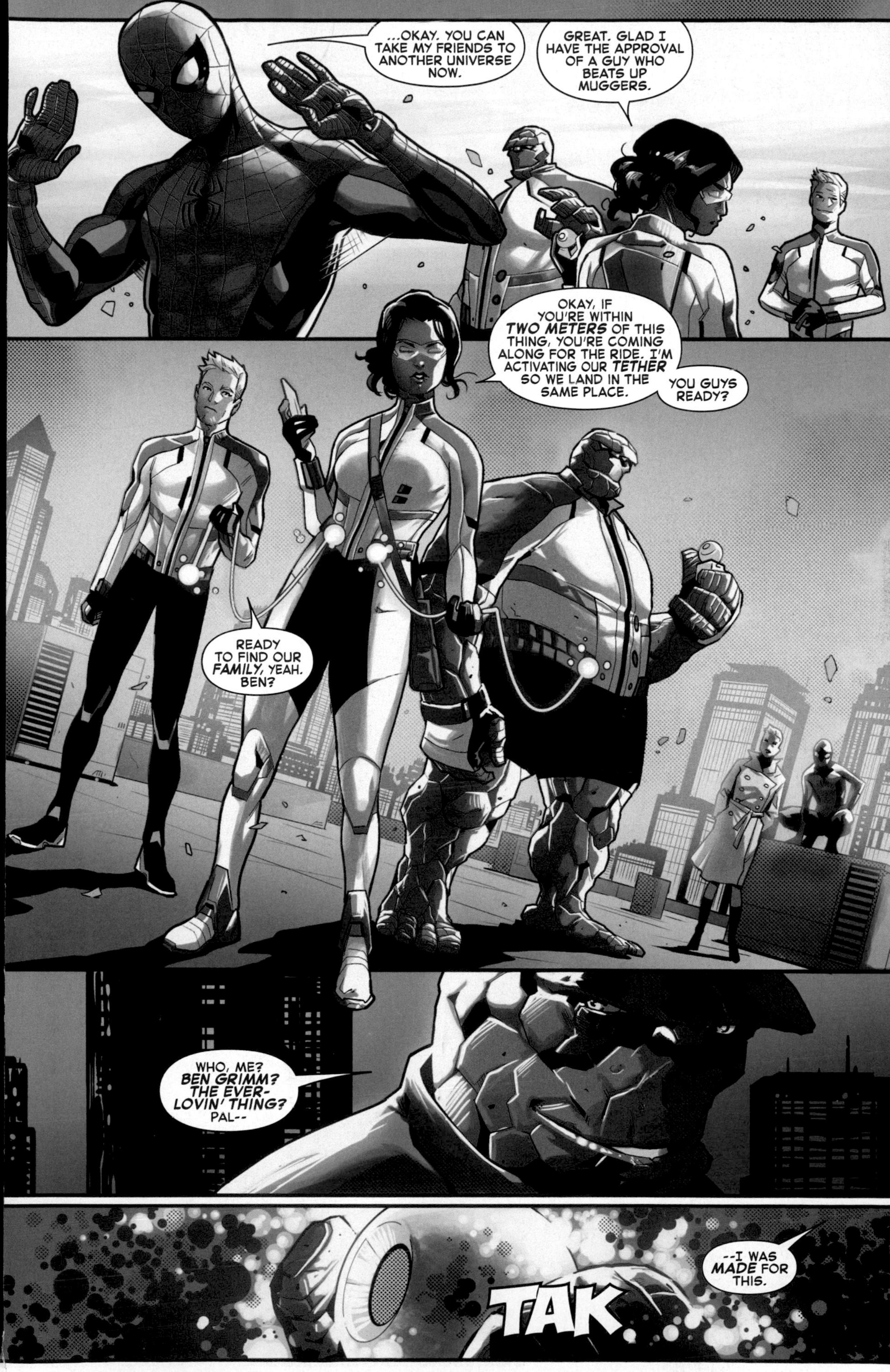
...OKAY. YOU CAN TAKE MY FRIENDS TO ANOTHER UNIVERSE NOW.
GREAT. GLAD I HAVE THE APPROVAL OF A GUY WHO BEATS UP MUGGERS.
OKAY, IF YOU'RE WITHIN TWO METERS OF THIS THING, YOU'RE COMING ALONG FOR THE RIDE. I'M ACTIVATING OUR TETHER SO WE LAND IN THE SAME PLACE.
YOU GUYS READY?
READY TO FIND OUR FAMILY, YEAH. BEN?
WHO, ME? BEN GRIMM? THE EVER-LOVIN' THING? PAL--
TAK
--I WAS MADE FOR THIS.

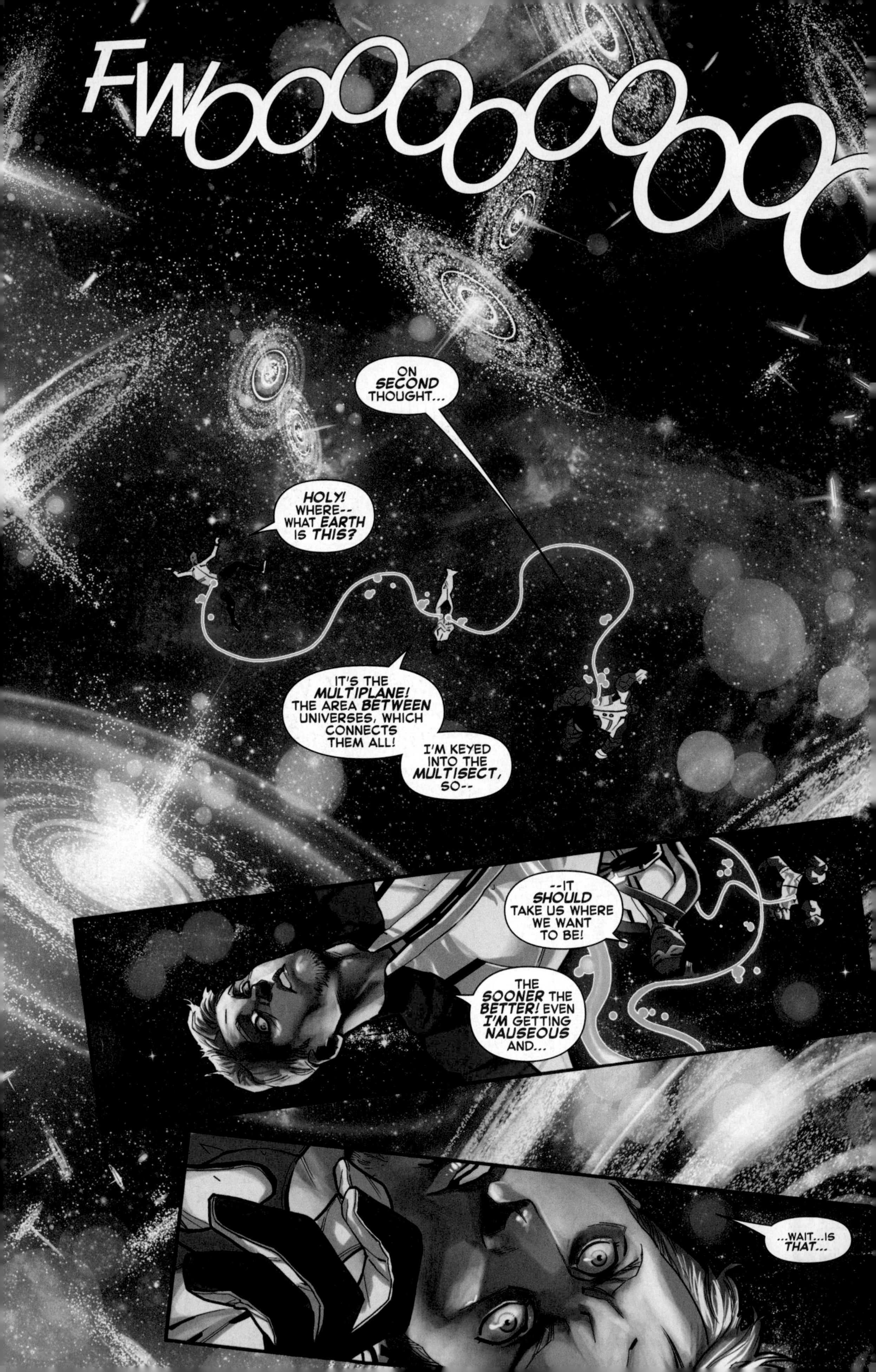
FWOOOOOOOOOOO
ON SECOND THOUGHT...
HOLY! WHERE-- WHAT EARTH IS THIS?
IT'S THE MULTIPLANE! THE AREA BETWEEN UNIVERSES, WHICH CONNECTS THEM ALL!
I'M KEYED INTO THE MULTISECT, SO--
--IT SHOULD TAKE US WHERE WE WANT TO BE!
THE SOONER THE BETTER! EVEN I'M GETTING NAUSEOUS AND...
...WAIT...IS THAT...

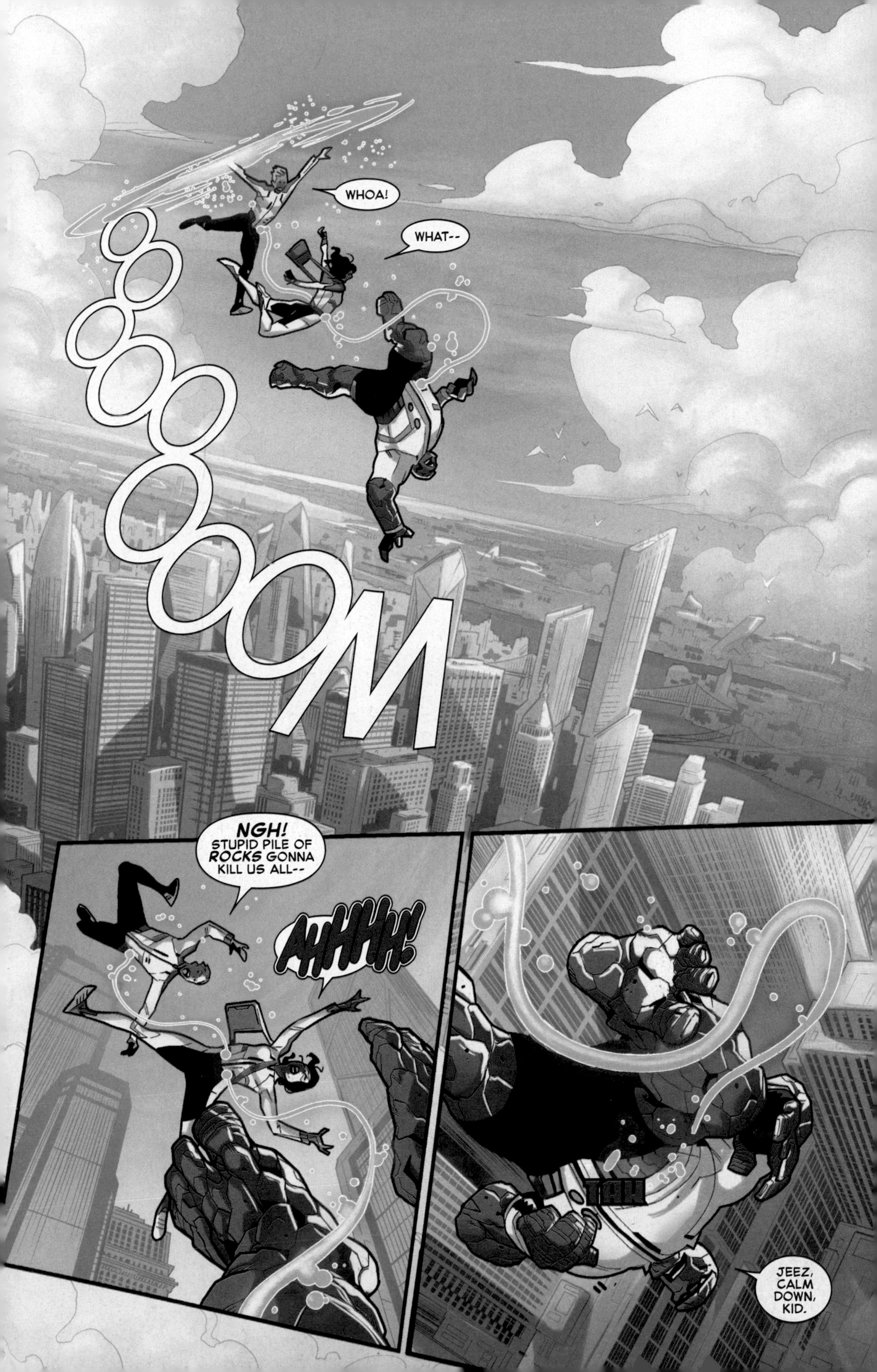

WHOA!
WHAT--
BOOOOOOOM
NGH! STUPID PILE OF ROCKS GONNA KILL US ALL--
AHHHH!
TAK
JEEZ, CALM DOWN, KID.

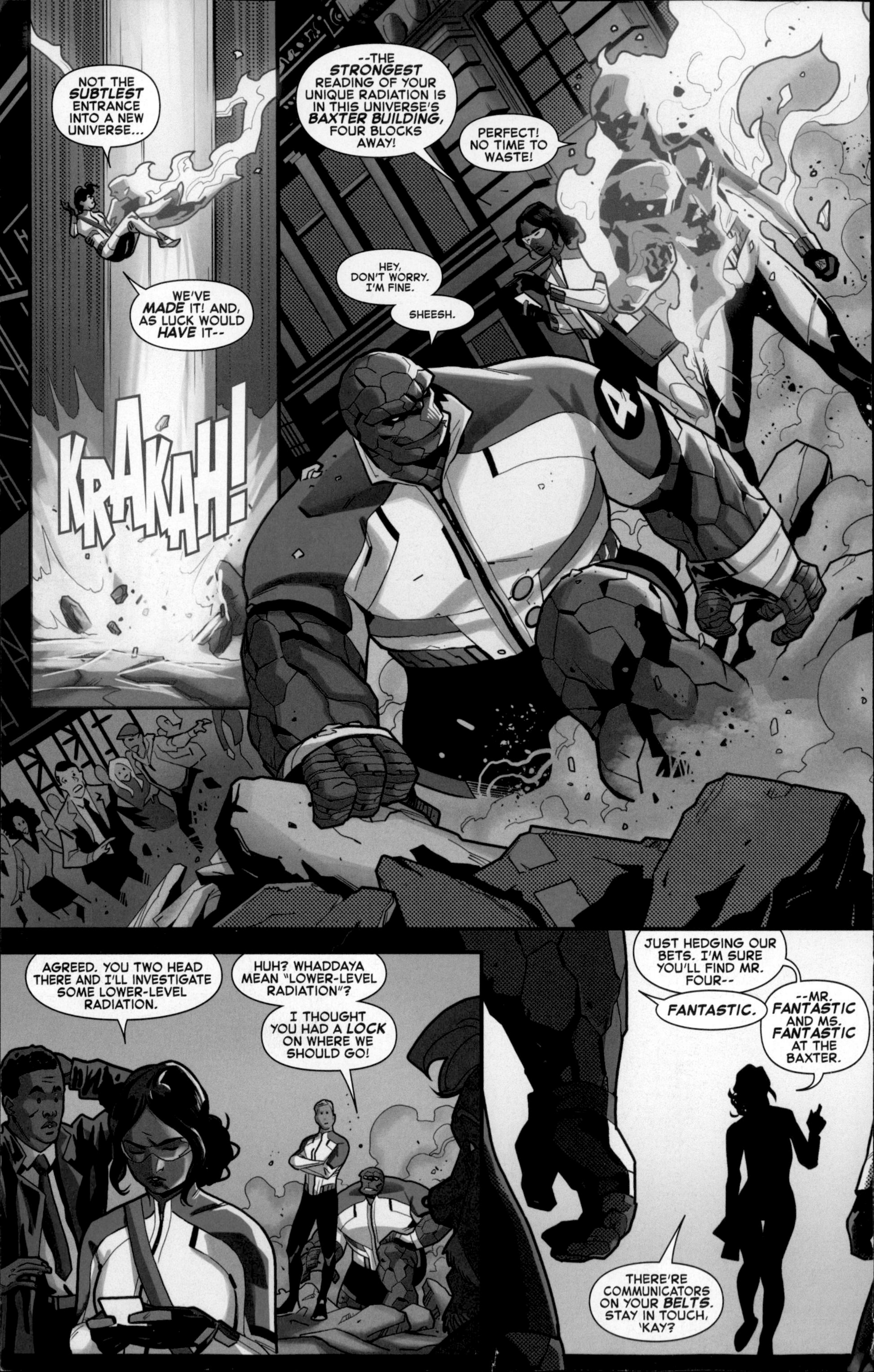
NOT THE SUBTLEST ENTRANCE INTO A NEW UNIVERSE...
WE'VE MADE IT! AND, AS LUCK WOULD HAVE IT--
KRAKAH!
--THE STRONGEST READING OF YOUR UNIQUE RADIATION IS IN THIS UNIVERSE'S BAXTER BUILDING, FOUR BLOCKS AWAY!
PERFECT! NO TIME TO WASTE!
HEY, DON'T WORRY. I'M FINE.
SHEESH.
AGREED. YOU TWO HEAD THERE AND I'LL INVESTIGATE SOME LOWER-LEVEL RADIATION.
HUH? WHADDAYA MEAN "LOWER-LEVEL RADIATION"?
I THOUGHT YOU HAD A LOCK ON WHERE WE SHOULD GO!
JUST HEDGING OUR BETS. I'M SURE YOU'LL FIND MR. FOUR--
FANTASTIC.
--MR. FANTASTIC AND MS. FANTASTIC AT THE BAXTER.
THERE'RE COMMUNICATORS ON YOUR BELTS. STAY IN TOUCH, 'KAY?

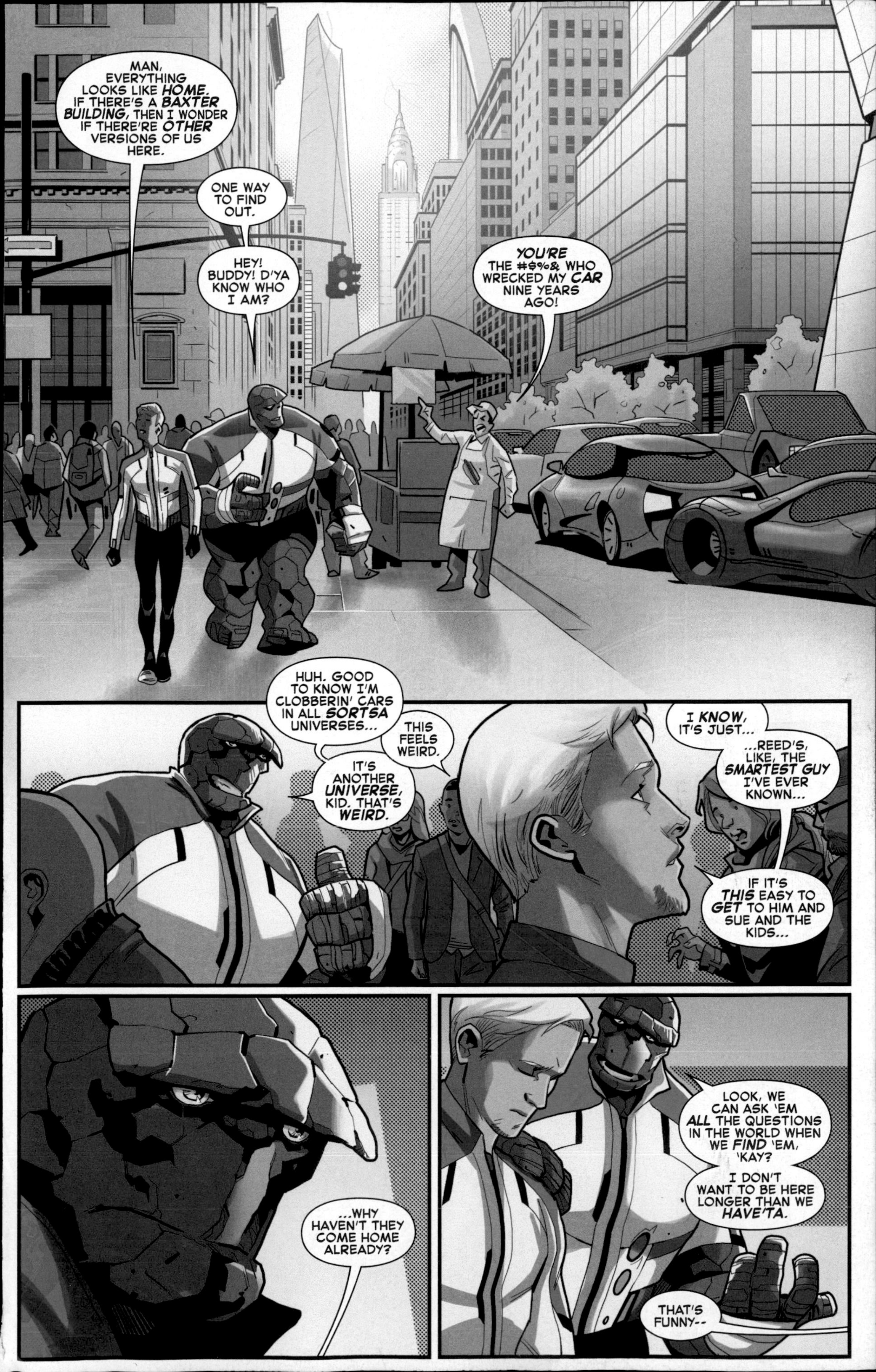
MAN, EVERYTHING LOOKS LIKE HOME. IF THERE'S A BAXTER BUILDING, THEN I WONDER IF THERE'RE OTHER VERSIONS OF US HERE.
ONE WAY TO FIND OUT.
HEY! BUDDY! D'YA KNOW WHO I AM?
YOU'RE THE #$%& WHO WRECKED MY CAR NINE YEARS AGO!
HUH. GOOD TO KNOW I'M CLOBBERIN' CARS IN ALL SORTSA UNIVERSES...
THIS FEELS WEIRD.
IT'S ANOTHER UNIVERSE, KID. THAT'S WEIRD.
I KNOW, IT'S JUST...
...REED'S, LIKE, THE SMARTEST GUY I'VE EVER KNOWN...
IF IT'S THIS EASY TO GET TO HIM AND SUE AND THE KIDS...
...WHY HAVEN'T THEY COME HOME ALREADY?
LOOK, WE CAN ASK 'EM ALL THE QUESTIONS IN THE WORLD WHEN WE FIND 'EM, 'KAY?
I DON'T WANT TO BE HERE LONGER THAN WE HAVE'TA.
THAT'S FUNNY--

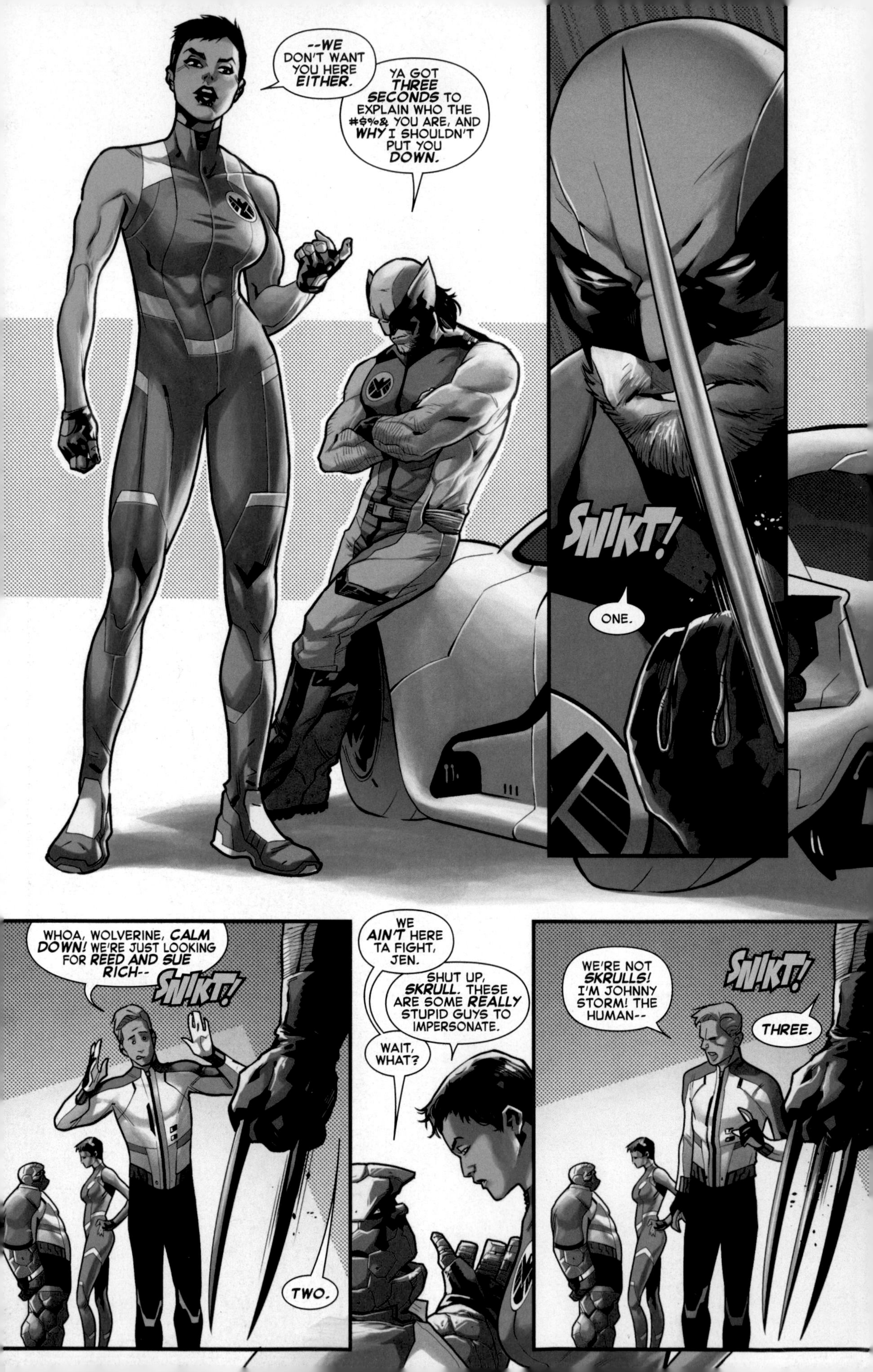
--WE DON'T WANT YOU HERE EITHER.
YA GOT THREE SECONDS TO EXPLAIN WHO THE #$%& YOU ARE, AND WHY I SHOULDN'T PUT YOU DOWN.
SNIKT!
ONE.
WHOA, WOLVERINE, CALM DOWN! WE'RE JUST LOOKING FOR REED AND SUE RICH--
SNIKT!
TWO.
WE AIN'T HERE TA FIGHT, JEN.
SHUT UP, SKRULL. THESE ARE SOME REALLY STUPID GUYS TO IMPERSONATE.
WAIT, WHAT?
WE'RE NOT SKRULLS! I'M JOHNNY STORM! THE HUMAN--
SNIKT!
THREE.

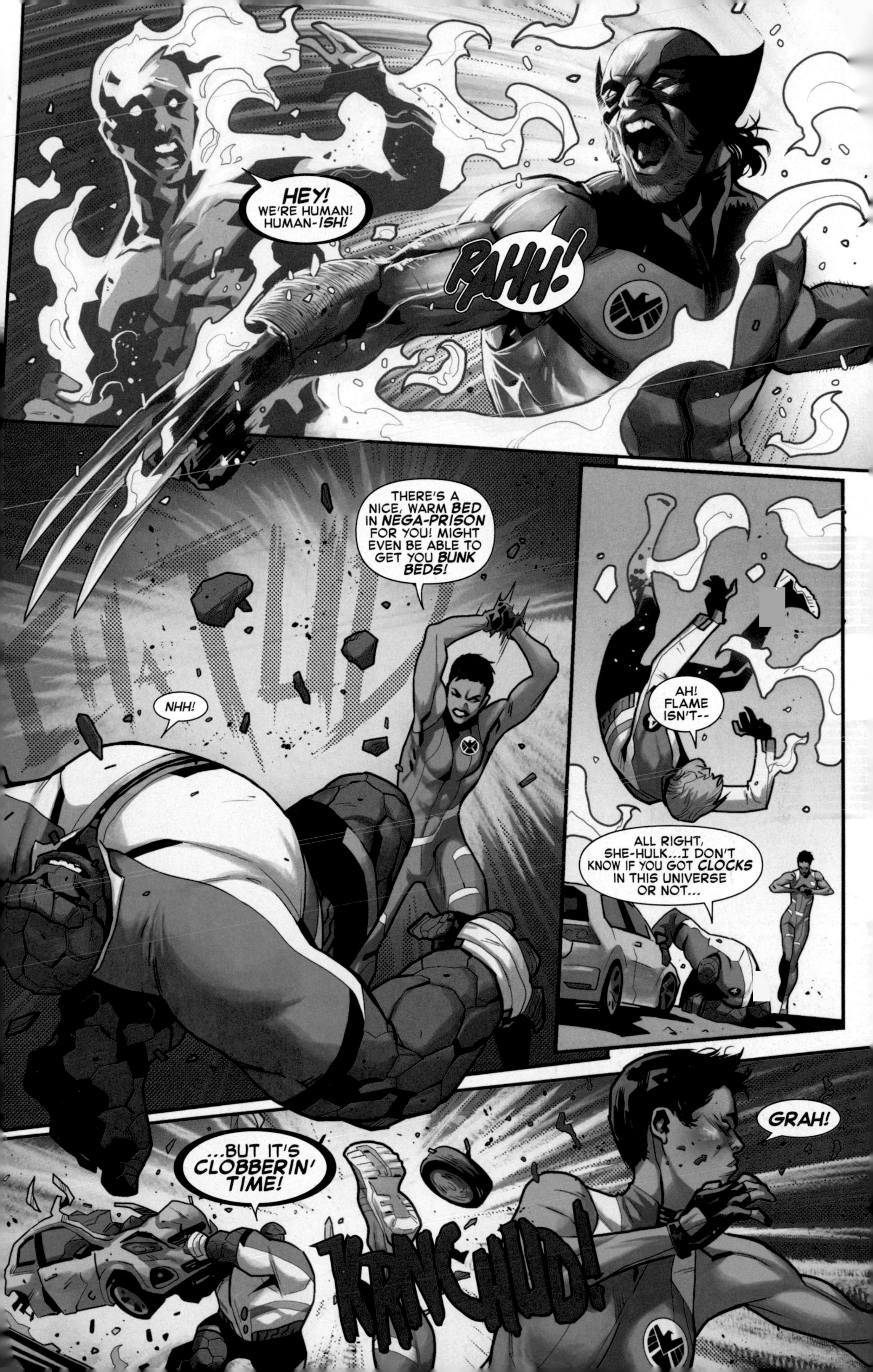
HEY! WE'RE HUMAN! HUMAN-ISH!
RAHH!
THERE'S A NICE, WARM BED IN NEGA-PRISON FOR YOU! MIGHT EVEN BE ABLE TO GET YOU BUNK BEDS!
NHH!
AH! FLAME ISN'T--
ALL RIGHT, SHE-HULK...I DON'T KNOW IF YOU GOT CLOCKS IN THIS UNIVERSE OR NOT...
...BUT IT'S CLOBBERIN' TIME!
GRAH!
KRRNCHUD!

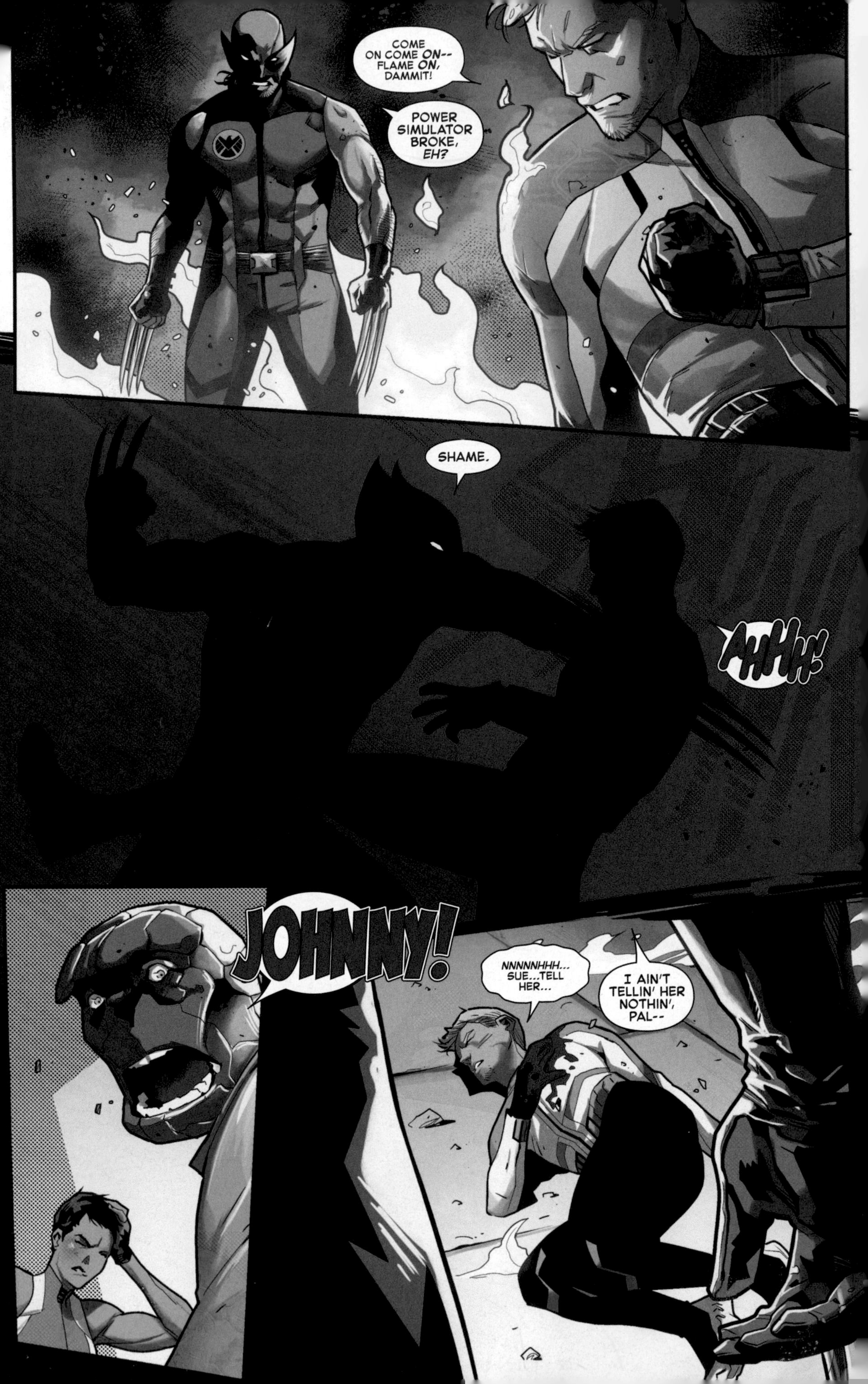
COME ON COME ON-- FLAME ON, DAMMIT!
POWER SIMULATOR BROKE, EH?
SHAME.
AHHH!
JOHNNY!
NNNNNHHH... SUE...TELL HER...
I AIN'T TELLIN' HER NOTHIN', PAL--

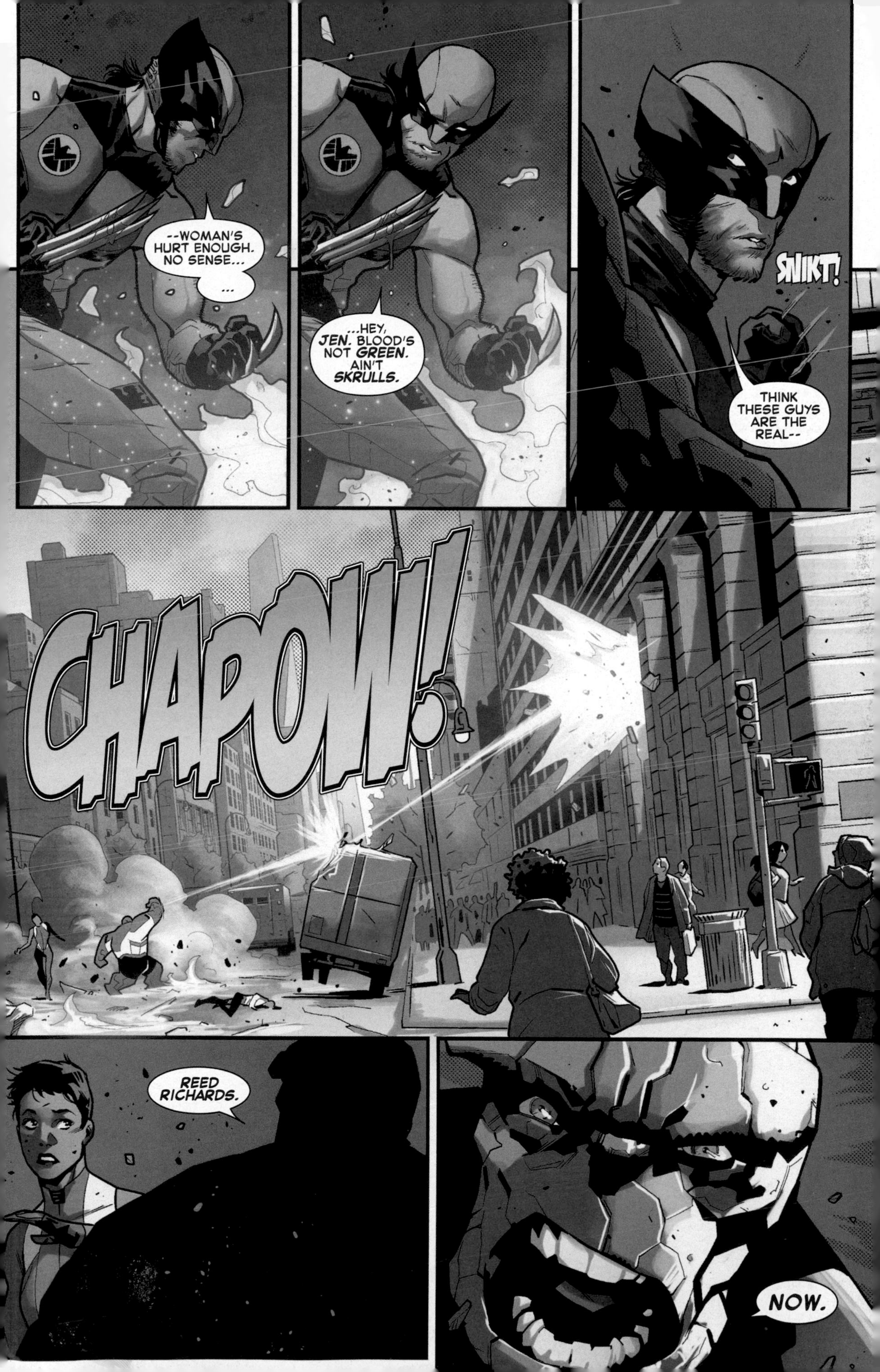
--WOMAN'S HURT ENOUGH. NO SENSE...
...
...HEY, JEN. BLOOD'S NOT GREEN. AIN'T SKRULLS.
SNIKT!
THINK THESE GUYS ARE THE REAL--
CHAPOW!
REED RICHARDS.
NOW.

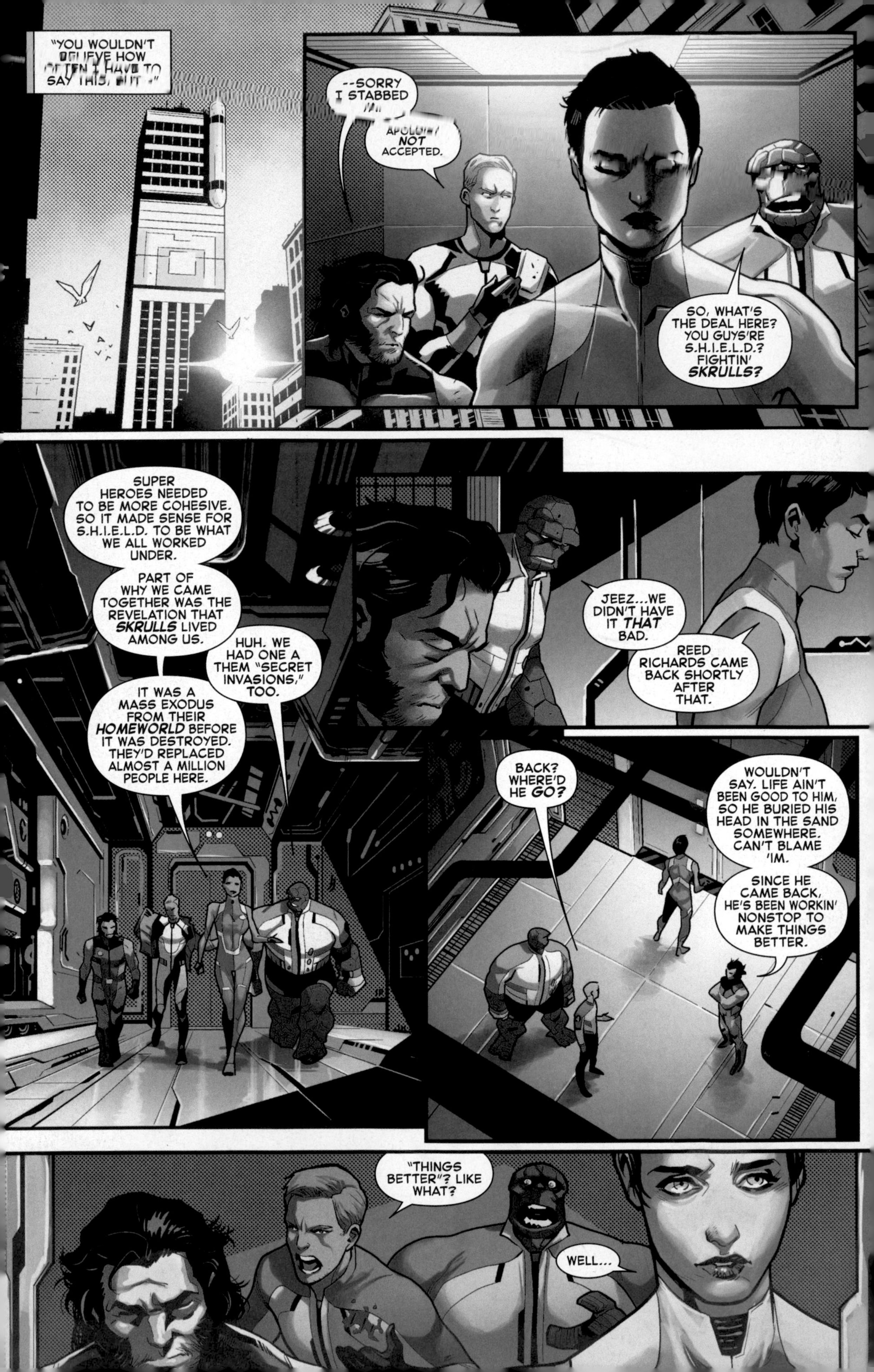
"YOU WOULDN'T BELIEVE HOW OFTEN I HAVE TO SAY THIS, BUT--"
--SORRY I STABBED
APOLOGY NOT ACCEPTED.
SO, WHAT'S THE DEAL HERE? YOU GUYS'RE S.H.I.E.L.D.? FIGHTIN' SKRULLS?
SUPER HEROES NEEDED TO BE MORE COHESIVE. SO IT MADE SENSE FOR S.H.I.E.L.D. TO BE WHAT WE ALL WORKED UNDER.
PART OF WHY WE CAME TOGETHER WAS THE REVELATION THAT SKRULLS LIVED AMONG US.
HUH. WE HAD ONE A THEM "SECRET INVASIONS," TOO.
IT WAS A MASS EXODUS FROM THEIR HOMEWORLD BEFORE IT WAS DESTROYED. THEY'D REPLACED ALMOST A MILLION PEOPLE HERE.
JEEZ...WE DIDN'T HAVE IT THAT BAD.
REED RICHARDS CAME BACK SHORTLY AFTER THAT.
BACK? WHERE'D HE GO?
WOULDN'T SAY. LIFE AIN'T BEEN GOOD TO HIM, SO HE BURIED HIS HEAD IN THE SAND SOMEWHERE. CAN'T BLAME 'IM.
SINCE HE CAME BACK, HE'S BEEN WORKIN' NONSTOP TO MAKE THINGS BETTER.
"THINGS BETTER"? LIKE WHAT?
WELL...

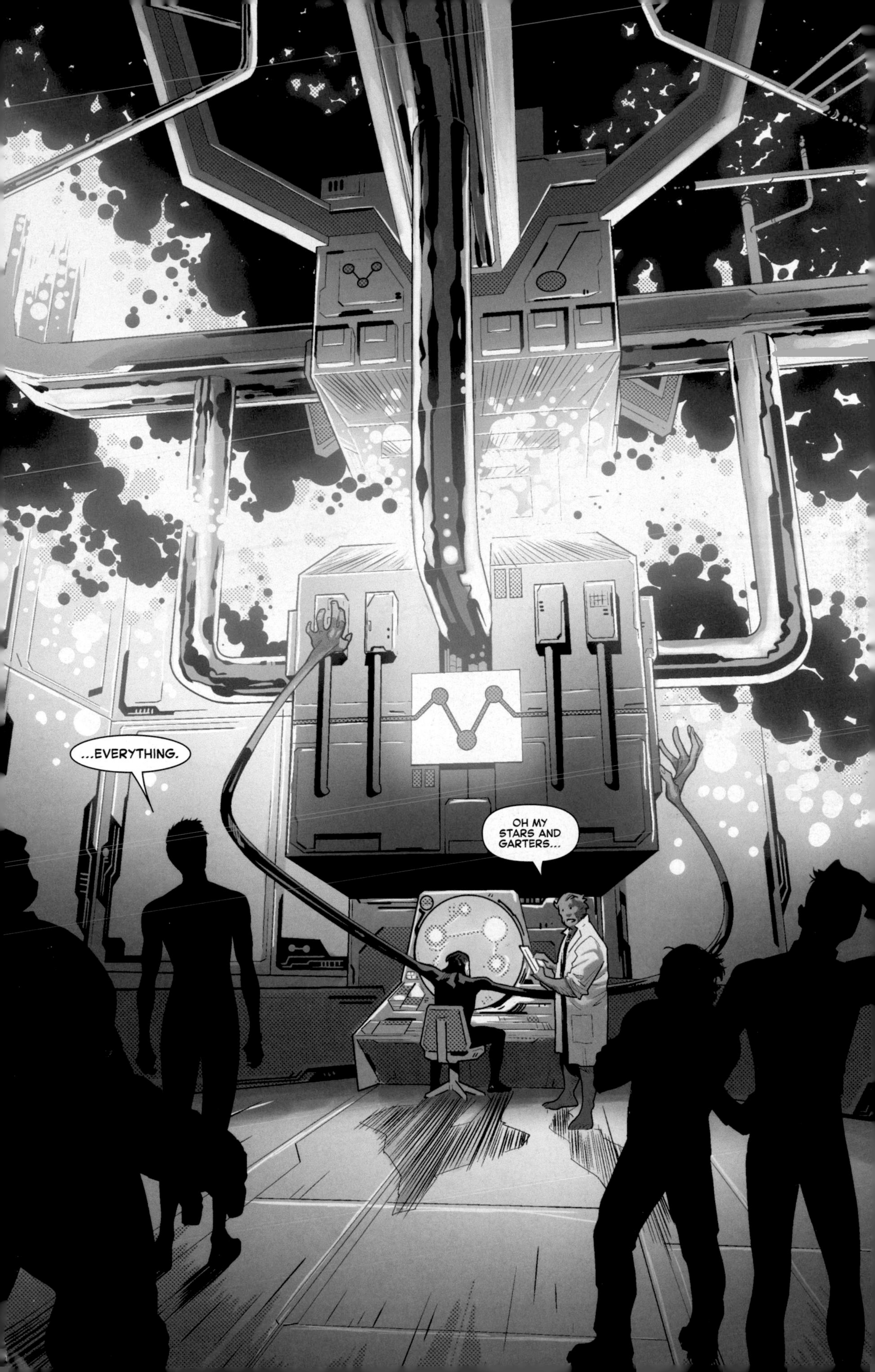
...EVERYTHING.
OH MY STARS AND GARTERS...

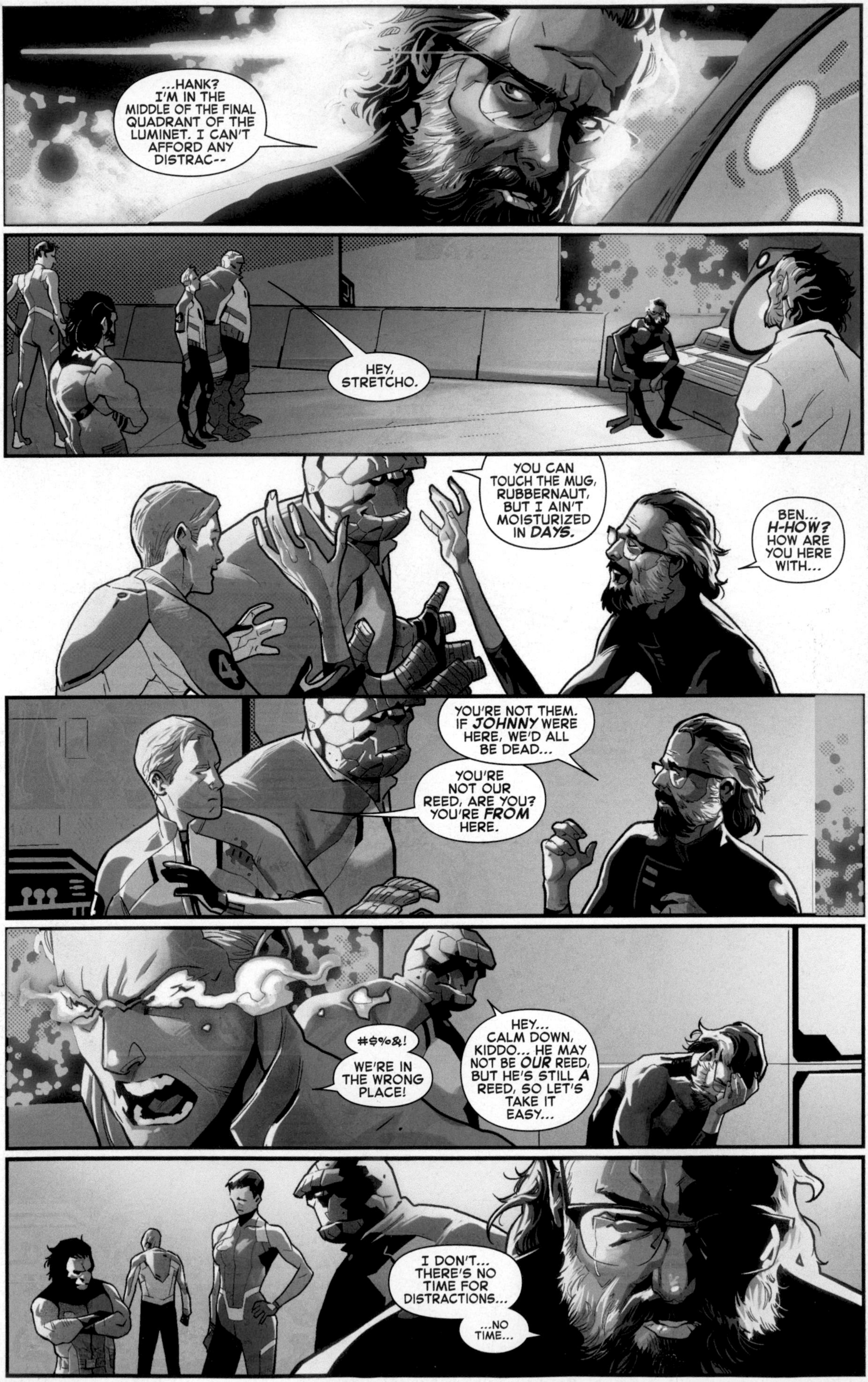
...HANK? I'M IN THE MIDDLE OF THE FINAL QUADRANT OF THE LUMINET. I CAN'T AFFORD ANY DISTRAC--
HEY, STRETCHO.
YOU CAN TOUCH THE MUG, RUBBERNAUT, BUT I AIN'T MOISTURIZED IN DAYS.
BEN... H-HOW? HOW ARE YOU HERE WITH...
YOU'RE NOT THEM. IF JOHNNY WERE HERE, WE'D ALL BE DEAD...
YOU'RE NOT OUR REED, ARE YOU? YOU'RE FROM HERE.
#$%&!
WE'RE IN THE WRONG PLACE!
HEY... CALM DOWN, KIDDO... HE MAY NOT BE OUR REED, BUT HE'S STILL A REED, SO LET'S TAKE IT EASY...
I DON'T... THERE'S NO TIME FOR DISTRACTIONS...
...NO TIME...

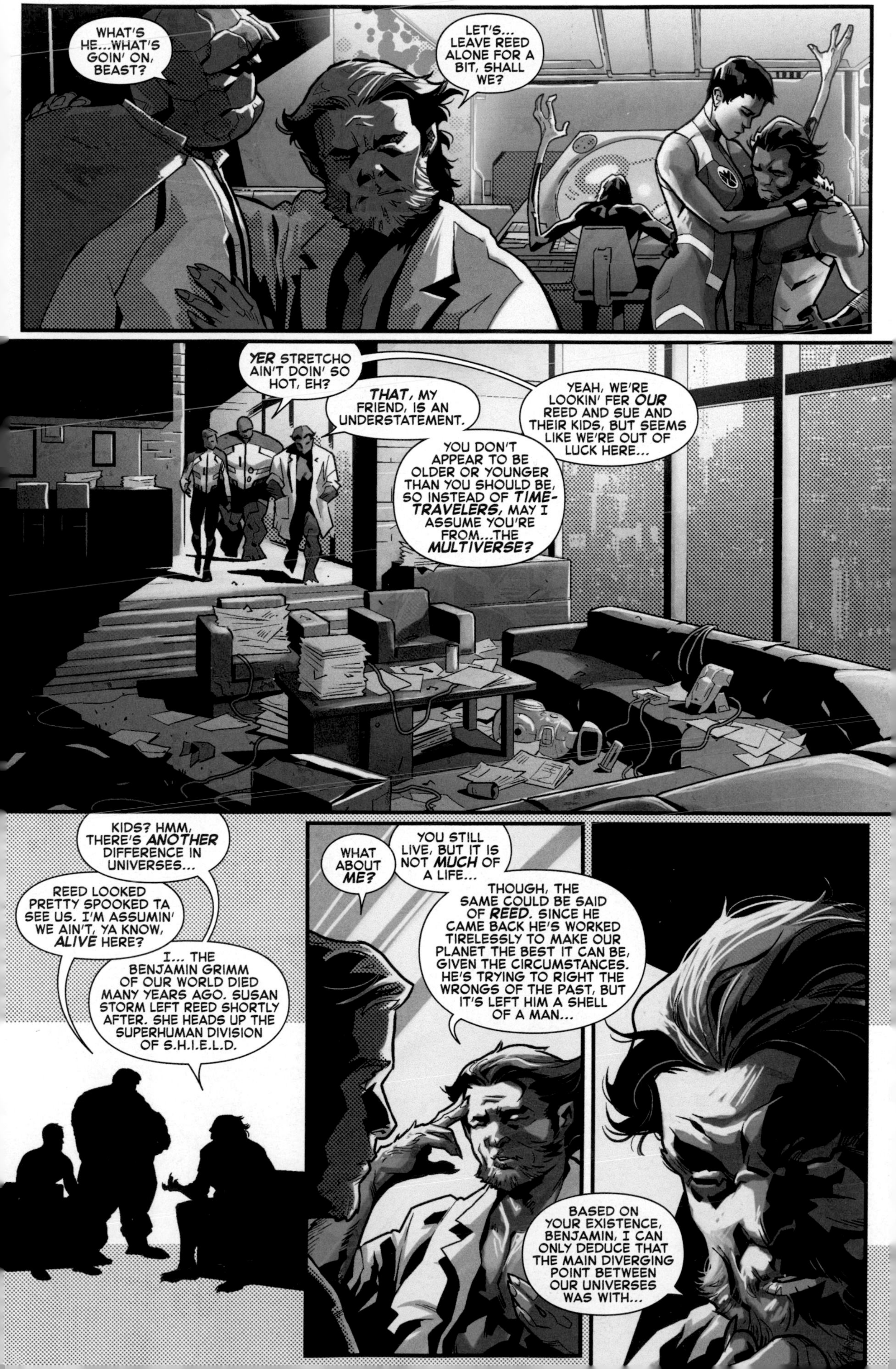
WHAT'S HE...WHAT'S GOIN' ON, BEAST?
LET'S... LEAVE REED ALONE FOR A BIT, SHALL WE?
YER STRETCHO AIN'T DOIN' SO HOT, EH?
THAT, MY FRIEND, IS AN UNDERSTATEMENT.
YEAH, WE'RE LOOKIN' FER OUR REED AND SUE AND THEIR KIDS, BUT SEEMS LIKE WE'RE OUT OF LUCK HERE...
YOU DON'T APPEAR TO BE OLDER OR YOUNGER THAN YOU SHOULD BE, SO INSTEAD OF TIME-TRAVELERS, MAY I ASSUME YOU'RE FROM...THE MULTIVERSE?
KIDS? HMM, THERE'S ANOTHER DIFFERENCE IN UNIVERSES...
REED LOOKED PRETTY SPOOKED TA SEE US. I'M ASSUMIN' WE AIN'T, YA KNOW, ALIVE HERE?
I... THE BENJAMIN GRIMM OF OUR WORLD DIED MANY YEARS AGO. SUSAN STORM LEFT REED SHORTLY AFTER. SHE HEADS UP THE SUPERHUMAN DIVISION OF S.H.I.E.L.D.
WHAT ABOUT ME?
YOU STILL LIVE, BUT IT IS NOT MUCH OF A LIFE...
THOUGH, THE SAME COULD BE SAID OF REED. SINCE HE CAME BACK HE'S WORKED TIRELESSLY TO MAKE OUR PLANET THE BEST IT CAN BE, GIVEN THE CIRCUMSTANCES. HE'S TRYING TO RIGHT THE WRONGS OF THE PAST, BUT IT'S LEFT HIM A SHELL OF A MAN...
BASED ON YOUR EXISTENCE, BENJAMIN, I CAN ONLY DEDUCE THAT THE MAIN DIVERGING POINT BETWEEN OUR UNIVERSES WAS WITH...

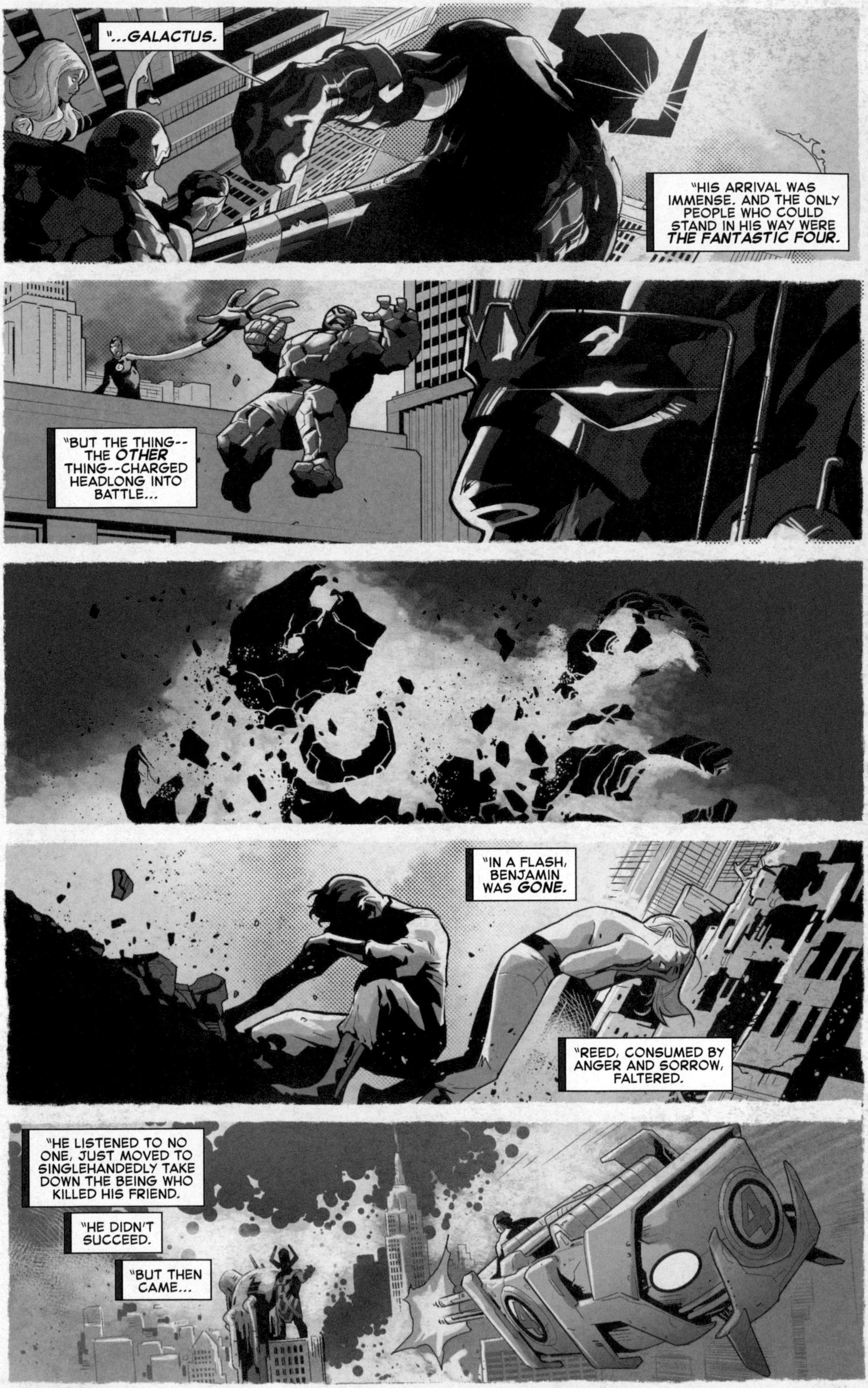
"...GALACTUS.
"HIS ARRIVAL WAS IMMENSE. AND THE ONLY PEOPLE WHO COULD STAND IN HIS WAY WERE THE FANTASTIC FOUR.
"BUT THE THING-- THE OTHER THING--CHARGED HEADLONG INTO BATTLE...
"IN A FLASH, BENJAMIN WAS GONE.
"REED, CONSUMED BY ANGER AND SORROW, FALTERED.
"HE LISTENED TO NO ONE, JUST MOVED TO SINGLEHANDEDLY TAKE DOWN THE BEING WHO KILLED HIS FRIEND.
"HE DIDN'T SUCCEED.
"BUT THEN CAME...

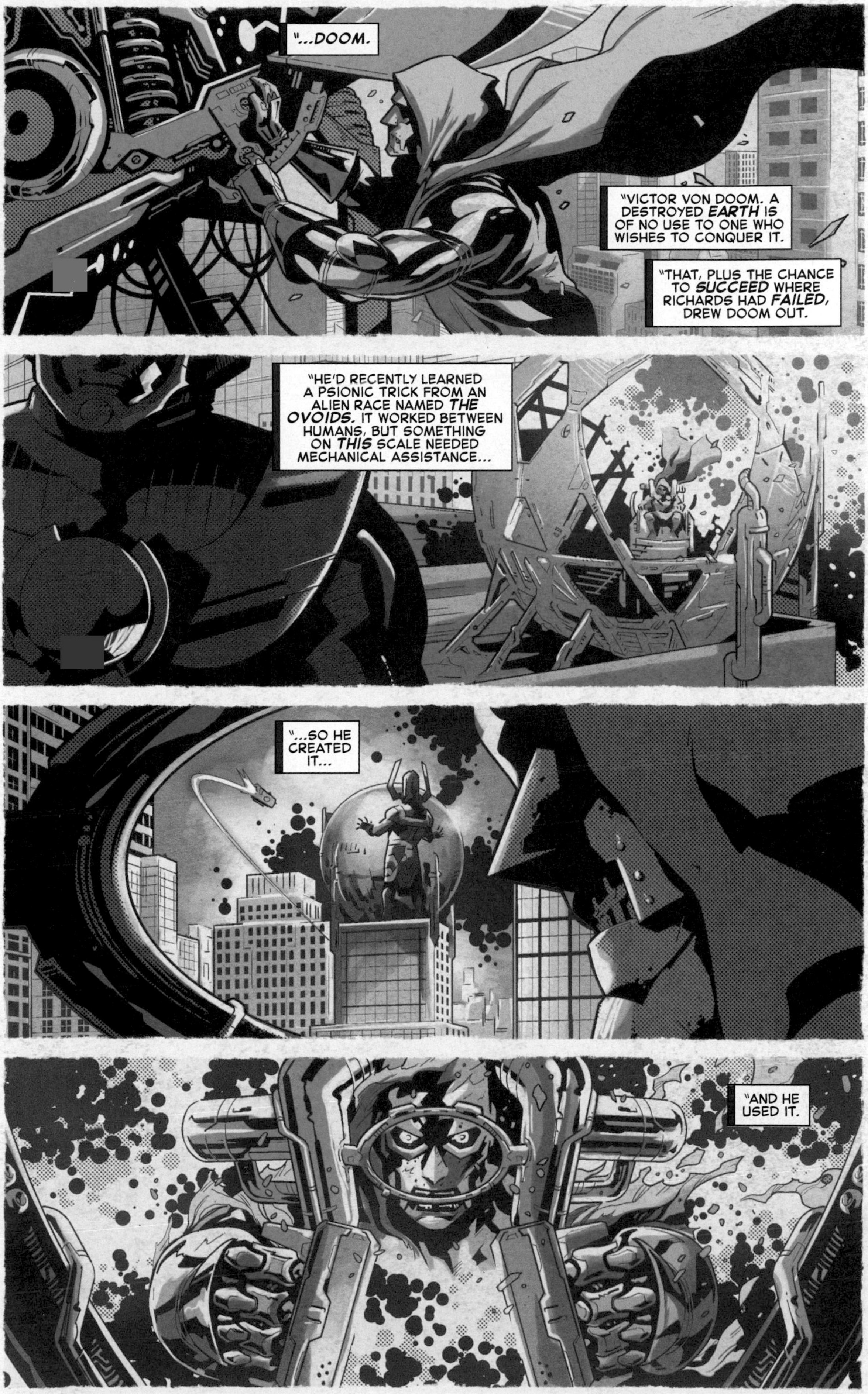
"...DOOM.
"VICTOR VON DOOM. A DESTROYED EARTH IS OF NO USE TO ONE WHO WISHES TO CONQUER IT.
"THAT, PLUS THE CHANCE TO SUCCEED WHERE RICHARDS HAD FAILED, DREW DOOM OUT.
"HE'D RECENTLY LEARNED A PSIONIC TRICK FROM AN ALIEN RACE NAMED THE OVOIDS. IT WORKED BETWEEN HUMANS, BUT SOMETHING ON THIS SCALE NEEDED MECHANICAL ASSISTANCE...
"...SO HE CREATED IT...
"AND HE USED IT.

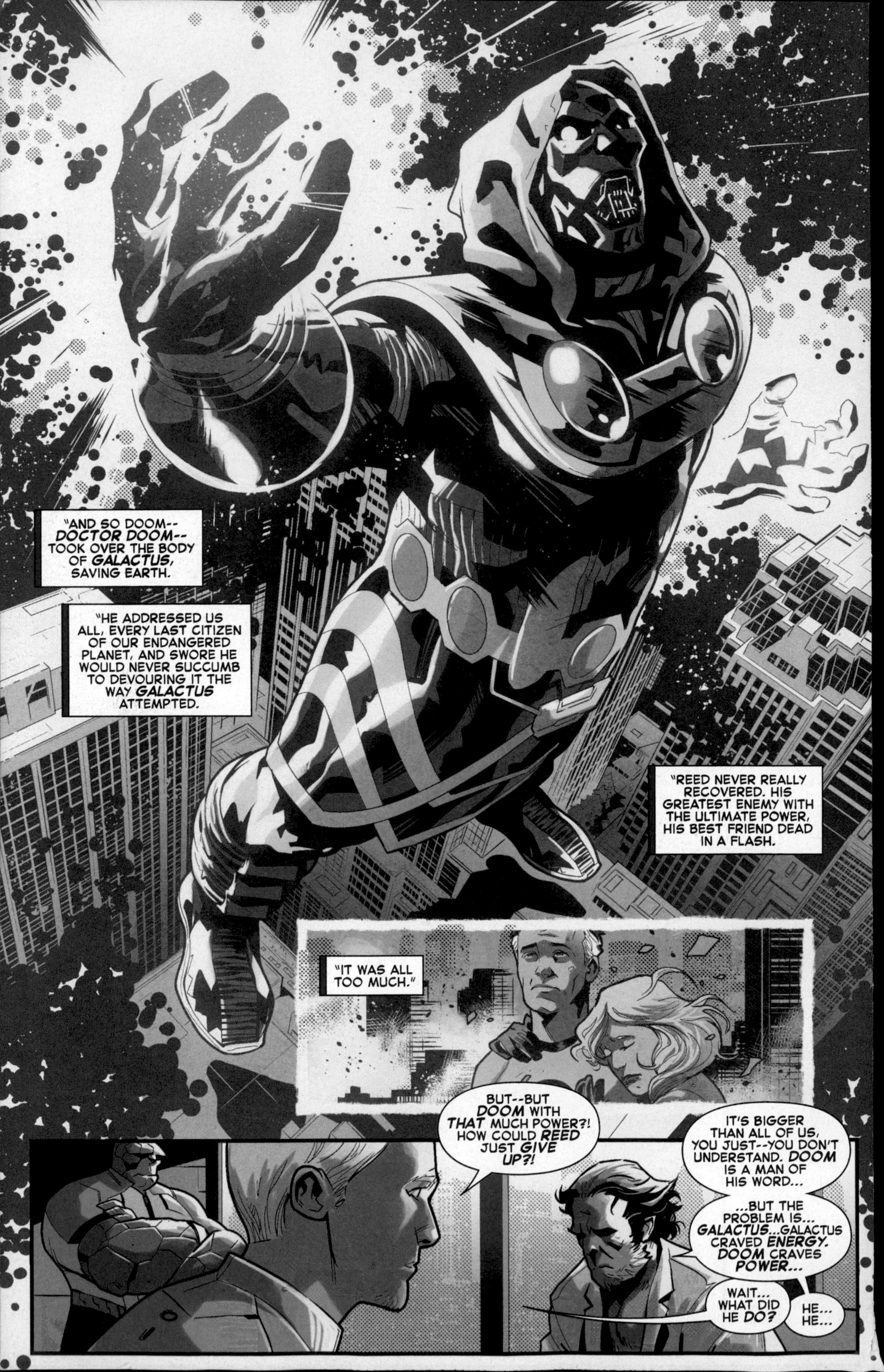
"AND SO DOOM-- DOCTOR DOOM-- TOOK OVER THE BODY OF GALACTUS, SAVING EARTH.
"HE ADDRESSED US ALL, EVERY LAST CITIZEN OF OUR ENDANGERED PLANET, AND SWORE HE WOULD NEVER SUCCUMB TO DEVOURING IT THE WAY GALACTUS ATTEMPTED.
"REED NEVER REALLY RECOVERED. HIS GREATEST ENEMY WITH THE ULTIMATE POWER, HIS BEST FRIEND DEAD IN A FLASH.
"IT WAS ALL TOO MUCH."
BUT--BUT DOOM WITH THAT MUCH POWER?! HOW COULD REED JUST GIVE UP?!
IT'S BIGGER THAN ALL OF US, YOU JUST--YOU DON'T UNDERSTAND. DOOM IS A MAN OF HIS WORD...
...BUT THE PROBLEM IS... GALACTUS...GALACTUS CRAVED ENERGY. DOOM CRAVES POWER...
WAIT... WHAT DID HE DO?
HE... HE...

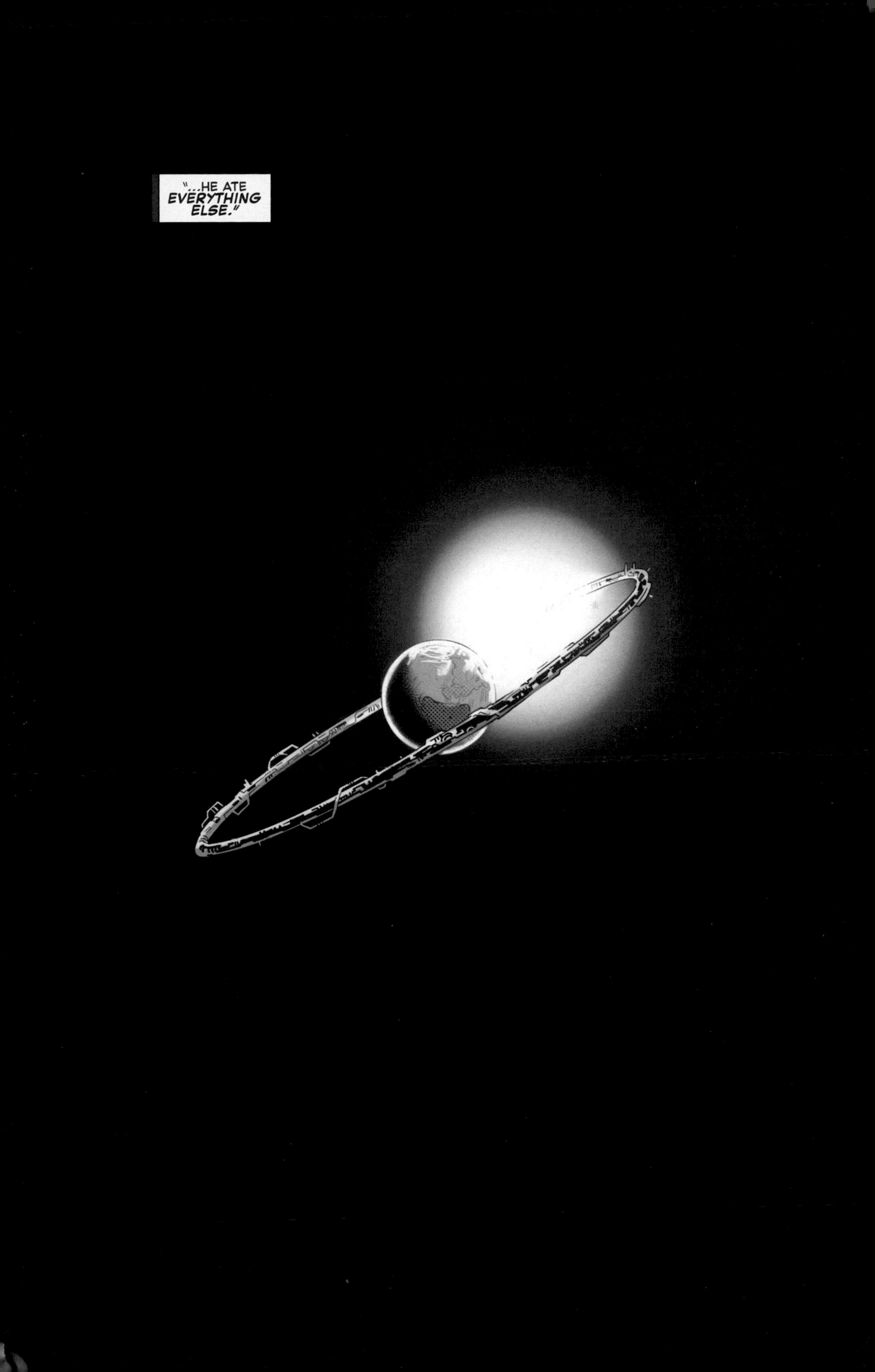
"...HE ATE *EVERYTHING* ELSE."

5

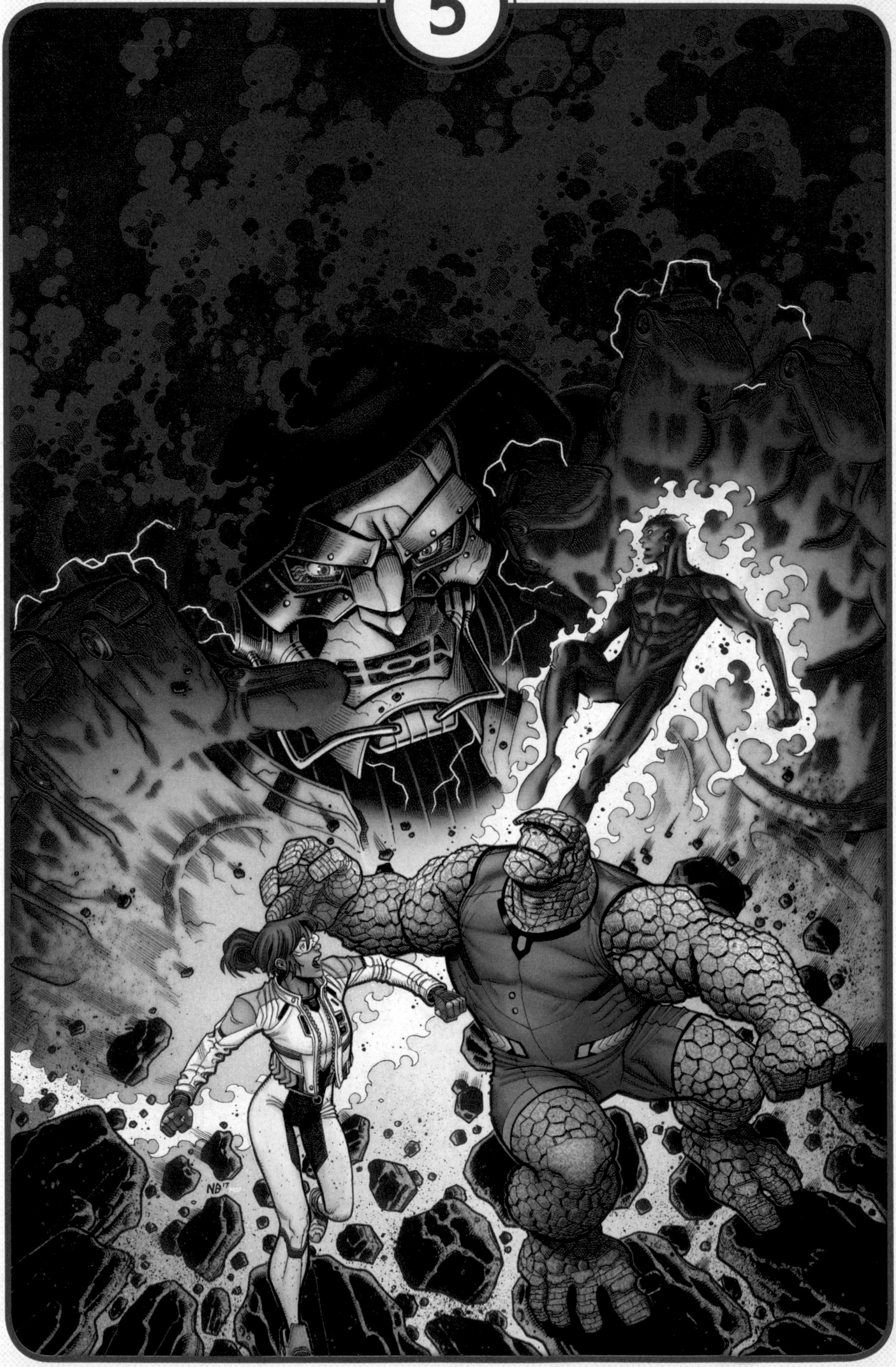

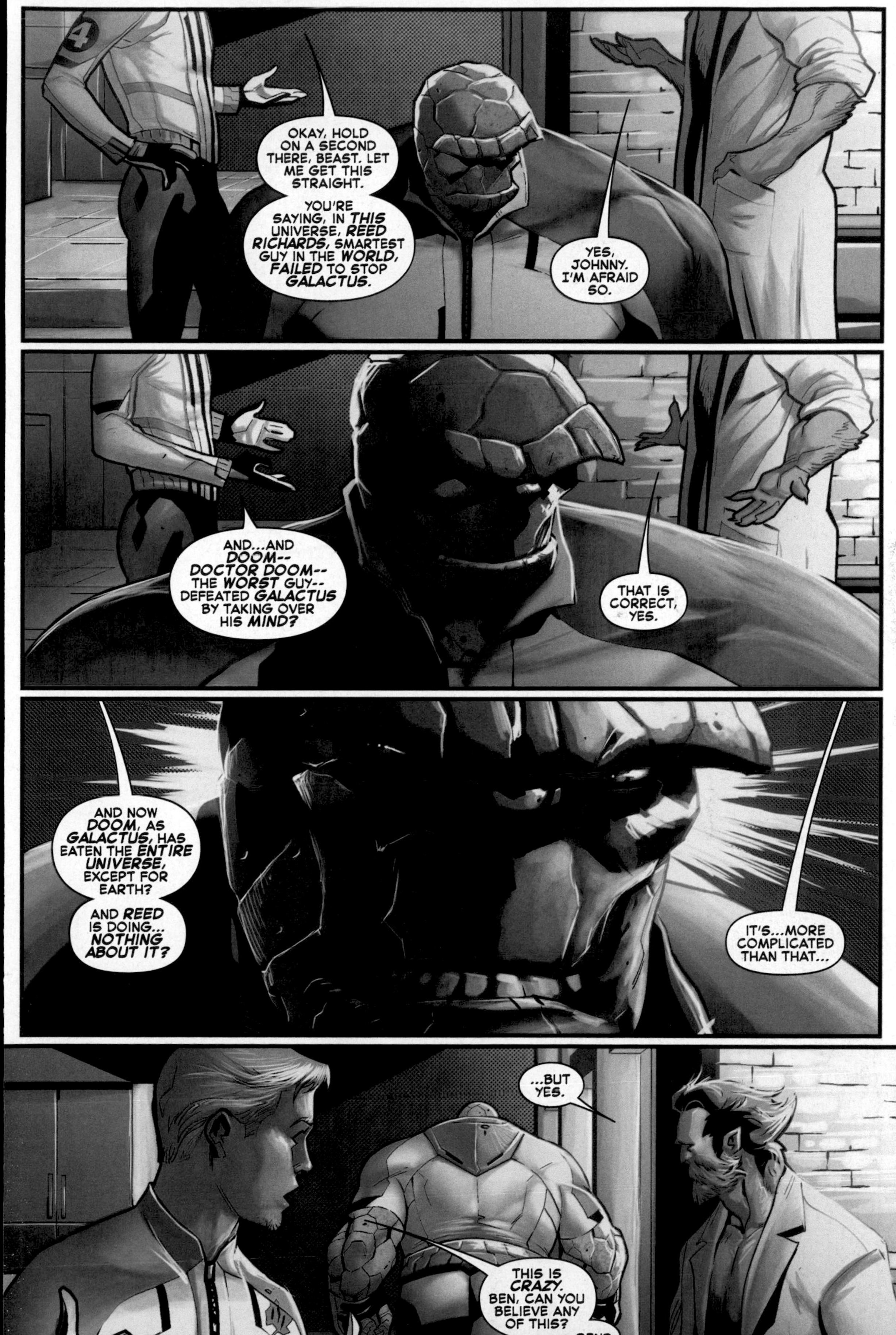
OKAY, HOLD ON A SECOND THERE, BEAST. LET ME GET THIS STRAIGHT.
YOU'RE SAYING, IN THIS UNIVERSE, REED RICHARDS, SMARTEST GUY IN THE WORLD, FAILED TO STOP GALACTUS.
YES, JOHNNY. I'M AFRAID SO.
AND...AND DOOM-- DOCTOR DOOM-- THE WORST GUY-- DEFEATED GALACTUS BY TAKING OVER HIS MIND?
THAT IS CORRECT, YES.
AND NOW DOOM, AS GALACTUS, HAS EATEN THE ENTIRE UNIVERSE, EXCEPT FOR EARTH?
AND REED IS DOING... NOTHING ABOUT IT?
IT'S...MORE COMPLICATED THAN THAT...
...BUT YES.
THIS IS CRAZY. BEN, CAN YOU BELIEVE ANY OF THIS?
BEN?

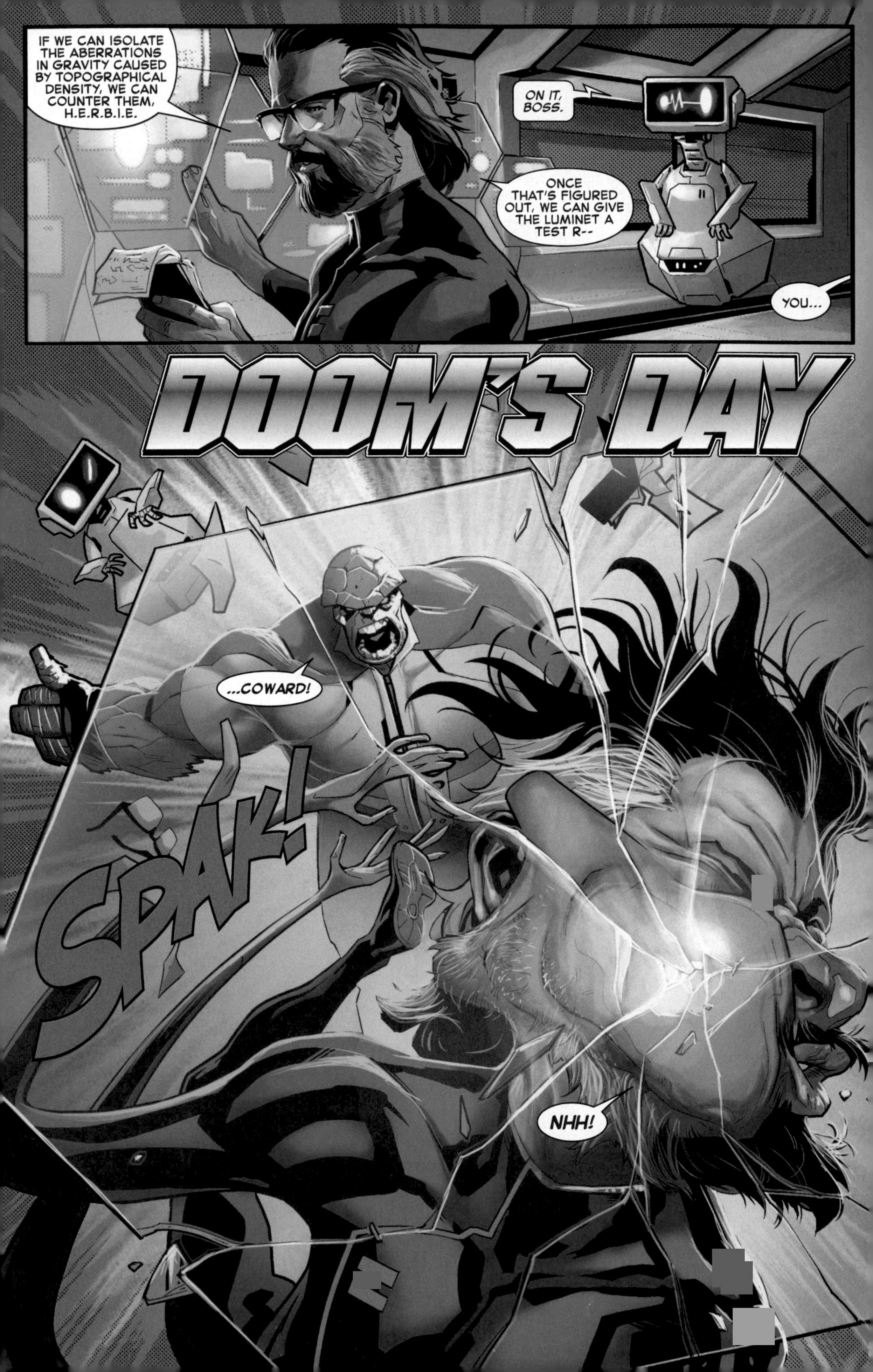
IF WE CAN ISOLATE THE ABERRATIONS IN GRAVITY CAUSED BY TOPOGRAPHICAL DENSITY, WE CAN COUNTER THEM, H.E.R.B.I.E.
ON IT, BOSS.
ONCE THAT'S FIGURED OUT, WE CAN GIVE THE LUMINET A TEST R--
YOU...
DOOM'S DAY
...COWARD!
SPAK!
NHH!

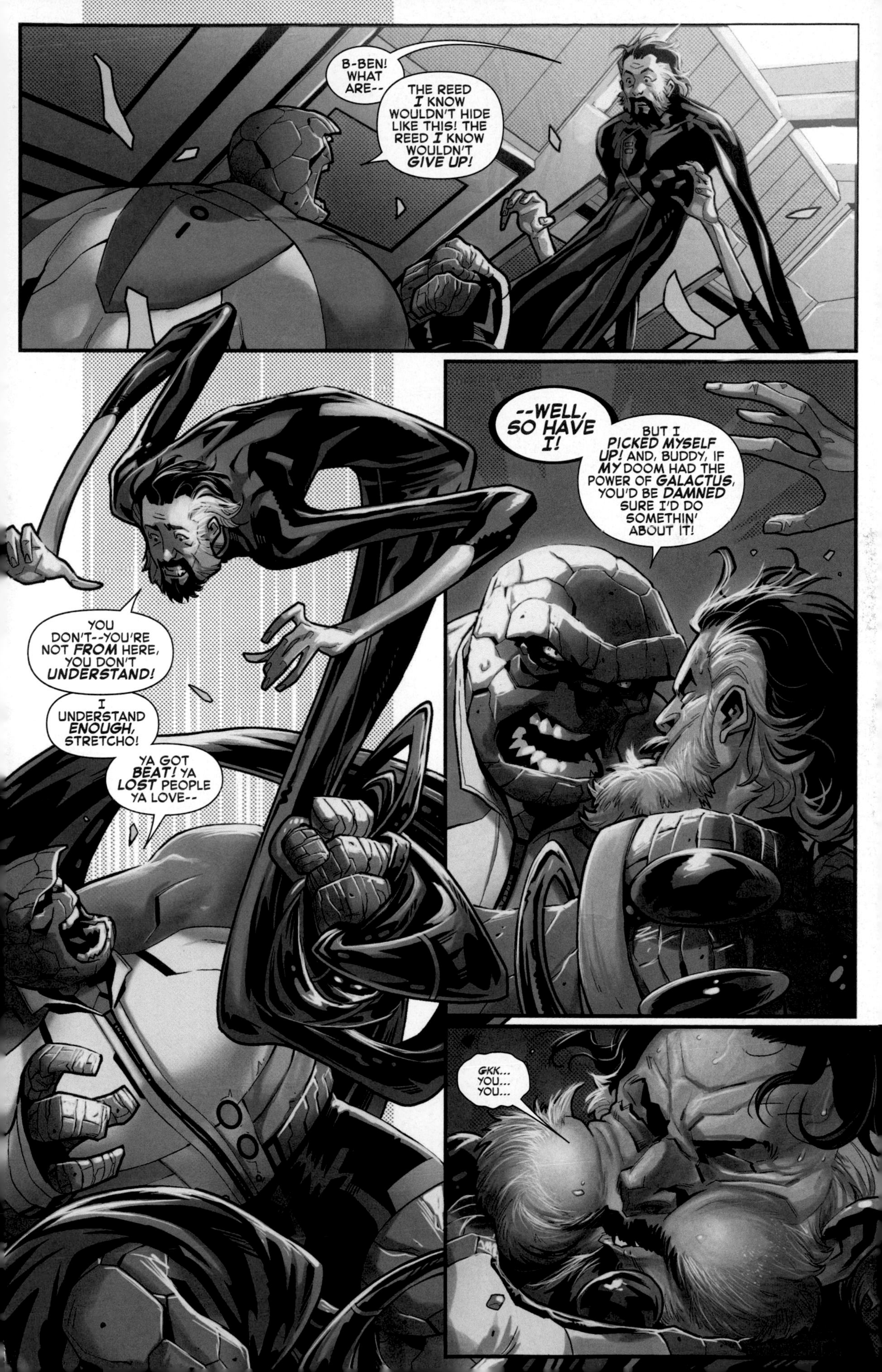
B-BEN! WHAT ARE--
THE REED I KNOW WOULDN'T HIDE LIKE THIS! THE REED I KNOW WOULDN'T GIVE UP!
YOU DON'T--YOU'RE NOT FROM HERE, YOU DON'T UNDERSTAND!
I UNDERSTAND ENOUGH, STRETCHO!
YA GOT BEAT! YA LOST PEOPLE YA LOVE--
--WELL, SO HAVE I!
BUT I PICKED MYSELF UP! AND, BUDDY, IF MY DOOM HAD THE POWER OF GALACTUS, YOU'D BE DAMNED SURE I'D DO SOMETHIN' ABOUT IT!
GKK... YOU... YOU...

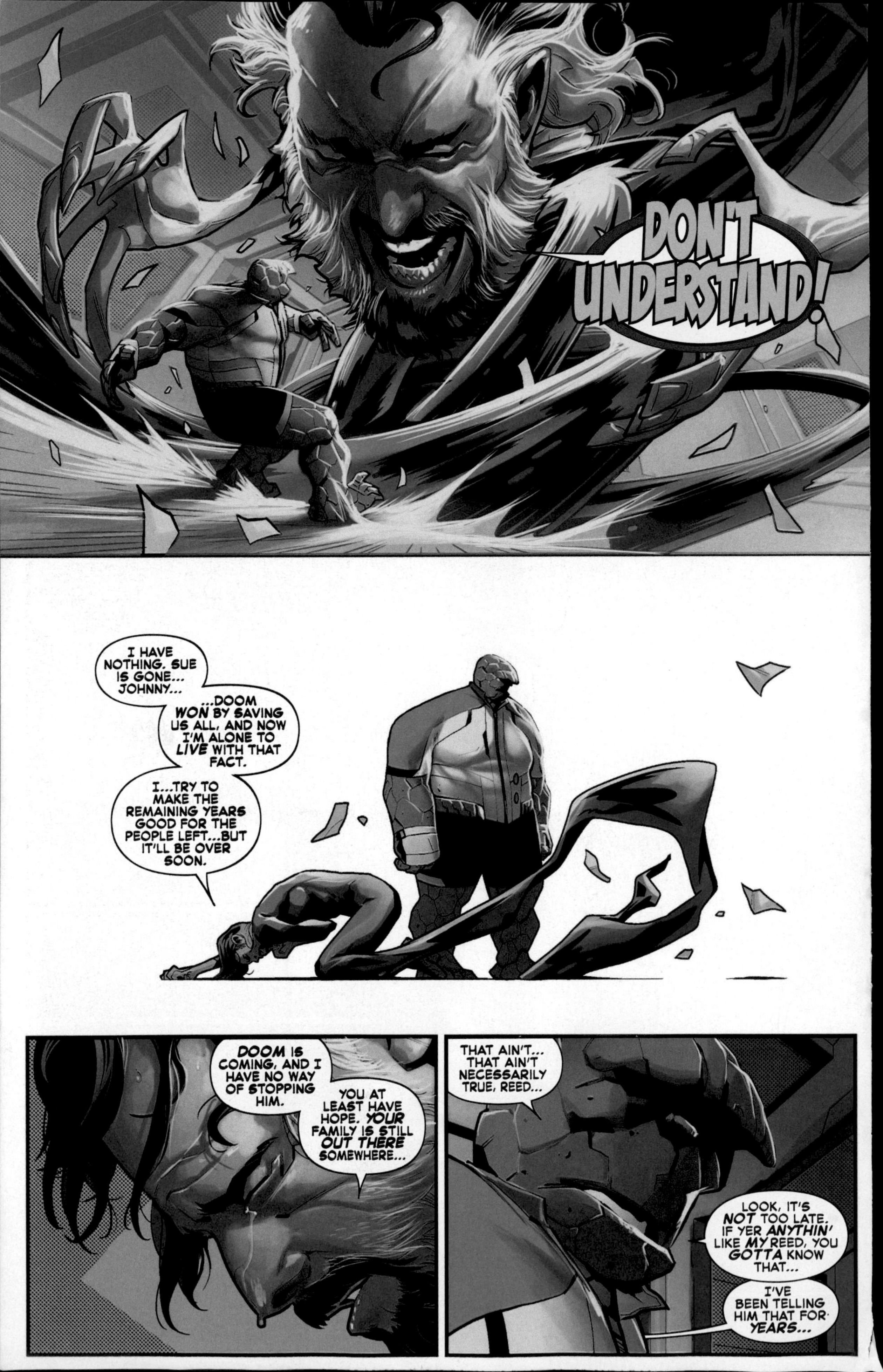
DON'T UNDERSTAND!
I HAVE NOTHING. SUE IS GONE... JOHNNY...
...DOOM WON BY SAVING US ALL, AND NOW I'M ALONE TO LIVE WITH THAT FACT.
I...TRY TO MAKE THE REMAINING YEARS GOOD FOR THE PEOPLE LEFT...BUT IT'LL BE OVER SOON.
DOOM IS COMING, AND I HAVE NO WAY OF STOPPING HIM.
YOU AT LEAST HAVE HOPE. YOUR FAMILY IS STILL OUT THERE SOMEWHERE...
THAT AIN'T... THAT AIN'T NECESSARILY TRUE, REED...
LOOK, IT'S NOT TOO LATE. IF YER ANYTHIN' LIKE MY REED, YOU GOTTA KNOW THAT...
I'VE BEEN TELLING HIM THAT FOR YEARS...

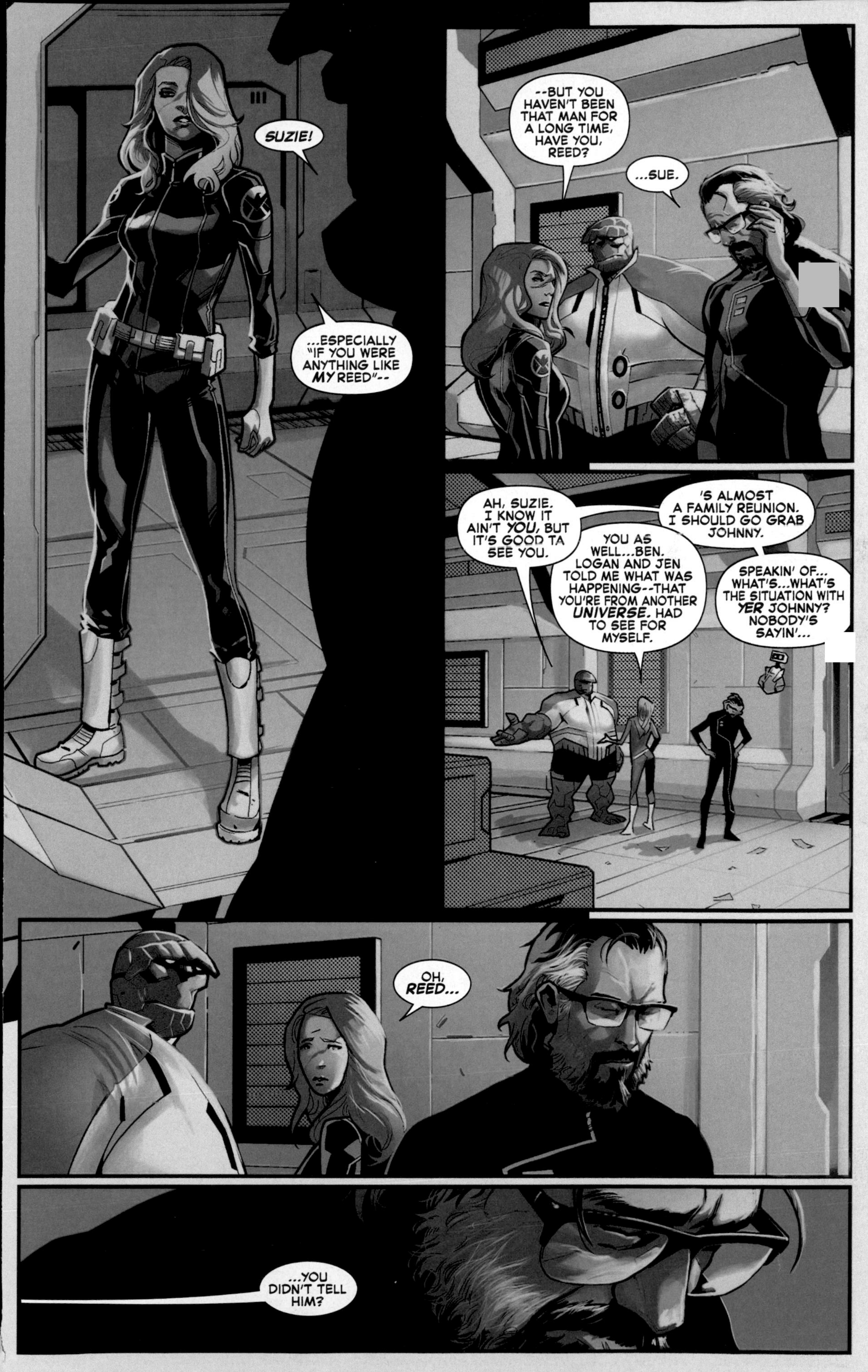
SUZIE!
...ESPECIALLY "IF YOU WERE ANYTHING LIKE MY REED"--
--BUT YOU HAVEN'T BEEN THAT MAN FOR A LONG TIME, HAVE YOU, REED?
...SUE.
AH, SUZIE. I KNOW IT AIN'T YOU, BUT IT'S GOOD TA SEE YOU.
YOU AS WELL...BEN. LOGAN AND JEN TOLD ME WHAT WAS HAPPENING--THAT YOU'RE FROM ANOTHER UNIVERSE. HAD TO SEE FOR MYSELF.
'S ALMOST A FAMILY REUNION. I SHOULD GO GRAB JOHNNY.
SPEAKIN' OF... WHAT'S...WHAT'S THE SITUATION WITH YER JOHNNY? NOBODY'S SAYIN'...
OH, REED...
...YOU DIDN'T TELL HIM?

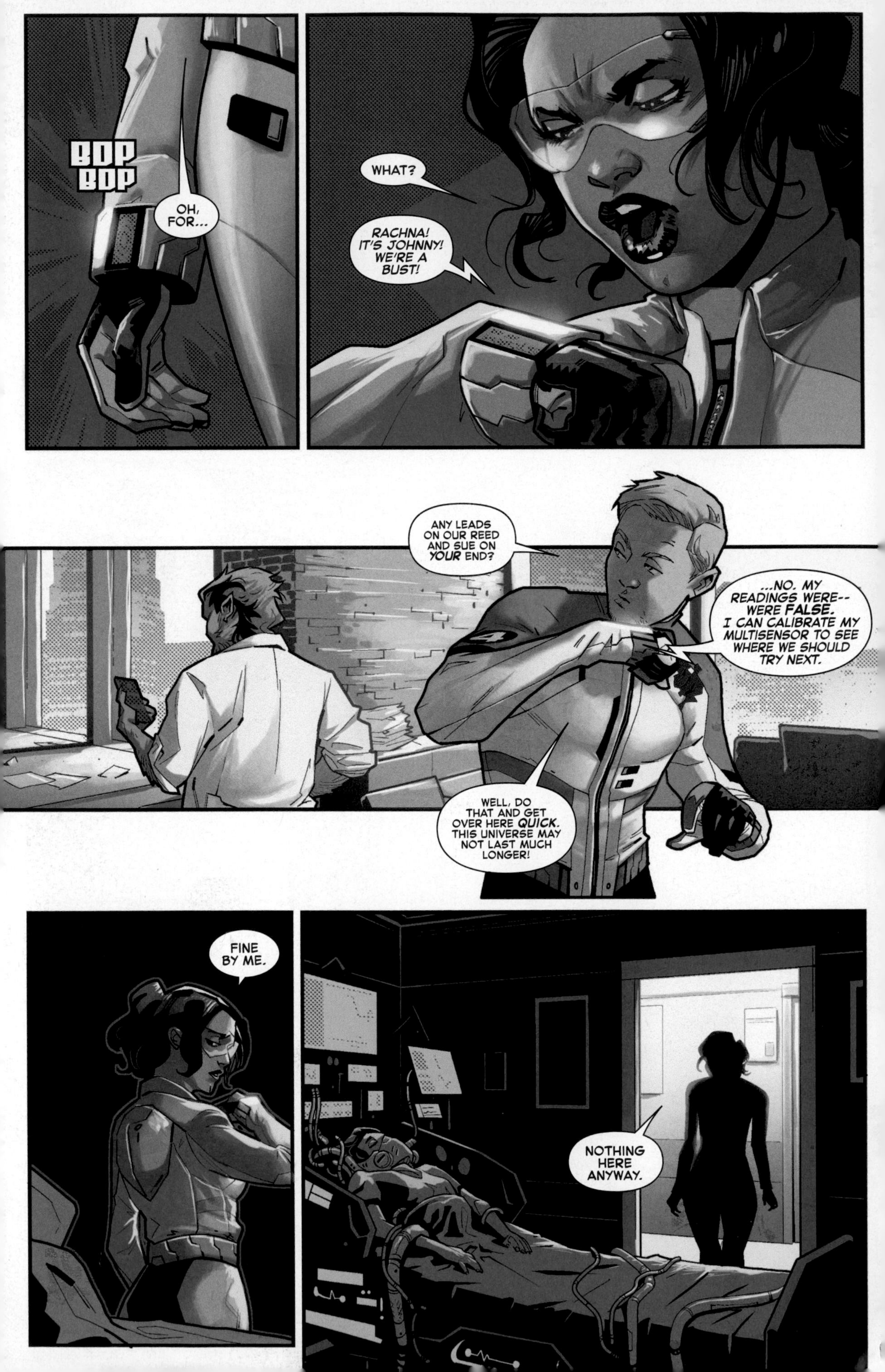
BOP
BOP
OH, FOR...
WHAT?
RACHNA! IT'S JOHNNY! WE'RE A BUST!
ANY LEADS ON OUR REED AND SUE ON YOUR END?
...NO. MY READINGS WERE-- WERE FALSE. I CAN CALIBRATE MY MULTISENSOR TO SEE WHERE WE SHOULD TRY NEXT.
WELL, DO THAT AND GET OVER HERE QUICK. THIS UNIVERSE MAY NOT LAST MUCH LONGER!
FINE BY ME.
NOTHING HERE ANYWAY.

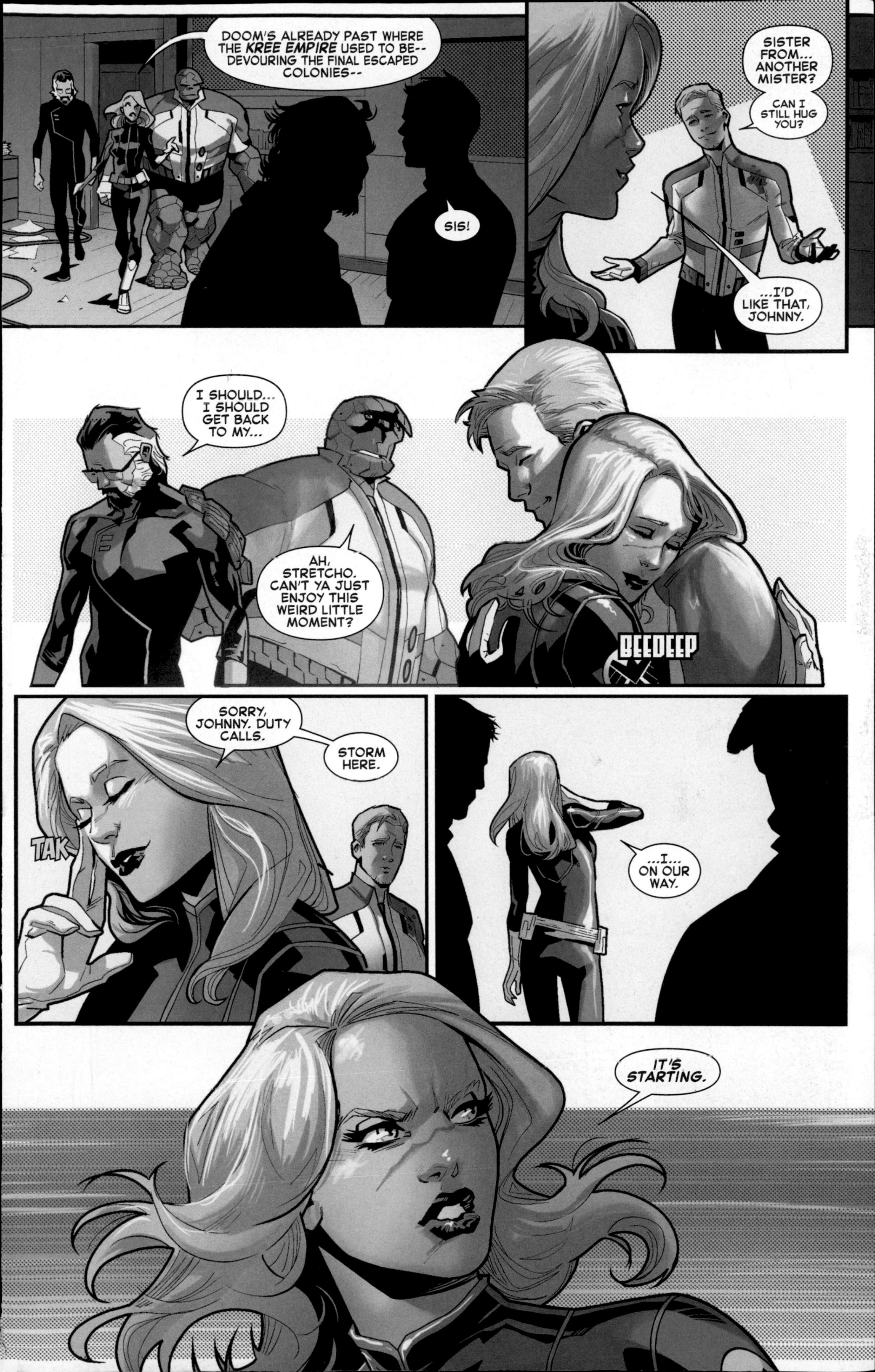
DOOM'S ALREADY PAST WHERE THE KREE EMPIRE USED TO BE-- DEVOURING THE FINAL ESCAPED COLONIES--
SIS!
SISTER FROM... ANOTHER MISTER?
CAN I STILL HUG YOU?
...I'D LIKE THAT, JOHNNY.
I SHOULD... I SHOULD GET BACK TO MY...
AH, STRETCHO. CAN'T YA JUST ENJOY THIS WEIRD LITTLE MOMENT?
BEEDEEP
SORRY, JOHNNY. DUTY CALLS.
STORM HERE.
TAK
...I... ON OUR WAY.
IT'S STARTING.

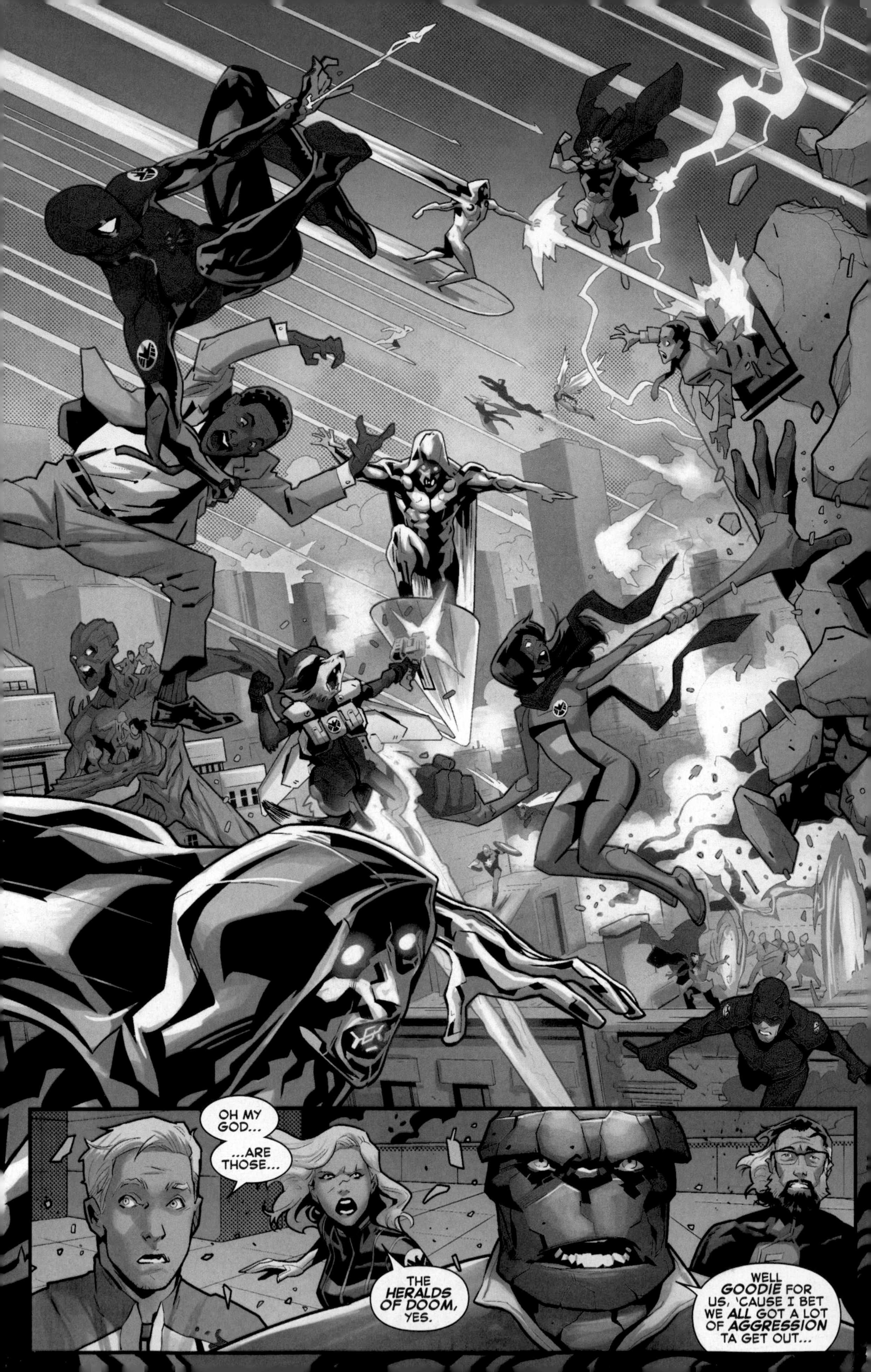
OH MY GOD...
...ARE THOSE...
THE HERALDS OF DOOM, YES.
WELL GOODIE FOR US, 'CAUSE I BET WE ALL GOT A LOT OF AGGRESSION TA GET OUT...

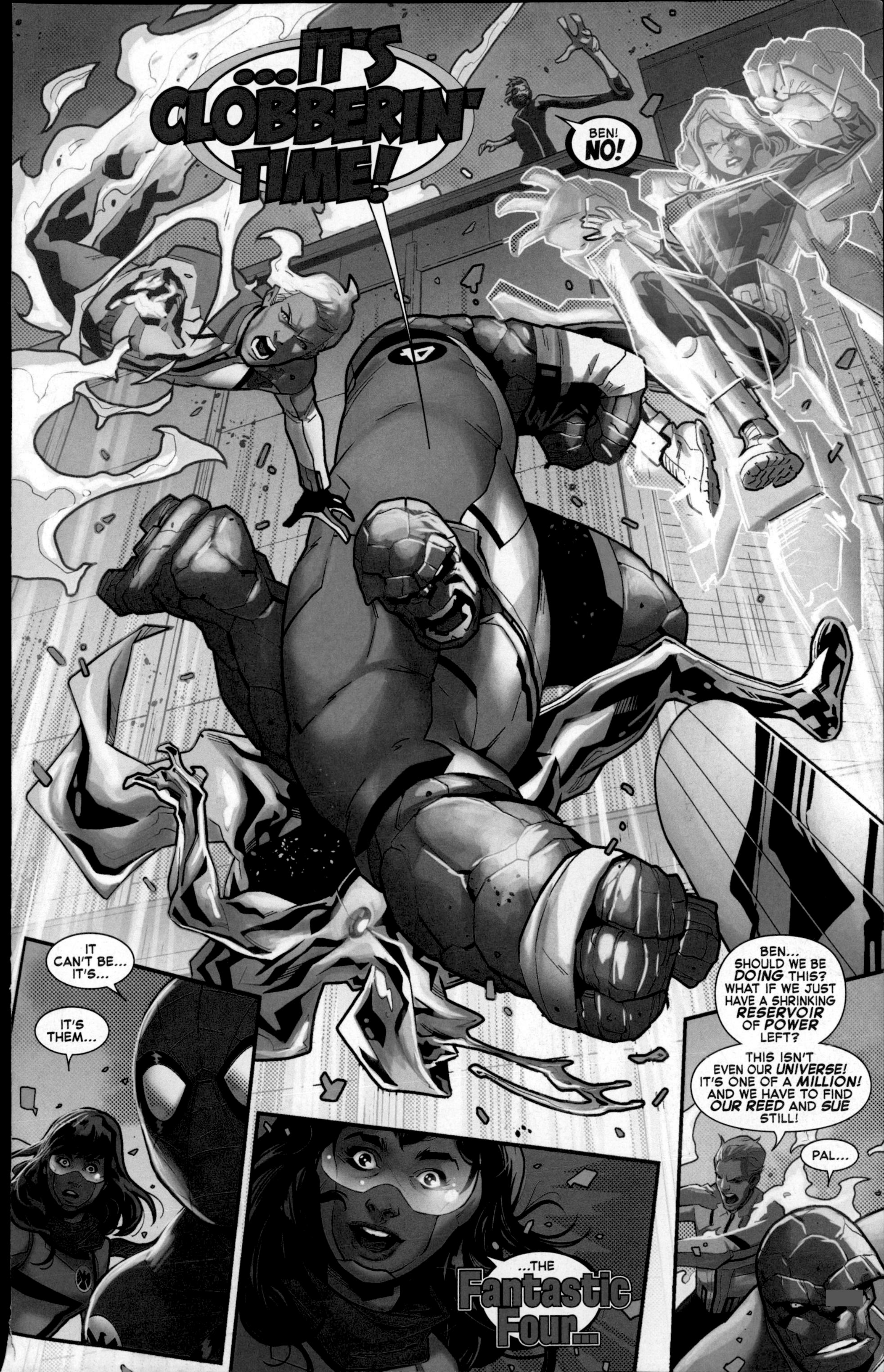

...IT'S CLOBBERIN' TIME!
BEN! NO!
IT CAN'T BE... IT'S...
IT'S THEM...
...THE
Fantastic Four...
BEN... SHOULD WE BE DOING THIS? WHAT IF WE JUST HAVE A SHRINKING RESERVOIR OF POWER LEFT?
THIS ISN'T EVEN OUR UNIVERSE! IT'S ONE OF A MILLION! AND WE HAVE TO FIND OUR REED AND SUE STILL!
PAL...

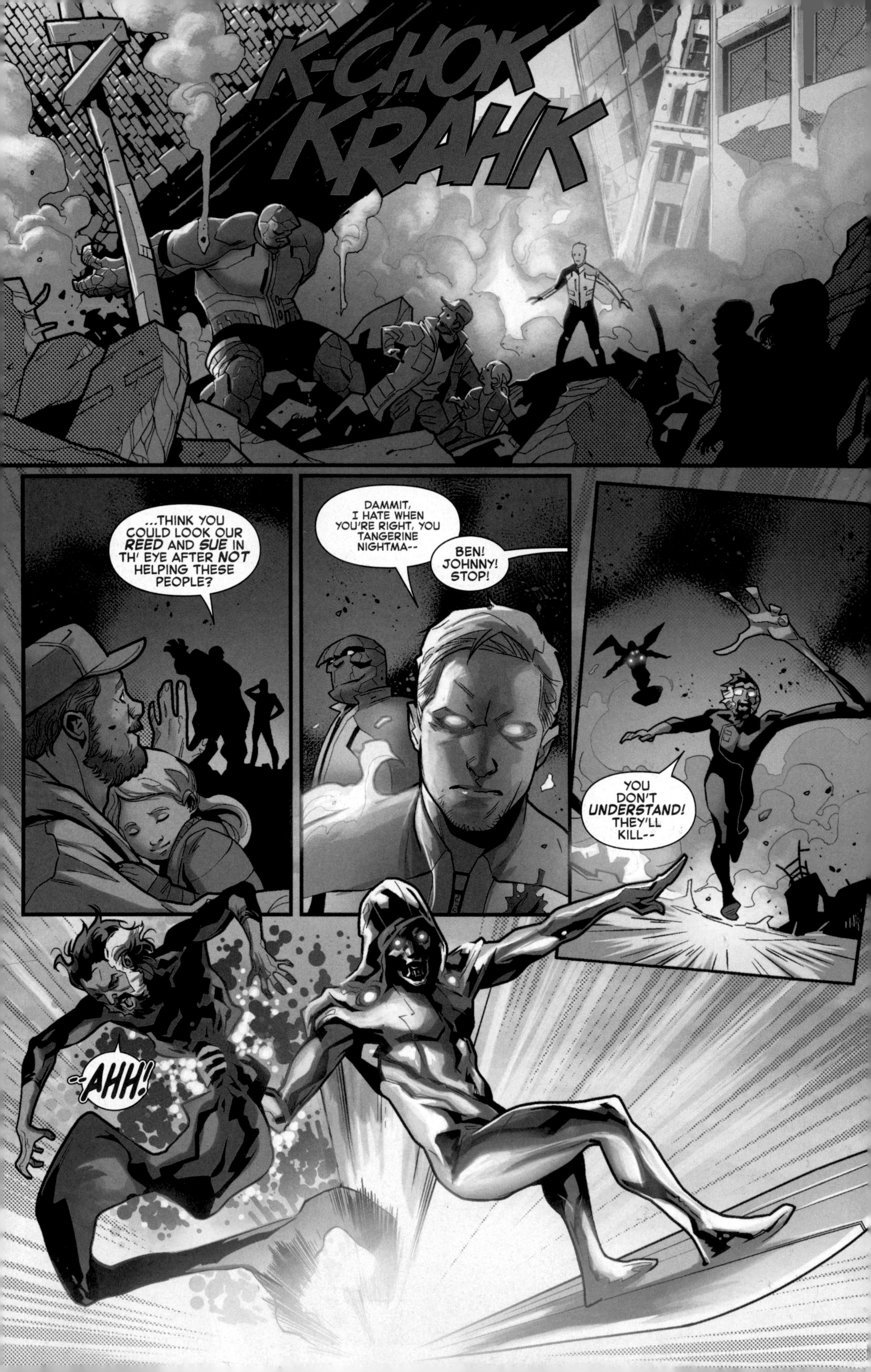

K-CHOK
KRAHK
...THINK YOU COULD LOOK OUR REED AND SUE IN TH' EYE AFTER NOT HELPING THESE PEOPLE?
DAMMIT, I HATE WHEN YOU'RE RIGHT, YOU TANGERINE NIGHTMA--
BEN! JOHNNY! STOP!
YOU DON'T UNDERSTAND! THEY'LL KILL--
-AHH!

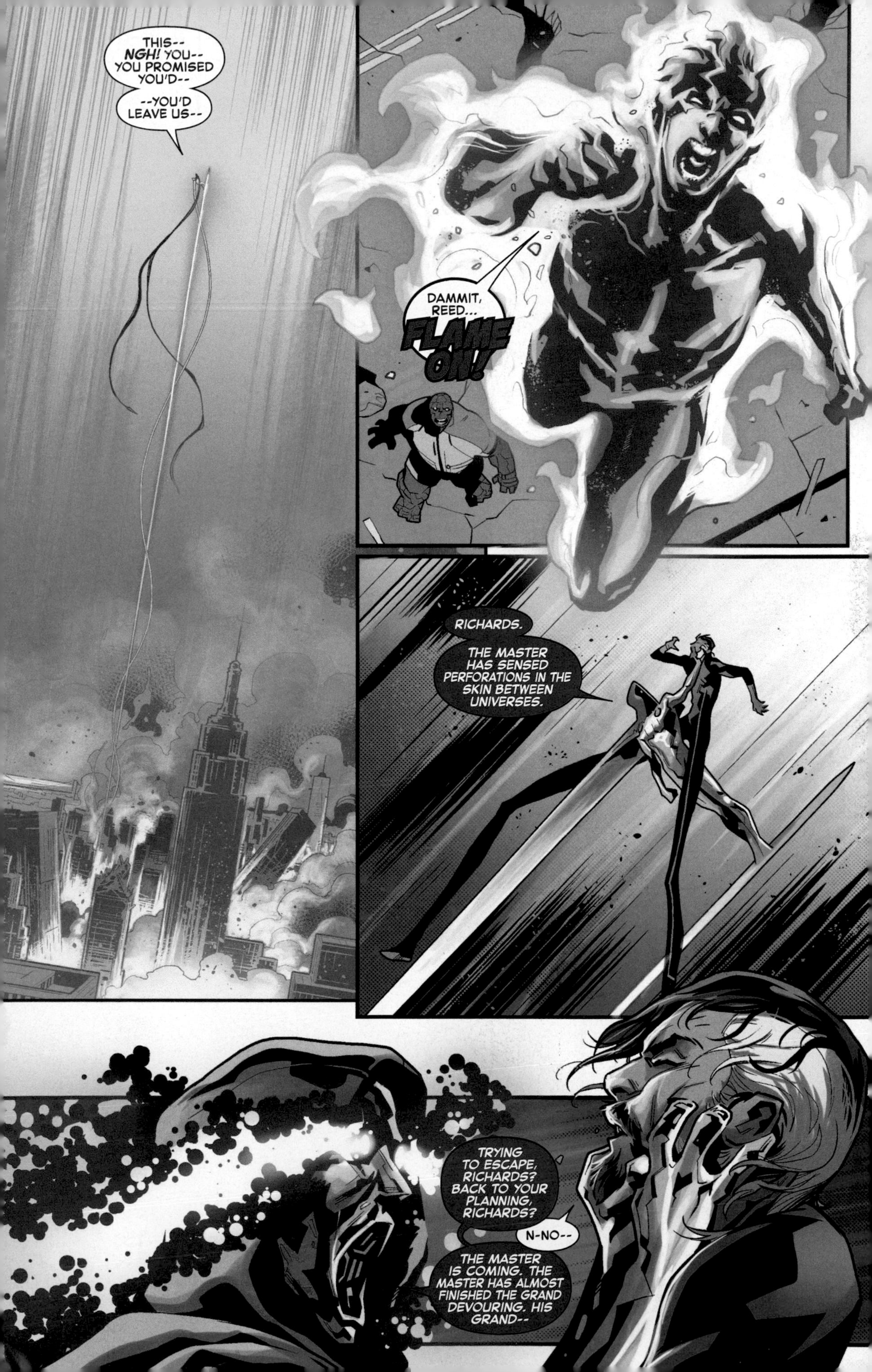
THIS-- NGH! YOU-- YOU PROMISED YOU'D--
--YOU'D LEAVE US--
DAMMIT, REED...
FLAME ON!
RICHARDS.
THE MASTER HAS SENSED PERFORATIONS IN THE SKIN BETWEEN UNIVERSES.
TRYING TO ESCAPE, RICHARDS? BACK TO YOUR PLANNING, RICHARDS?
N-NO--
THE MASTER IS COMING. THE MASTER HAS ALMOST FINISHED THE GRAND DEVOURING. HIS GRAND--

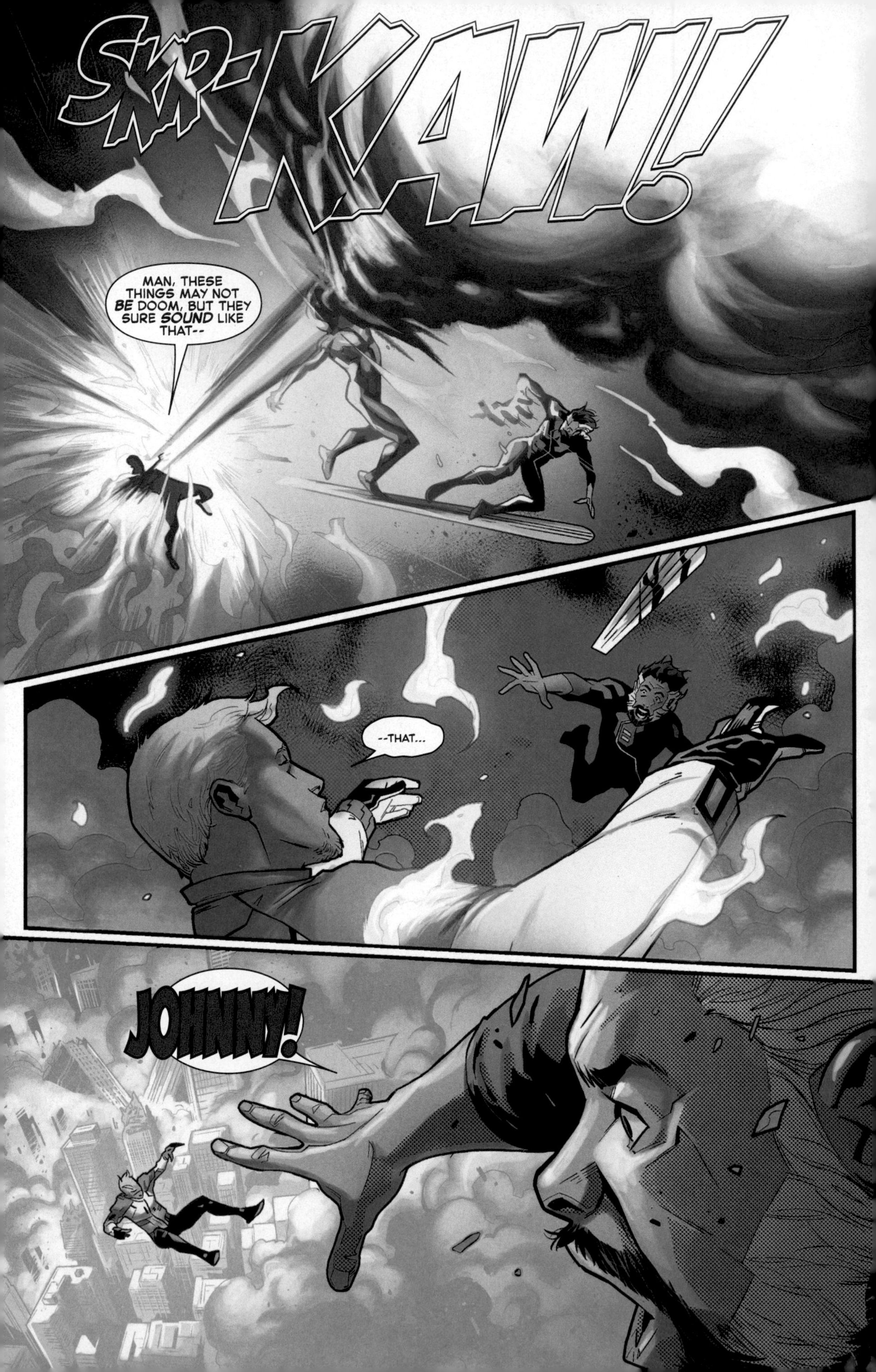
SKID-KAW!
MAN, THESE THINGS MAY NOT BE DOOM, BUT THEY SURE SOUND LIKE THAT--
--THAT...
JOHNNY!

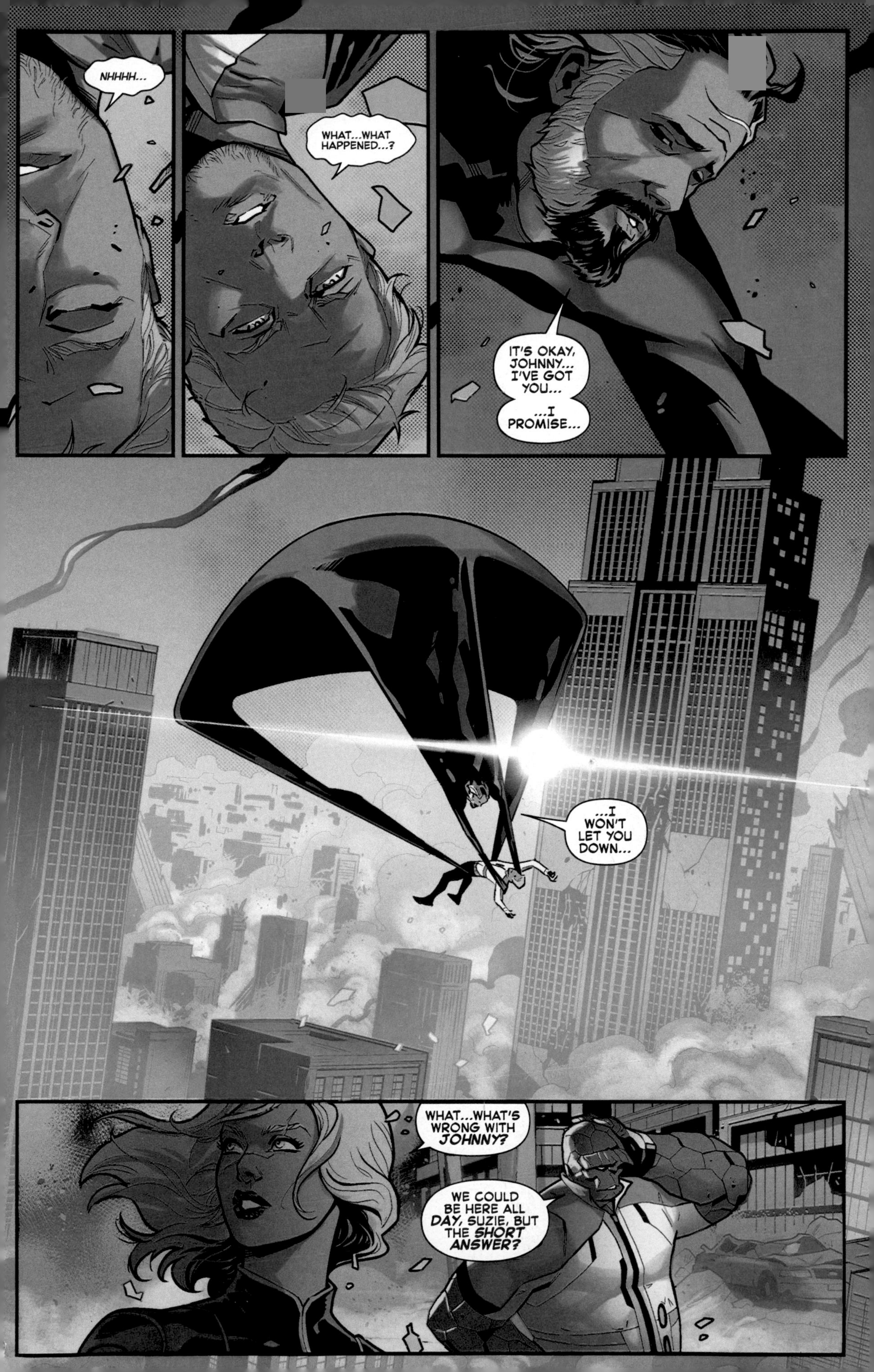
NHHHH...
WHAT...WHAT HAPPENED...?
IT'S OKAY, JOHNNY... I'VE GOT YOU...
...I PROMISE...
...I WON'T LET YOU DOWN...
WHAT...WHAT'S WRONG WITH JOHNNY?
WE COULD BE HERE ALL DAY, SUZIE, BUT THE SHORT ANSWER?

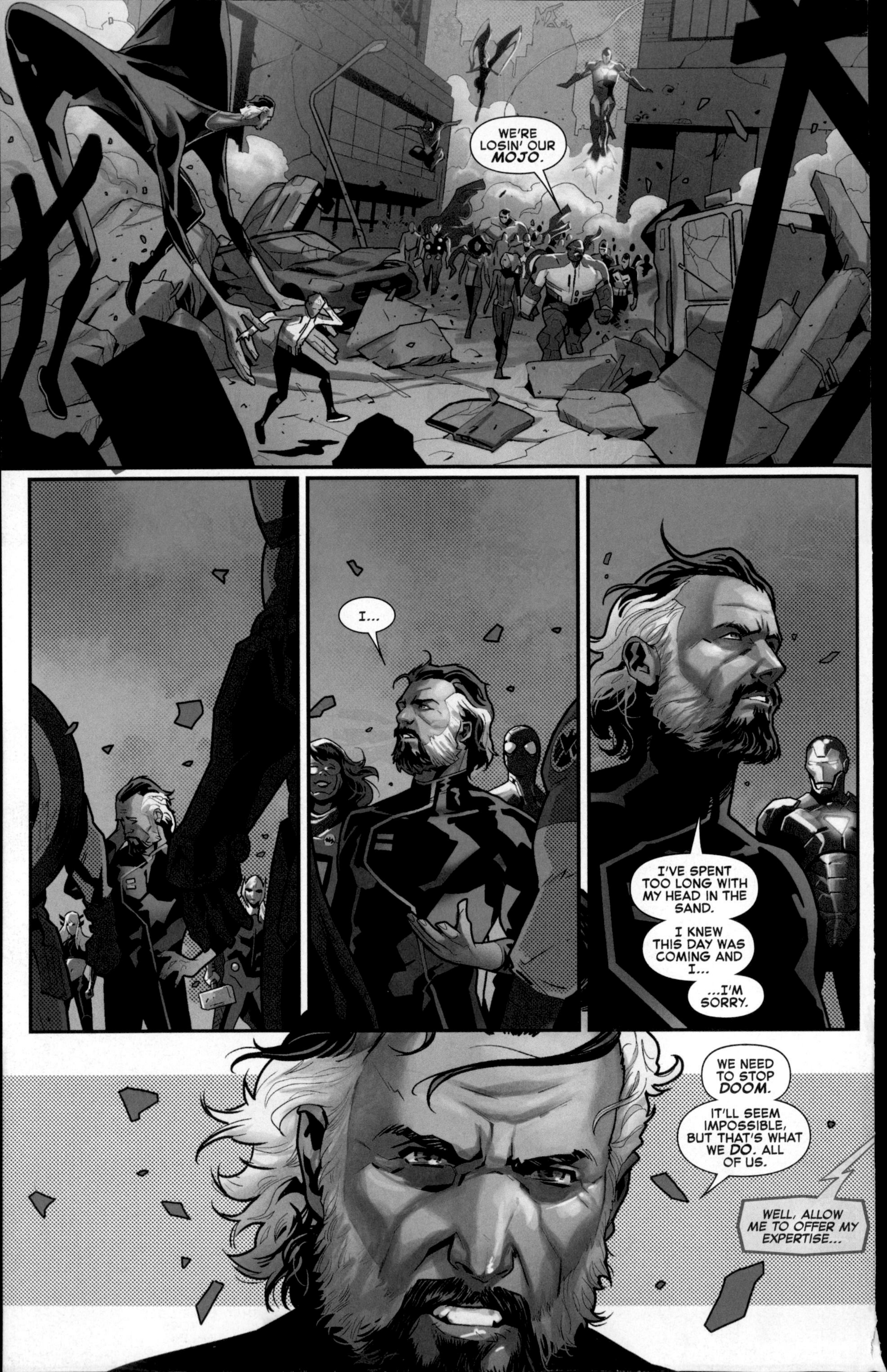
WE'RE LOSIN' OUR MOJO.
I...
I'VE SPENT TOO LONG WITH MY HEAD IN THE SAND.
I KNEW THIS DAY WAS COMING AND I...
...I'M SORRY.
WE NEED TO STOP DOOM.
IT'LL SEEM IMPOSSIBLE, BUT THAT'S WHAT WE DO. ALL OF US.
WELL, ALLOW ME TO OFFER MY EXPERTISE...

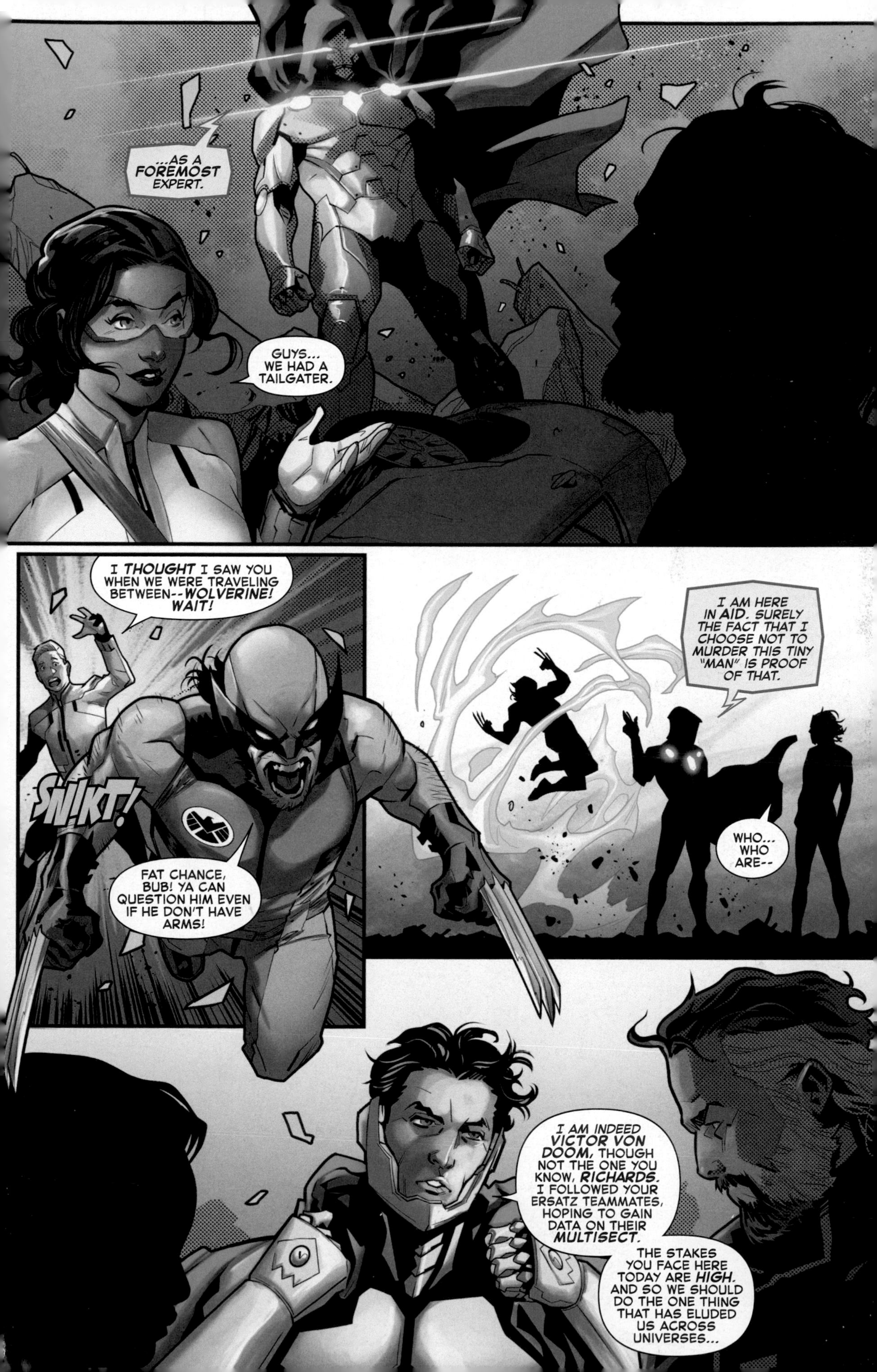

...AS A FOREMOST EXPERT.
GUYS... WE HAD A TAILGATER.
I THOUGHT I SAW YOU WHEN WE WERE TRAVELING BETWEEN--WOLVERINE! WAIT!
SNIKT!
FAT CHANCE, BUB! YA CAN QUESTION HIM EVEN IF HE DON'T HAVE ARMS!
I AM HERE IN AID. SURELY THE FACT THAT I CHOOSE NOT TO MURDER THIS TINY "MAN" IS PROOF OF THAT.
WHO... WHO ARE--
I AM INDEED VICTOR VON DOOM, THOUGH NOT THE ONE YOU KNOW, RICHARDS. I FOLLOWED YOUR ERSATZ TEAMMATES, HOPING TO GAIN DATA ON THEIR MULTISECT.
THE STAKES YOU FACE HERE TODAY ARE HIGH. AND SO WE SHOULD DO THE ONE THING THAT HAS ELUDED US ACROSS UNIVERSES...

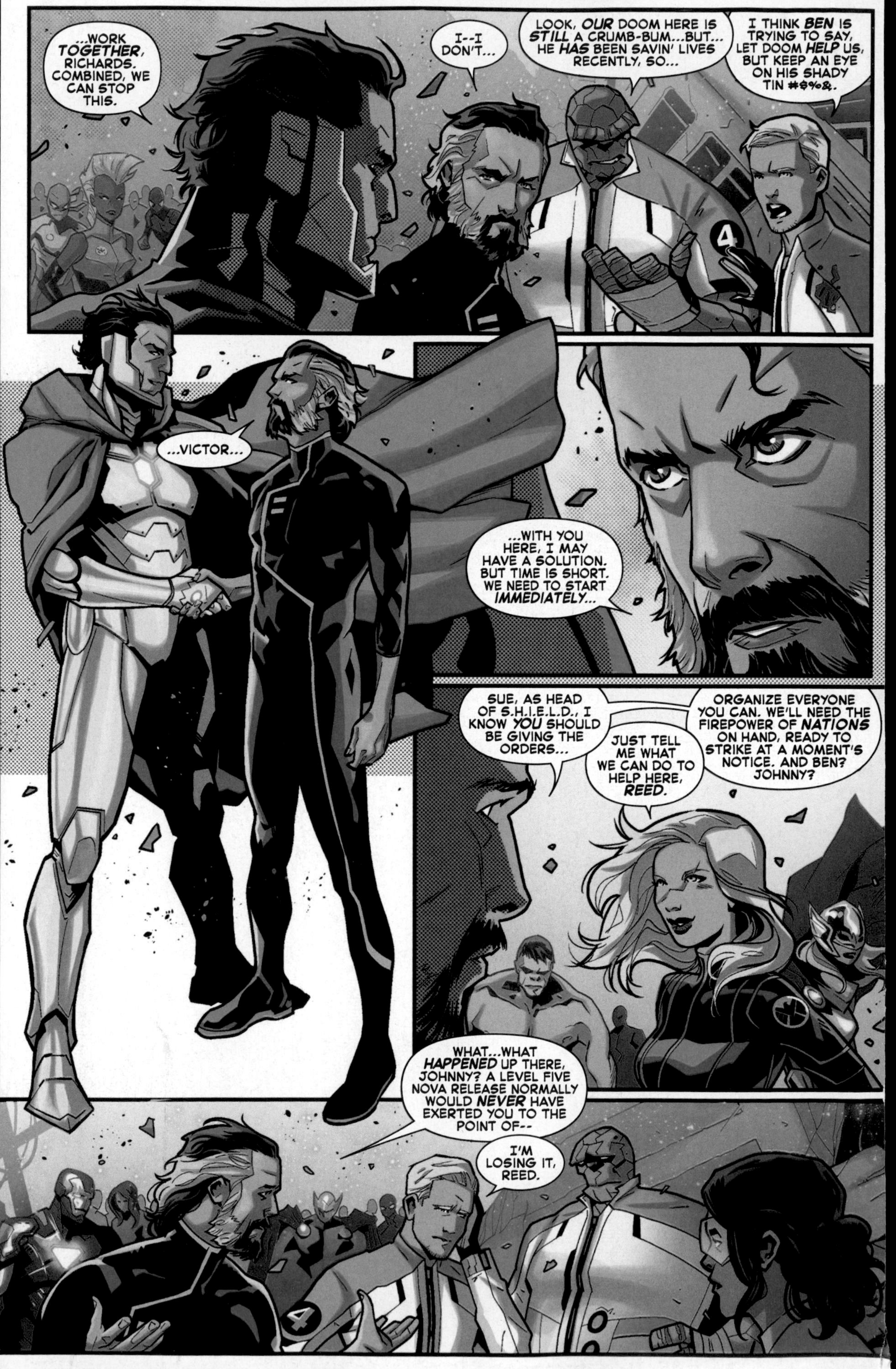
...WORK TOGETHER, RICHARDS. COMBINED, WE CAN STOP THIS.
I--I DON'T...
LOOK, OUR DOOM HERE IS STILL A CRUMB-BUM...BUT... HE HAS BEEN SAVIN' LIVES RECENTLY, SO...
I THINK BEN IS TRYING TO SAY, LET DOOM HELP US, BUT KEEP AN EYE ON HIS SHADY TIN #$%&.
...VICTOR...
...WITH YOU HERE, I MAY HAVE A SOLUTION. BUT TIME IS SHORT. WE NEED TO START IMMEDIATELY...
SUE, AS HEAD OF S.H.I.E.L.D., I KNOW YOU SHOULD BE GIVING THE ORDERS...
JUST TELL ME WHAT WE CAN DO TO HELP HERE, REED.
ORGANIZE EVERYONE YOU CAN. WE'LL NEED THE FIREPOWER OF NATIONS ON HAND, READY TO STRIKE AT A MOMENT'S NOTICE. AND BEN? JOHNNY?
WHAT...WHAT HAPPENED UP THERE, JOHNNY? A LEVEL FIVE NOVA RELEASE NORMALLY WOULD NEVER HAVE EXERTED YOU TO THE POINT OF--
I'M LOSING IT, REED.

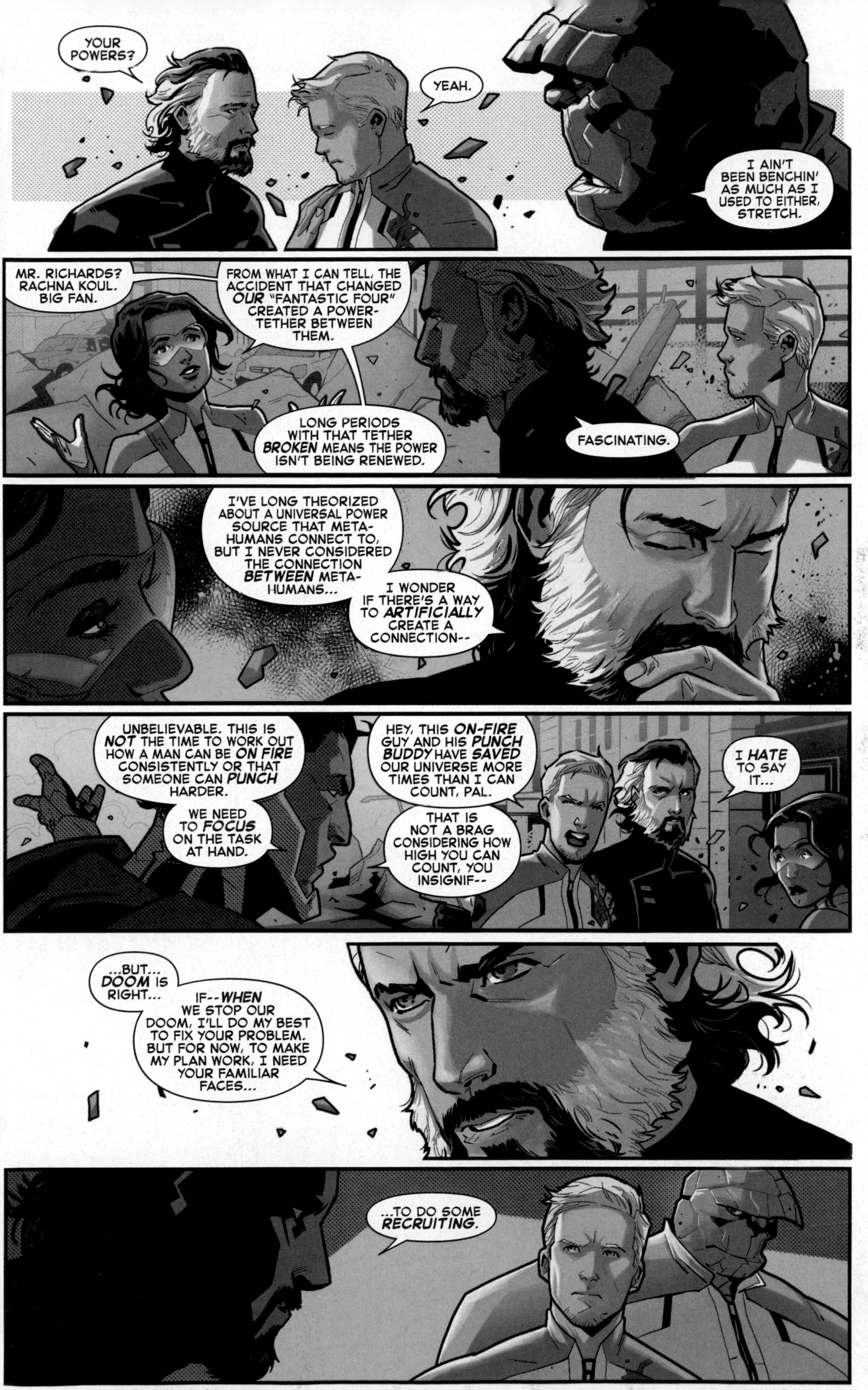
YOUR POWERS?
YEAH.
I AIN'T BEEN BENCHIN' AS MUCH AS I USED TO EITHER, STRETCH.
MR. RICHARDS? RACHNA KOUL. BIG FAN.
FROM WHAT I CAN TELL, THE ACCIDENT THAT CHANGED OUR "FANTASTIC FOUR" CREATED A POWER-TETHER BETWEEN THEM.
LONG PERIODS WITH THAT TETHER BROKEN MEANS THE POWER ISN'T BEING RENEWED.
FASCINATING.
I'VE LONG THEORIZED ABOUT A UNIVERSAL POWER SOURCE THAT META-HUMANS CONNECT TO, BUT I NEVER CONSIDERED THE CONNECTION BETWEEN META-HUMANS...
I WONDER IF THERE'S A WAY TO ARTIFICIALLY CREATE A CONNECTION--
UNBELIEVABLE. THIS IS NOT THE TIME TO WORK OUT HOW A MAN CAN BE ON FIRE CONSISTENTLY OR THAT SOMEONE CAN PUNCH HARDER.
WE NEED TO FOCUS ON THE TASK AT HAND.
HEY, THIS ON-FIRE GUY AND HIS PUNCH BUDDY HAVE SAVED OUR UNIVERSE MORE TIMES THAN I CAN COUNT, PAL.
THAT IS NOT A BRAG CONSIDERING HOW HIGH YOU CAN COUNT, YOU INSIGNIF--
I HATE TO SAY IT...
...BUT... DOOM IS RIGHT...
IF--WHEN WE STOP OUR DOOM, I'LL DO MY BEST TO FIX YOUR PROBLEM. BUT FOR NOW, TO MAKE MY PLAN WORK, I NEED YOUR FAMILIAR FACES...
...TO DO SOME RECRUITING.

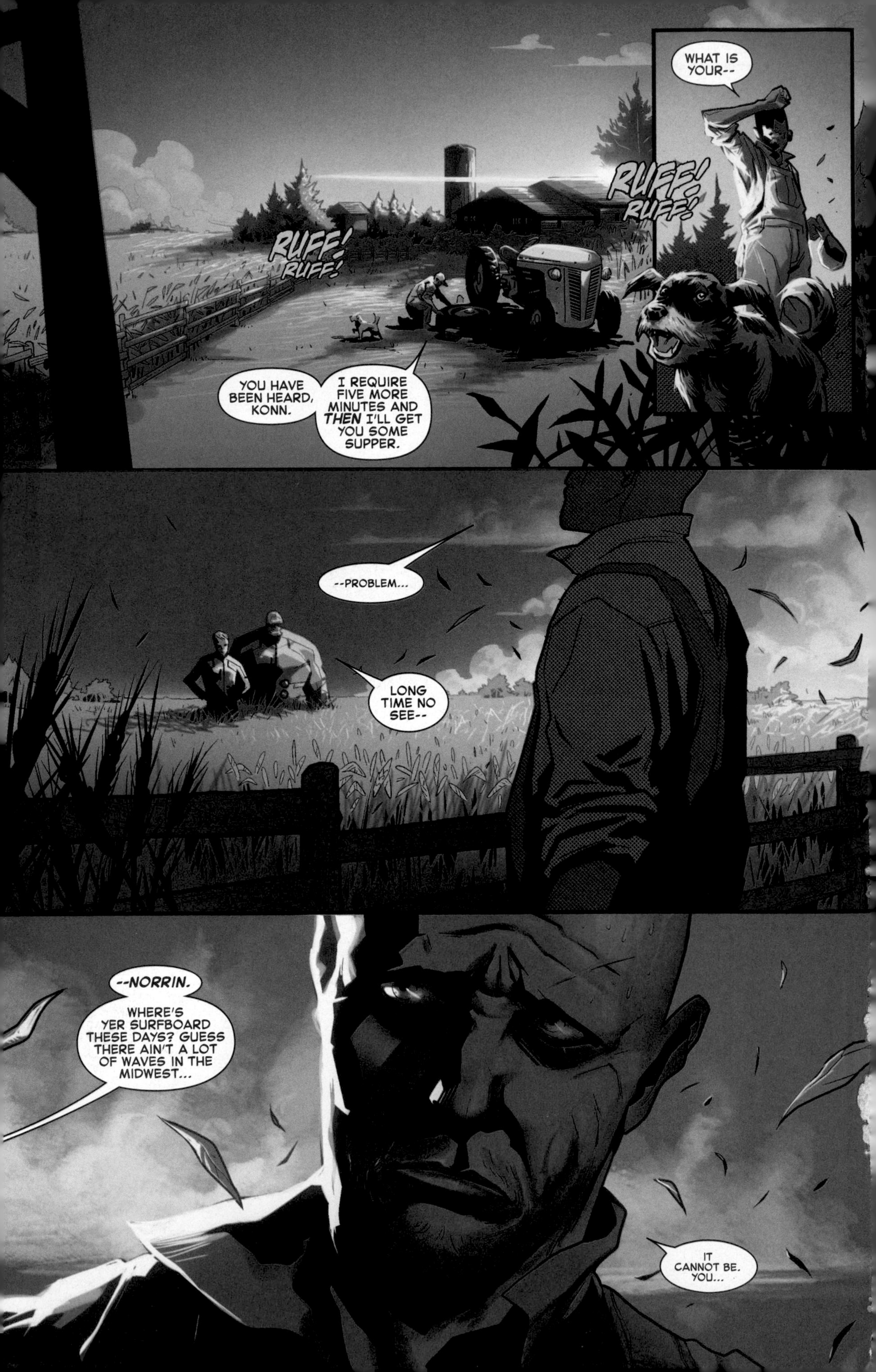

RUFF! RUFF!
YOU HAVE BEEN HEARD, KONN.
I REQUIRE FIVE MORE MINUTES AND THEN I'LL GET YOU SOME SUPPER.
WHAT IS YOUR--
RUFF! RUFF!
--PROBLEM...
LONG TIME NO SEE--
--NORRIN.
WHERE'S YER SURFBOARD THESE DAYS? GUESS THERE AIN'T A LOT OF WAVES IN THE MIDWEST...
IT CANNOT BE. YOU...

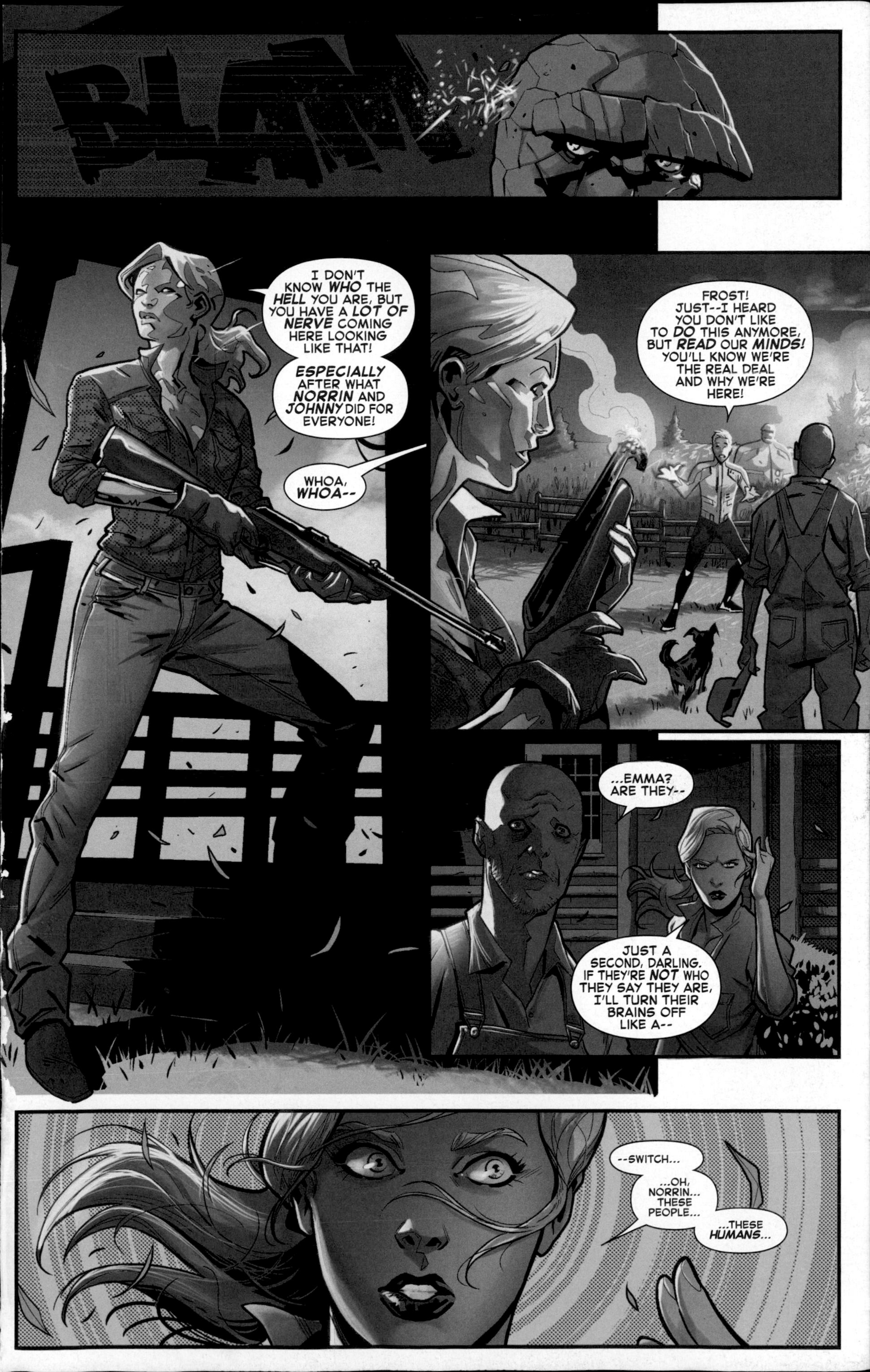
BLAM
I DON'T KNOW WHO THE HELL YOU ARE, BUT YOU HAVE A LOT OF NERVE COMING HERE LOOKING LIKE THAT!
ESPECIALLY AFTER WHAT NORRIN AND JOHNNY DID FOR EVERYONE!
WHOA, WHOA--
FROST! JUST--I HEARD YOU DON'T LIKE TO DO THIS ANYMORE, BUT READ OUR MINDS! YOU'LL KNOW WE'RE THE REAL DEAL AND WHY WE'RE HERE!
...EMMA? ARE THEY--
JUST A SECOND, DARLING. IF THEY'RE NOT WHO THEY SAY THEY ARE, I'LL TURN THEIR BRAINS OFF LIKE A--
--SWITCH...
...OH, NORRIN... THESE PEOPLE...
...THESE HUMANS...

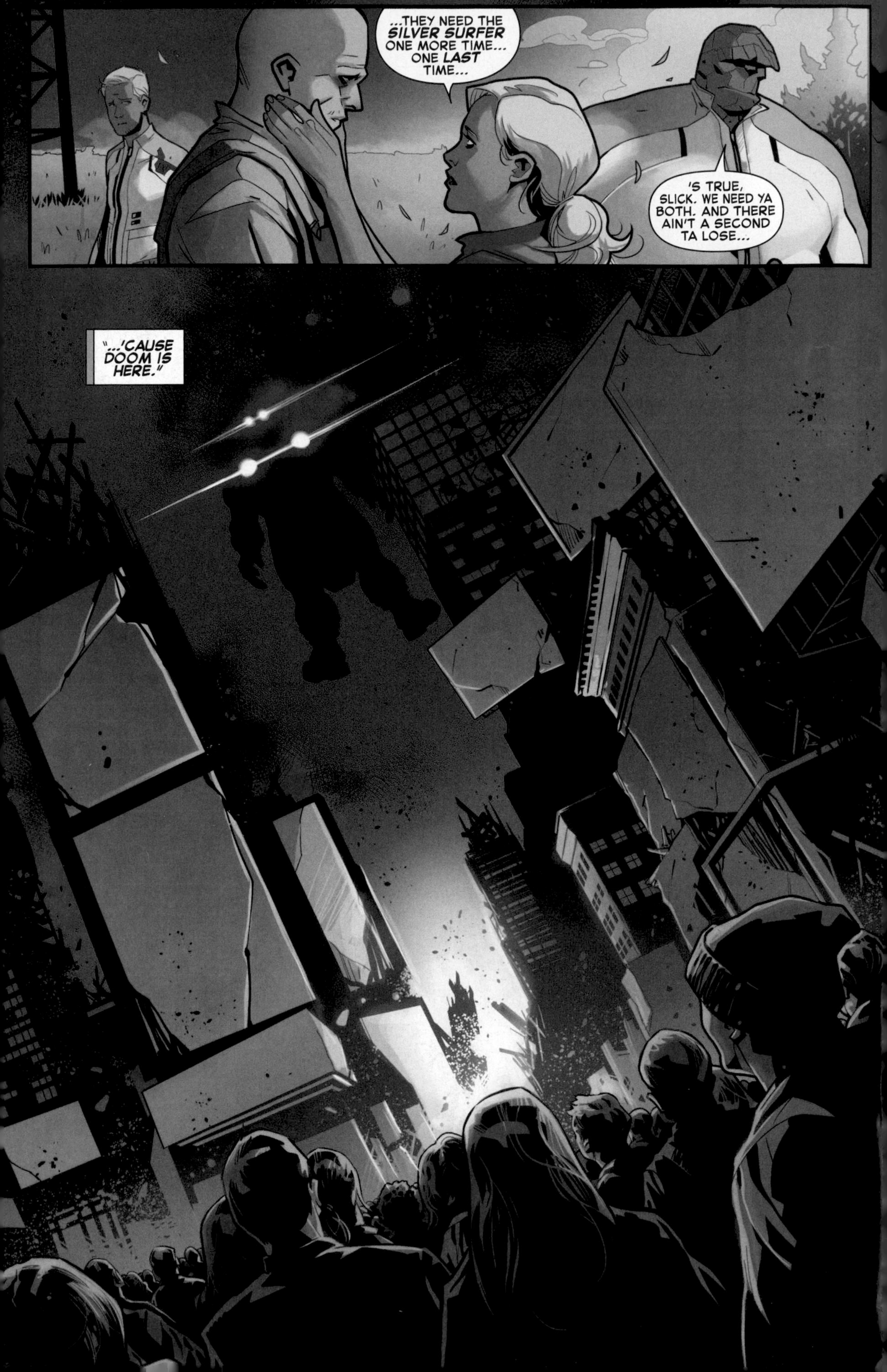
...THEY NEED THE SILVER SURFER ONE MORE TIME... ONE LAST TIME...
'S TRUE, SLICK. WE NEED YA BOTH. AND THERE AIN'T A SECOND TA LOSE...
"...'CAUSE DOOM IS HERE."

6

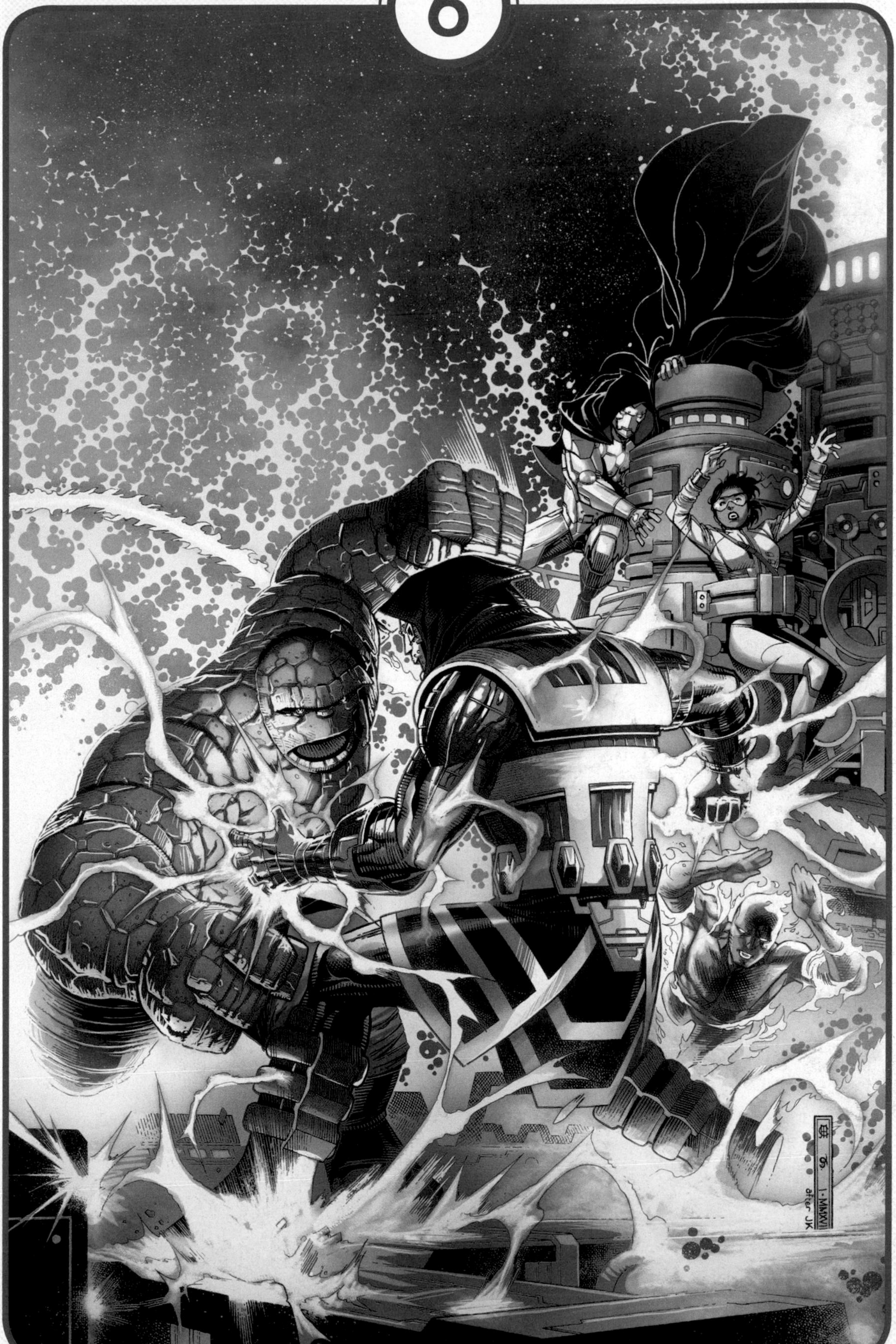

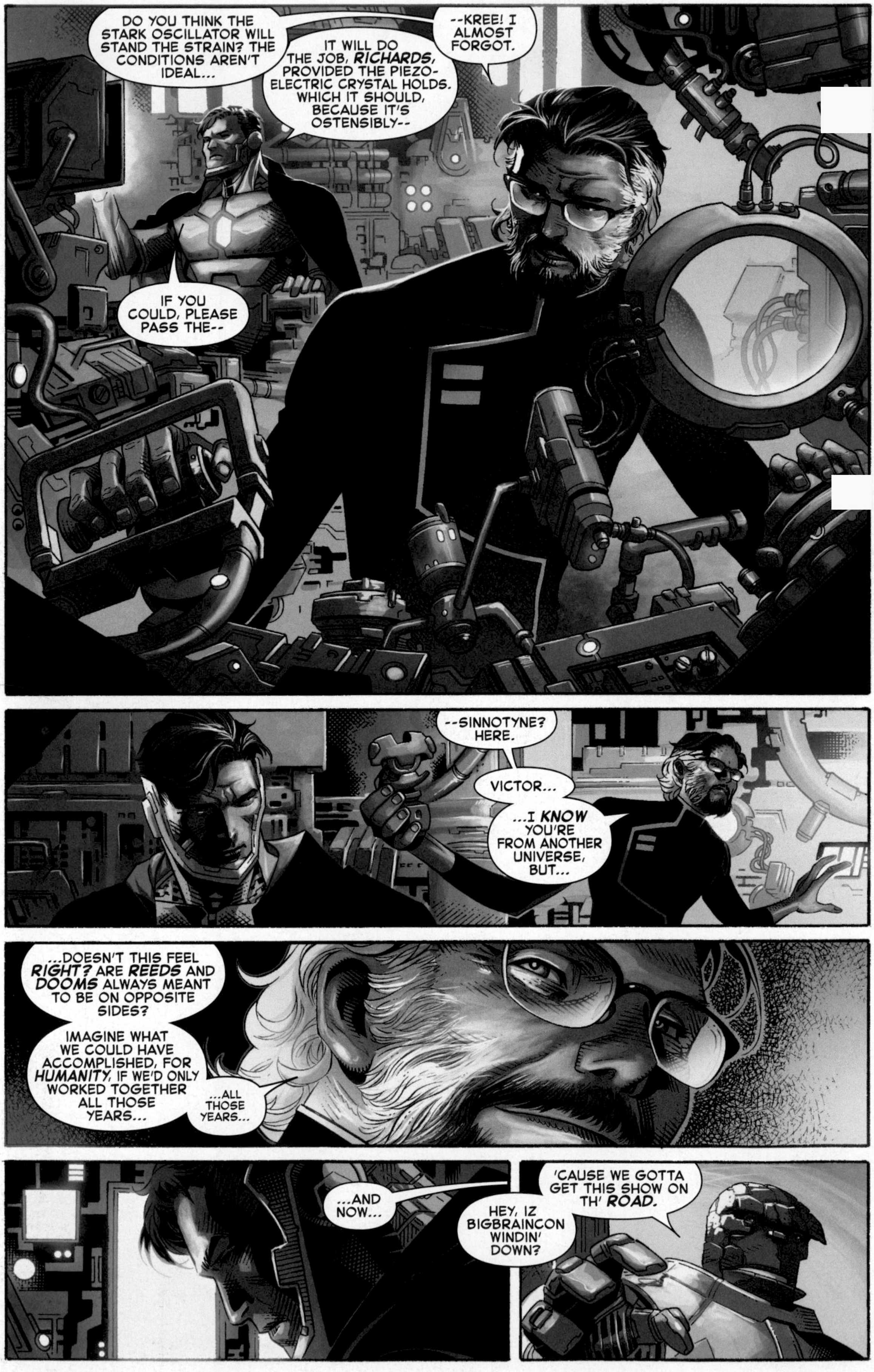
DO YOU THINK THE STARK OSCILLATOR WILL STAND THE STRAIN? THE CONDITIONS AREN'T IDEAL...
IT WILL DO THE JOB, RICHARDS, PROVIDED THE PIEZO-ELECTRIC CRYSTAL HOLDS. WHICH IT SHOULD, BECAUSE IT'S OSTENSIBLY--
--KREE! I ALMOST FORGOT.
IF YOU COULD, PLEASE PASS THE--
--SINNOTYNE? HERE.
VICTOR...
...I KNOW YOU'RE FROM ANOTHER UNIVERSE, BUT...
...DOESN'T THIS FEEL RIGHT? ARE REEDS AND DOOMS ALWAYS MEANT TO BE ON OPPOSITE SIDES?
IMAGINE WHAT WE COULD HAVE ACCOMPLISHED, FOR HUMANITY, IF WE'D ONLY WORKED TOGETHER ALL THOSE YEARS...
...ALL THOSE YEARS...
...AND NOW...
HEY, IZ BIGBRAINCON WINDIN' DOWN?
'CAUSE WE GOTTA GET THIS SHOW ON TH' ROAD.

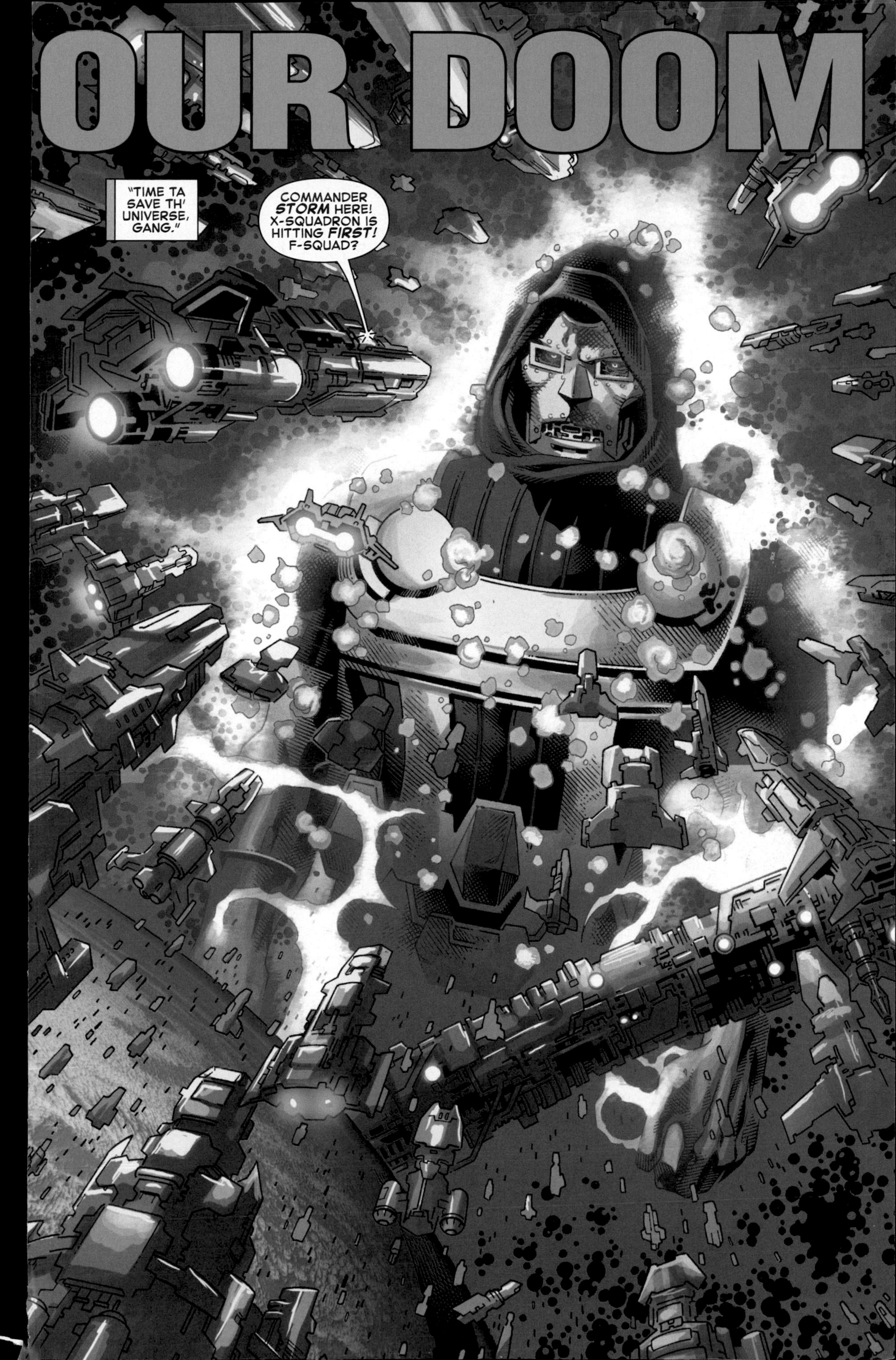
OUR DOOM
"TIME TA SAVE TH' UNIVERSE, GANG."
COMMANDER STORM HERE! X-SQUADRON IS HITTING FIRST! F-SQUAD?

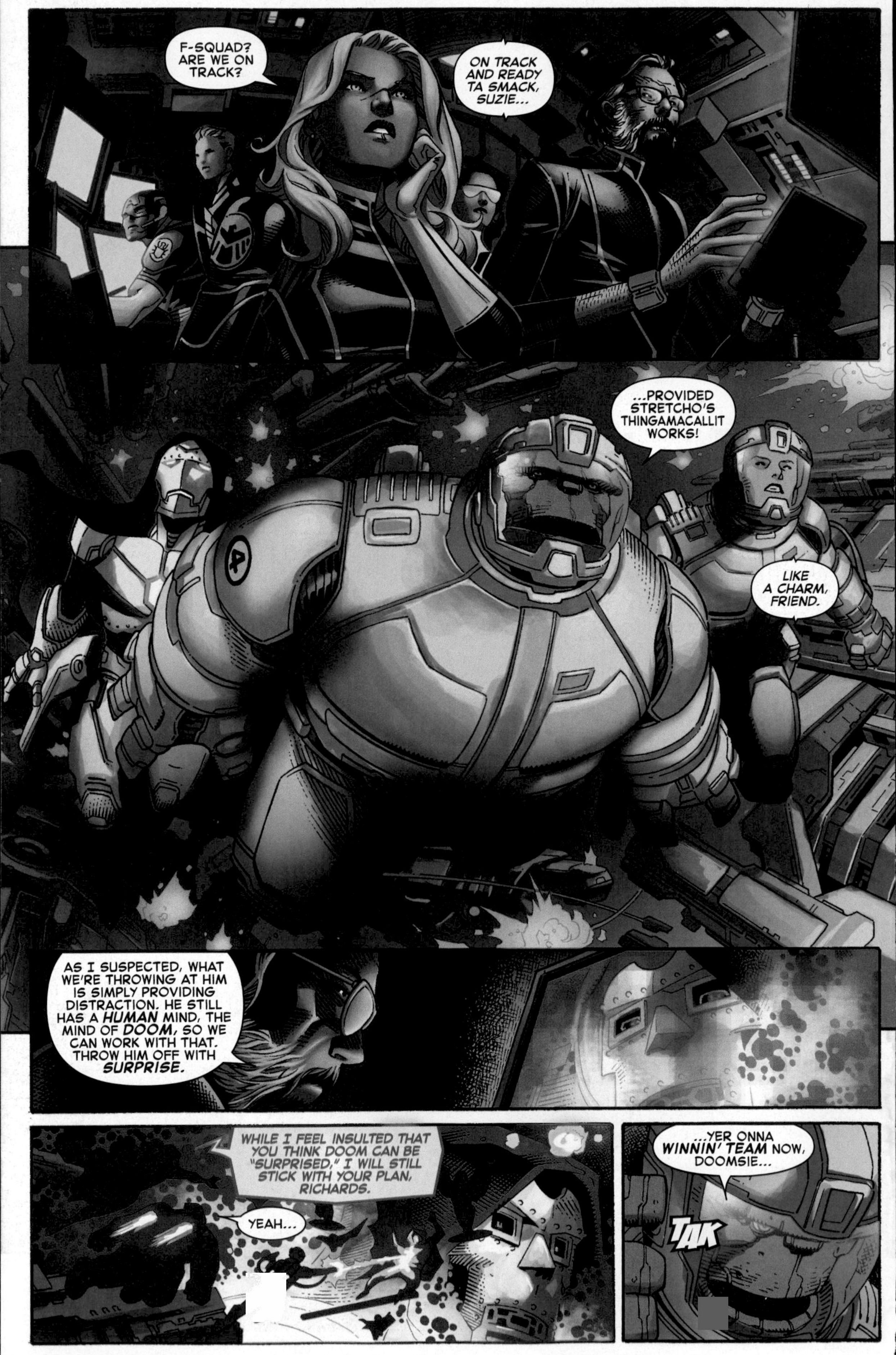
F-SQUAD? ARE WE ON TRACK?
ON TRACK AND READY TA SMACK, SUZIE...
...PROVIDED STRETCHO'S THINGAMACALLIT WORKS!
LIKE A CHARM, FRIEND.
AS I SUSPECTED, WHAT WE'RE THROWING AT HIM IS SIMPLY PROVIDING DISTRACTION. HE STILL HAS A HUMAN MIND, THE MIND OF DOOM, SO WE CAN WORK WITH THAT. THROW HIM OFF WITH SURPRISE.
WHILE I FEEL INSULTED THAT YOU THINK DOOM CAN BE "SURPRISED," I WILL STILL STICK WITH YOUR PLAN, RICHARDS.
YEAH...
...YER ONNA WINNIN' TEAM NOW, DOOMSIE...
TAK

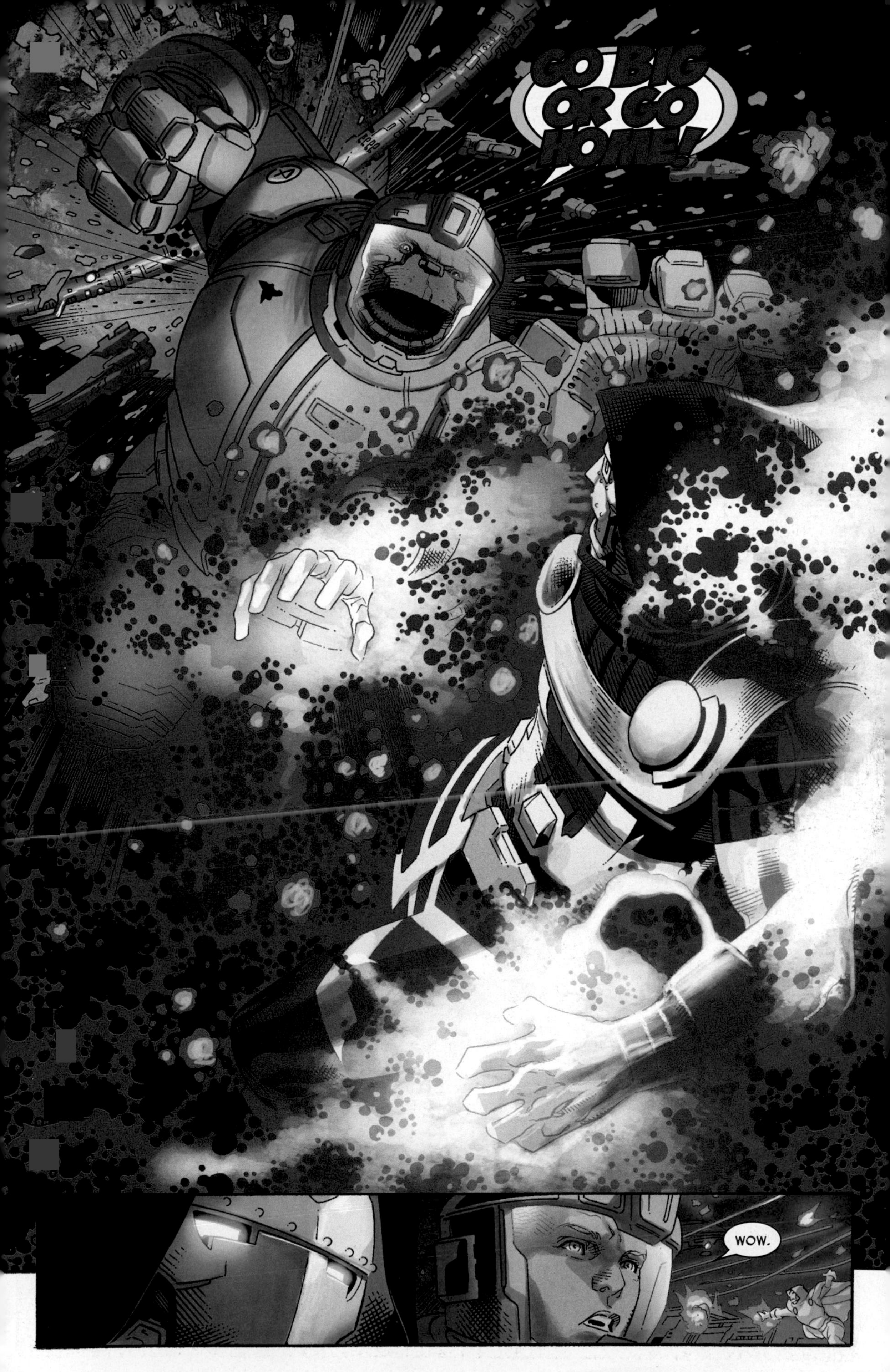
GO BIG OR GO HOME!
WOW.

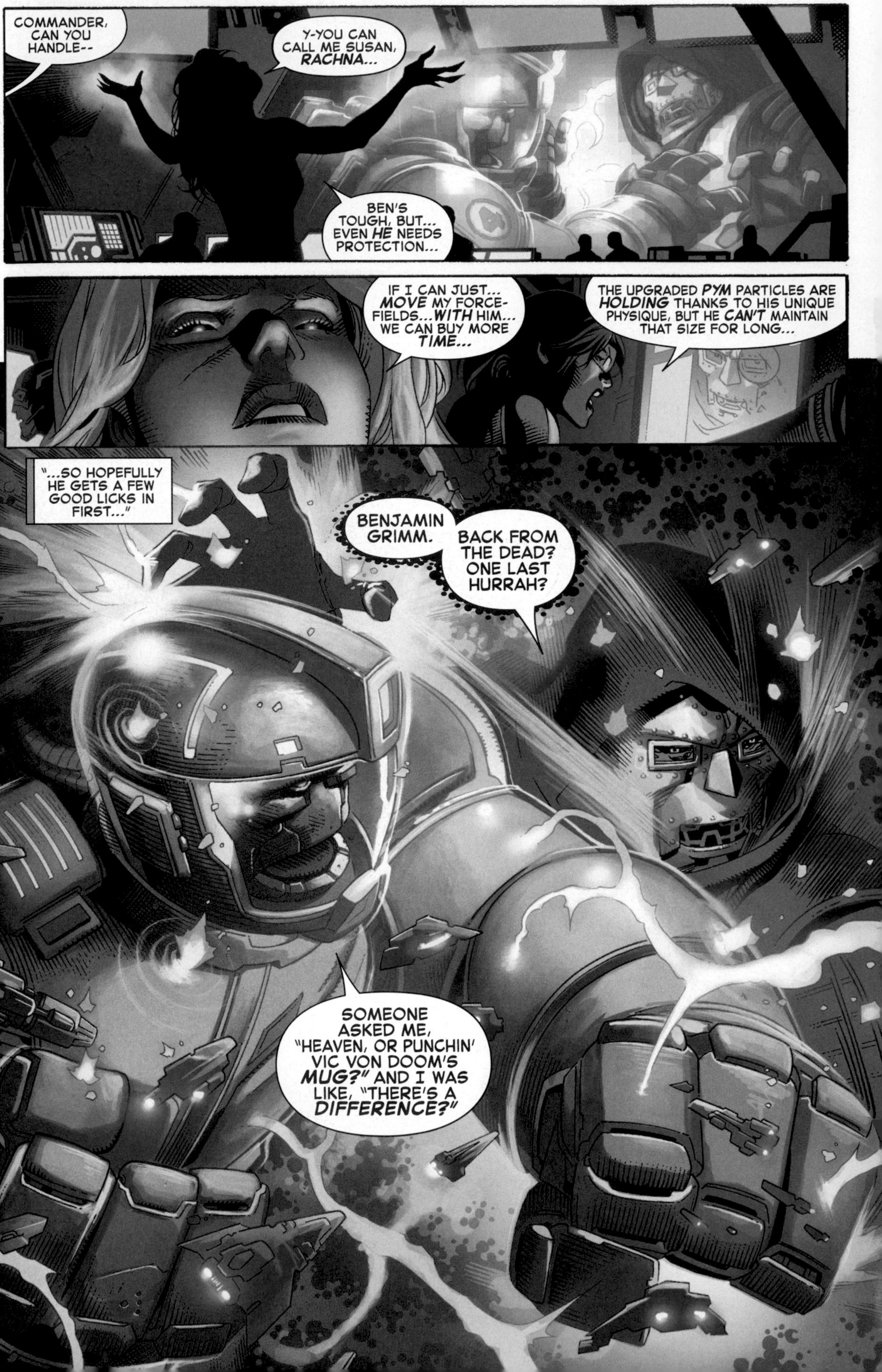

COMMANDER, CAN YOU HANDLE--
Y-YOU CAN CALL ME SUSAN, RACHNA...
BEN'S TOUGH, BUT... EVEN HE NEEDS PROTECTION...
IF I CAN JUST... MOVE MY FORCE-FIELDS...WITH HIM... WE CAN BUY MORE TIME...
THE UPGRADED PYM PARTICLES ARE HOLDING THANKS TO HIS UNIQUE PHYSIQUE, BUT HE CAN'T MAINTAIN THAT SIZE FOR LONG...
"...SO HOPEFULLY HE GETS A FEW GOOD LICKS IN FIRST..."
BENJAMIN GRIMM.
BACK FROM THE DEAD? ONE LAST HURRAH?
SOMEONE ASKED ME, "HEAVEN, OR PUNCHIN' VIC VON DOOM'S MUG?" AND I WAS LIKE, "THERE'S A DIFFERENCE?"

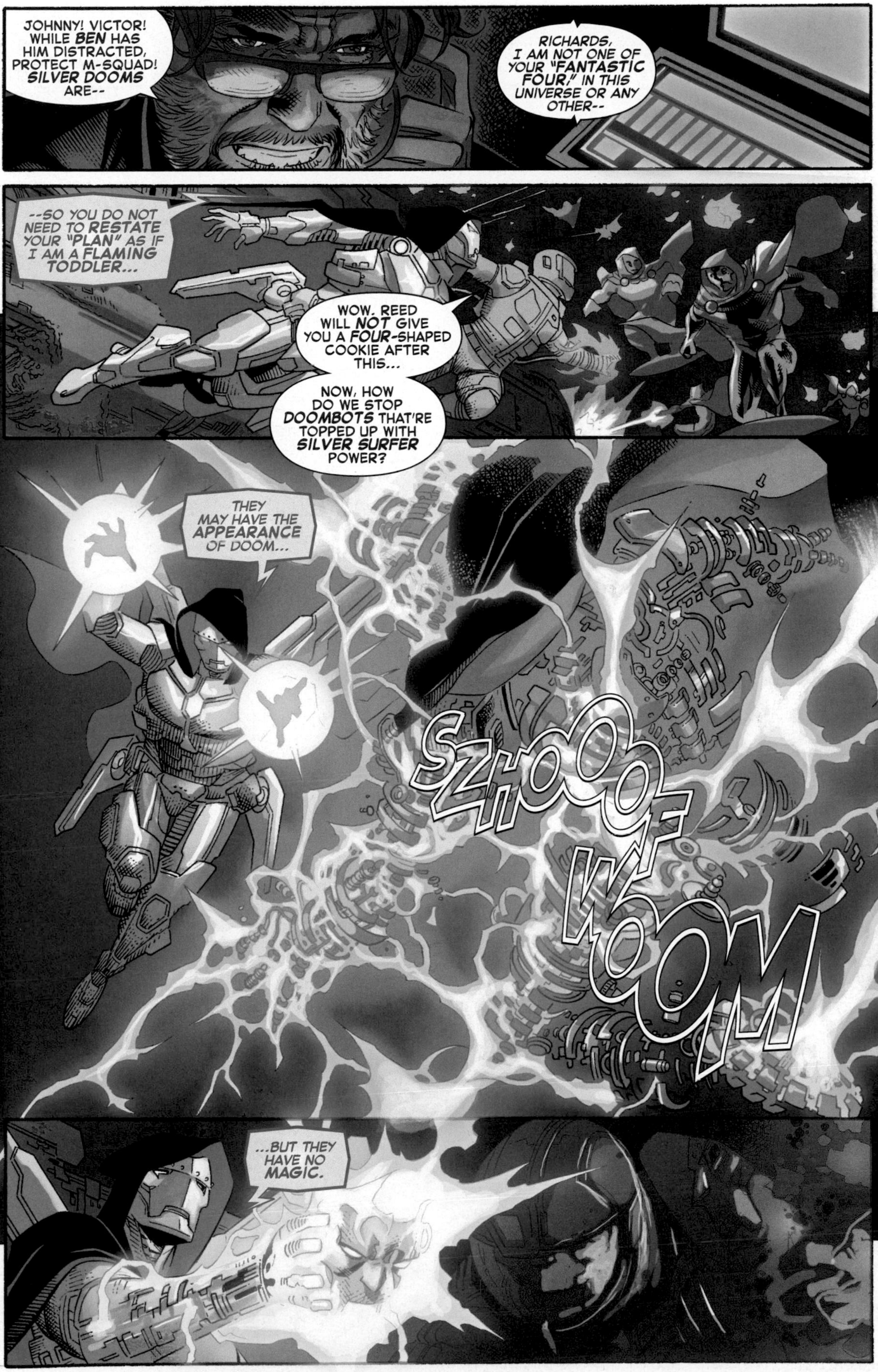
JOHNNY! VICTOR! WHILE BEN HAS HIM DISTRACTED, PROTECT M-SQUAD! SILVER DOOMS ARE--
RICHARDS, I AM NOT ONE OF YOUR "FANTASTIC FOUR," IN THIS UNIVERSE OR ANY OTHER--
--SO YOU DO NOT NEED TO RESTATE YOUR "PLAN" AS IF I AM A FLAMING TODDLER...
WOW. REED WILL NOT GIVE YOU A FOUR-SHAPED COOKIE AFTER THIS...
NOW, HOW DO WE STOP DOOMBOTS THAT'RE TOPPED UP WITH SILVER SURFER POWER?
THEY MAY HAVE THE APPEARANCE OF DOOM...
SZHOOOF
WOOOM
...BUT THEY HAVE NO MAGIC.

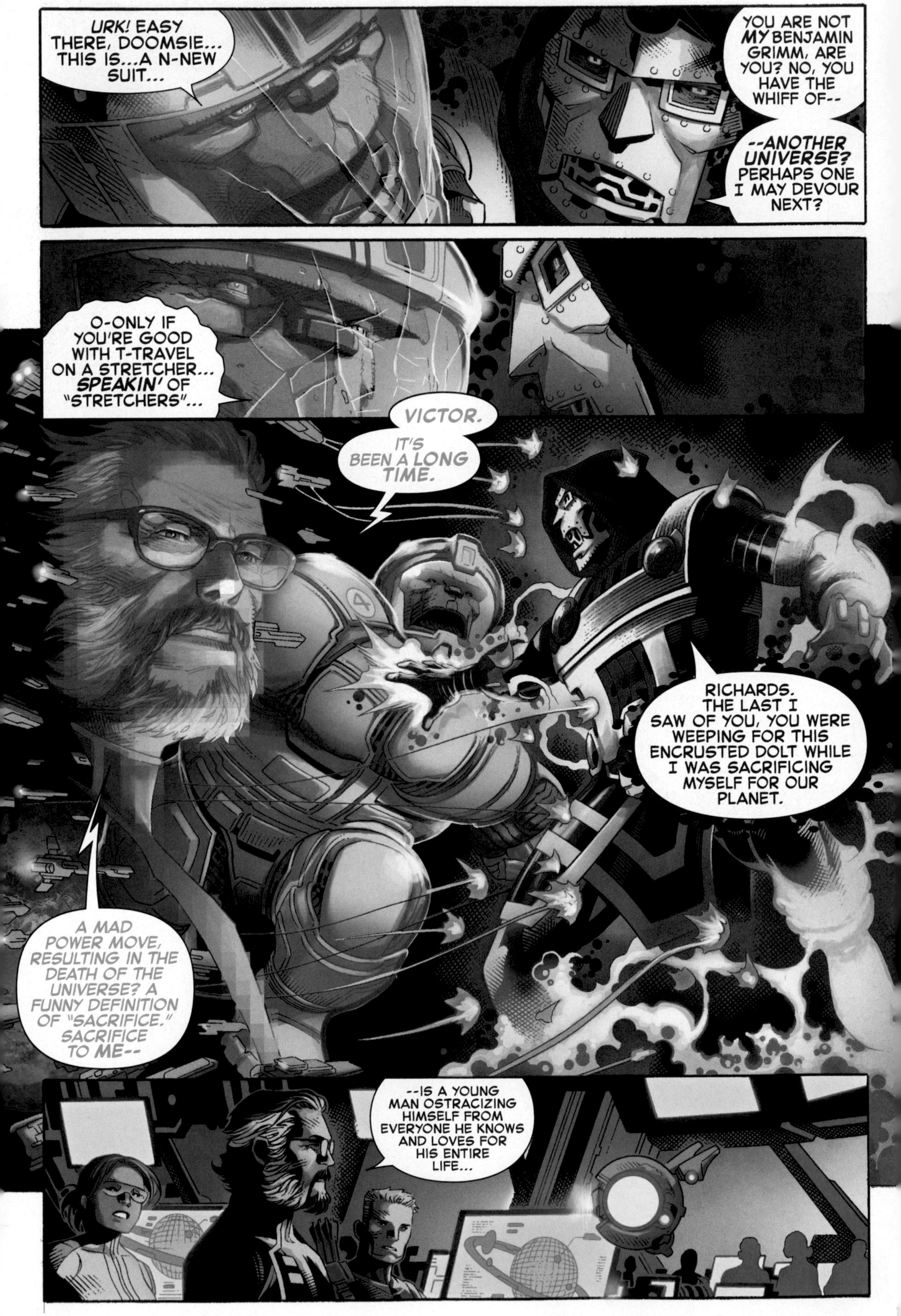
URK! EASY THERE, DOOMSIE... THIS IS...A N-NEW SUIT...
YOU ARE NOT MY BENJAMIN GRIMM, ARE YOU? NO, YOU HAVE THE WHIFF OF--
--ANOTHER UNIVERSE? PERHAPS ONE I MAY DEVOUR NEXT?
O-ONLY IF YOU'RE GOOD WITH T-TRAVEL ON A STRETCHER... SPEAKIN' OF "STRETCHERS"...
VICTOR.
IT'S BEEN A LONG TIME.
RICHARDS. THE LAST I SAW OF YOU, YOU WERE WEEPING FOR THIS ENCRUSTED DOLT WHILE I WAS SACRIFICING MYSELF FOR OUR PLANET.
A MAD POWER MOVE, RESULTING IN THE DEATH OF THE UNIVERSE? A FUNNY DEFINITION OF "SACRIFICE." SACRIFICE TO ME--
--IS A YOUNG MAN OSTRACIZING HIMSELF FROM EVERYONE HE KNOWS AND LOVES FOR HIS ENTIRE LIFE...

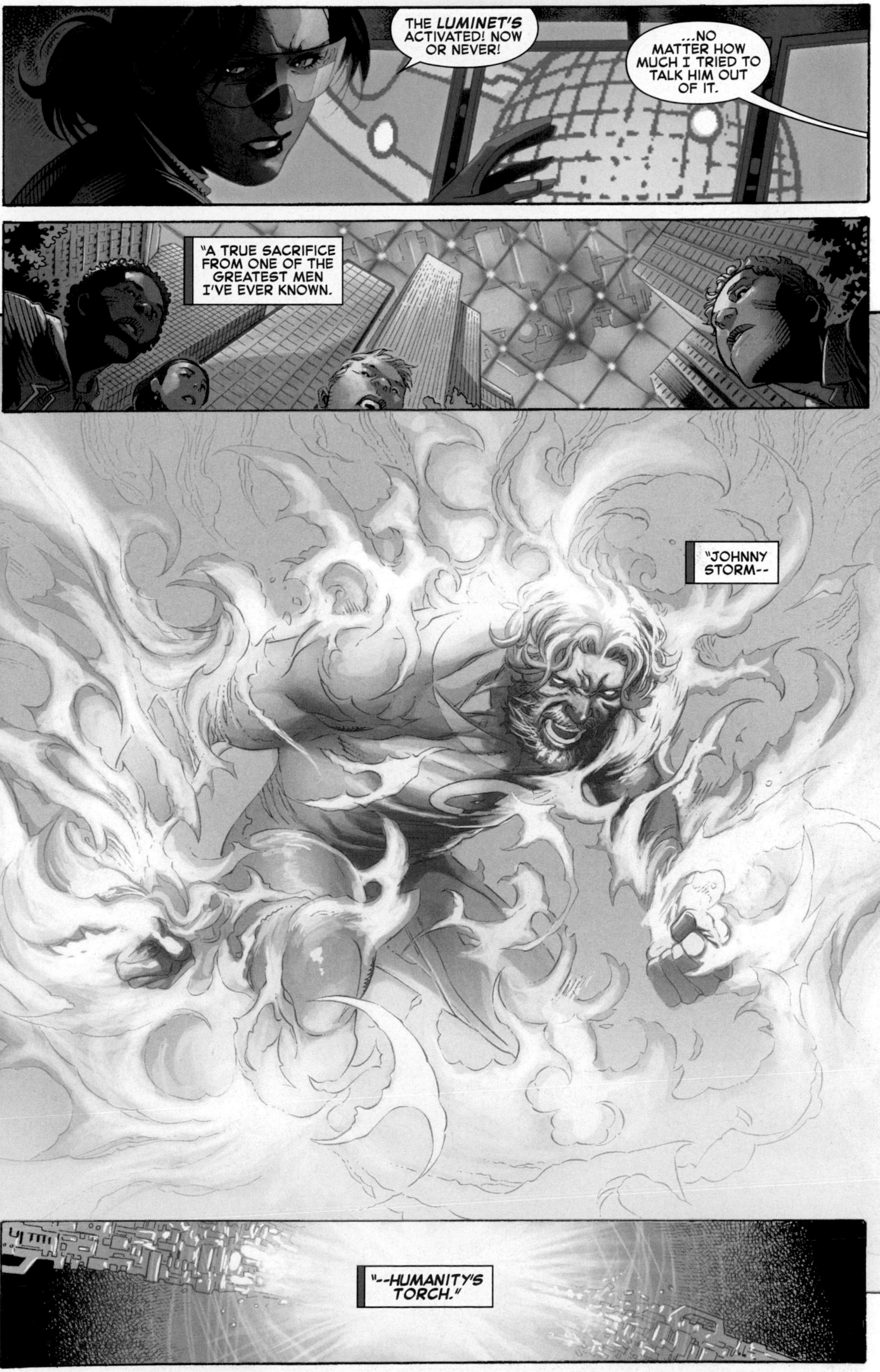
THE LUMINET'S ACTIVATED! NOW OR NEVER!
...NO MATTER HOW MUCH I TRIED TO TALK HIM OUT OF IT.
"A TRUE SACRIFICE FROM ONE OF THE GREATEST MEN I'VE EVER KNOWN.
"JOHNNY STORM--
"--HUMANITY'S TORCH."

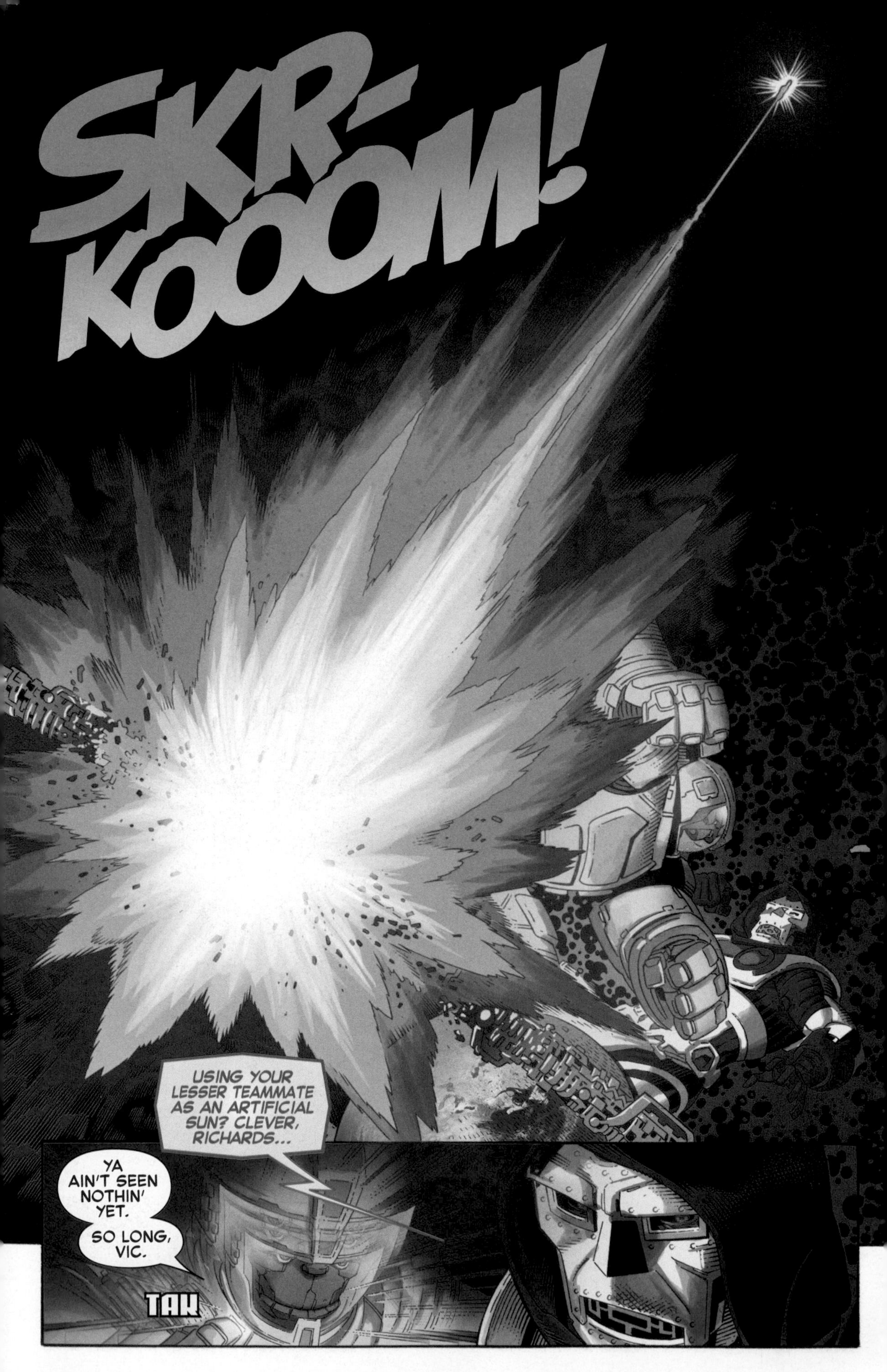
SKR-KOOOM!
USING YOUR LESSER TEAMMATE AS AN ARTIFICIAL SUN? CLEVER, RICHARDS...
YA AIN'T SEEN NOTHIN' YET.
SO LONG, VIC.
TAK

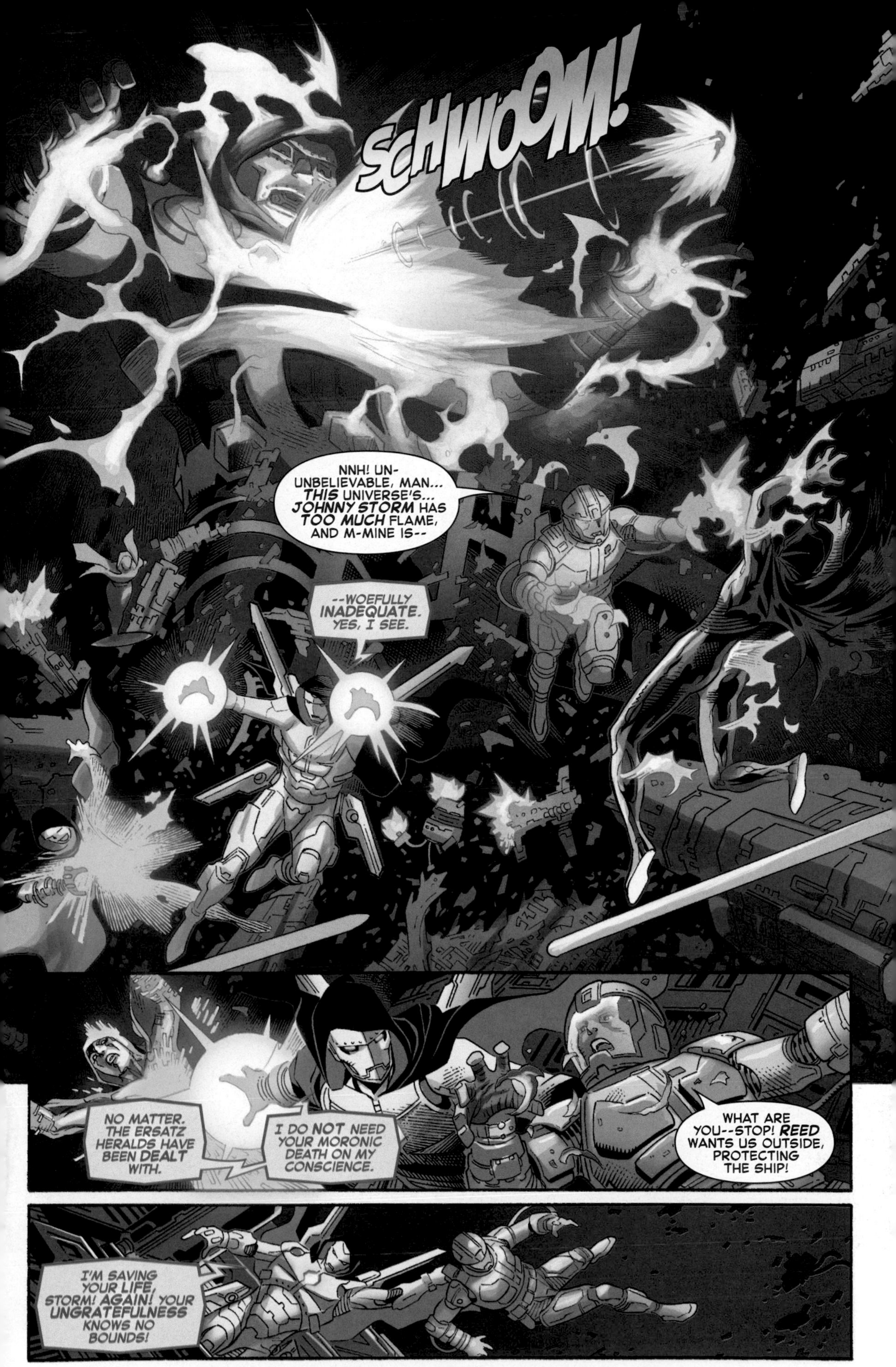
SCHWOOM!
NNH! UN-UNBELIEVABLE, MAN... THIS UNIVERSE'S... JOHNNY STORM HAS TOO MUCH FLAME, AND M-MINE IS--
--WOEFULLY INADEQUATE. YES, I SEE.
NO MATTER. THE ERSATZ HERALDS HAVE BEEN DEALT WITH.
I DO NOT NEED YOUR MORONIC DEATH ON MY CONSCIENCE.
WHAT ARE YOU--STOP! REED WANTS US OUTSIDE, PROTECTING THE SHIP!
I'M SAVING YOUR LIFE, STORM! AGAIN! YOUR UNGRATEFULNESS KNOWS NO BOUNDS!

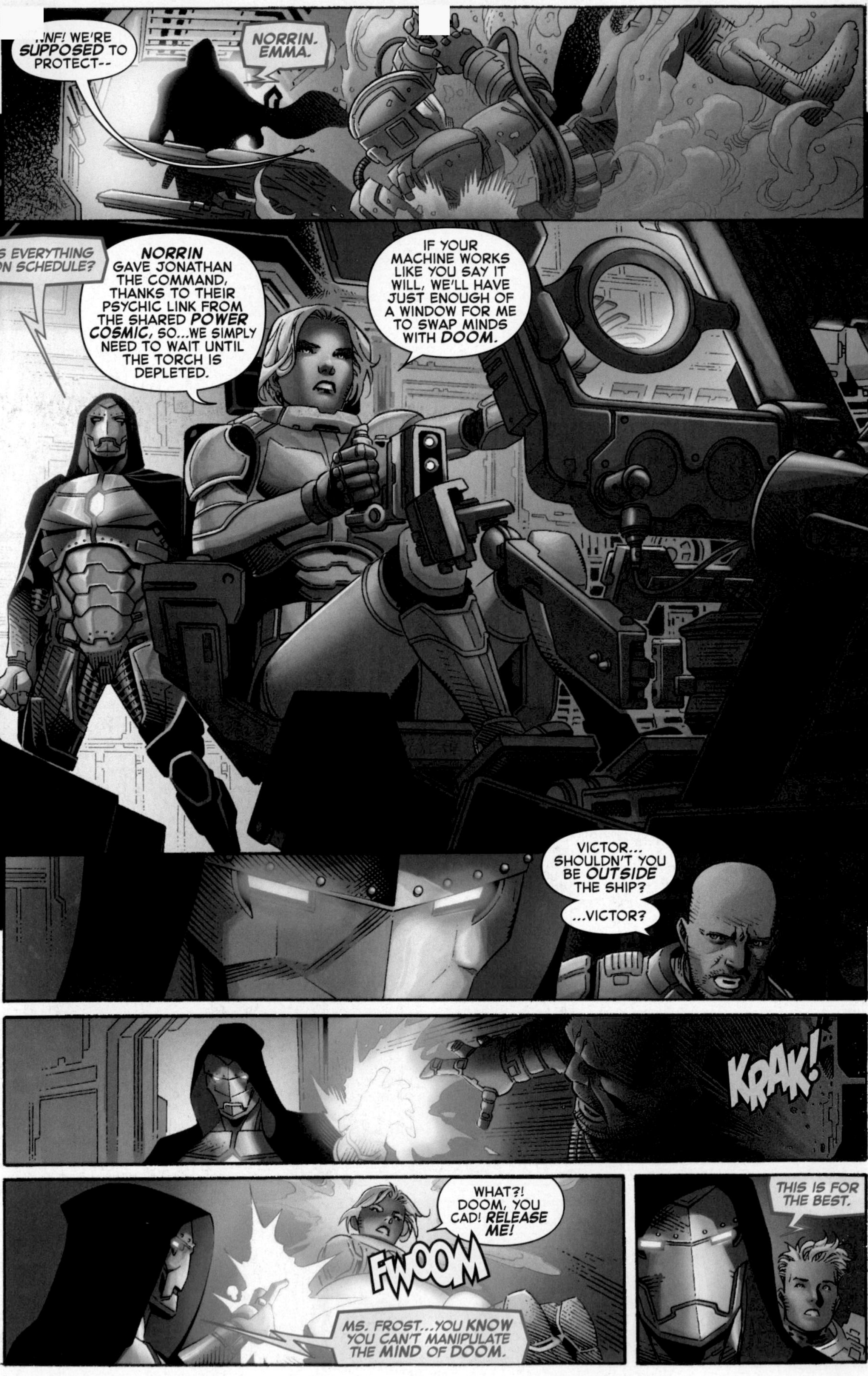
NNF! WE'RE SUPPOSED TO PROTECT--
NORRIN. EMMA.
IS EVERYTHING ON SCHEDULE?
NORRIN GAVE JONATHAN THE COMMAND, THANKS TO THEIR PSYCHIC LINK FROM THE SHARED POWER COSMIC, SO...WE SIMPLY NEED TO WAIT UNTIL THE TORCH IS DEPLETED.
IF YOUR MACHINE WORKS LIKE YOU SAY IT WILL, WE'LL HAVE JUST ENOUGH OF A WINDOW FOR ME TO SWAP MINDS WITH DOOM.
VICTOR... SHOULDN'T YOU BE OUTSIDE THE SHIP?
...VICTOR?
KRAK!
WHAT?! DOOM, YOU CAD! RELEASE ME!
FWOOM
MS. FROST...YOU KNOW YOU CAN'T MANIPULATE THE MIND OF DOOM.
THIS IS FOR THE BEST.

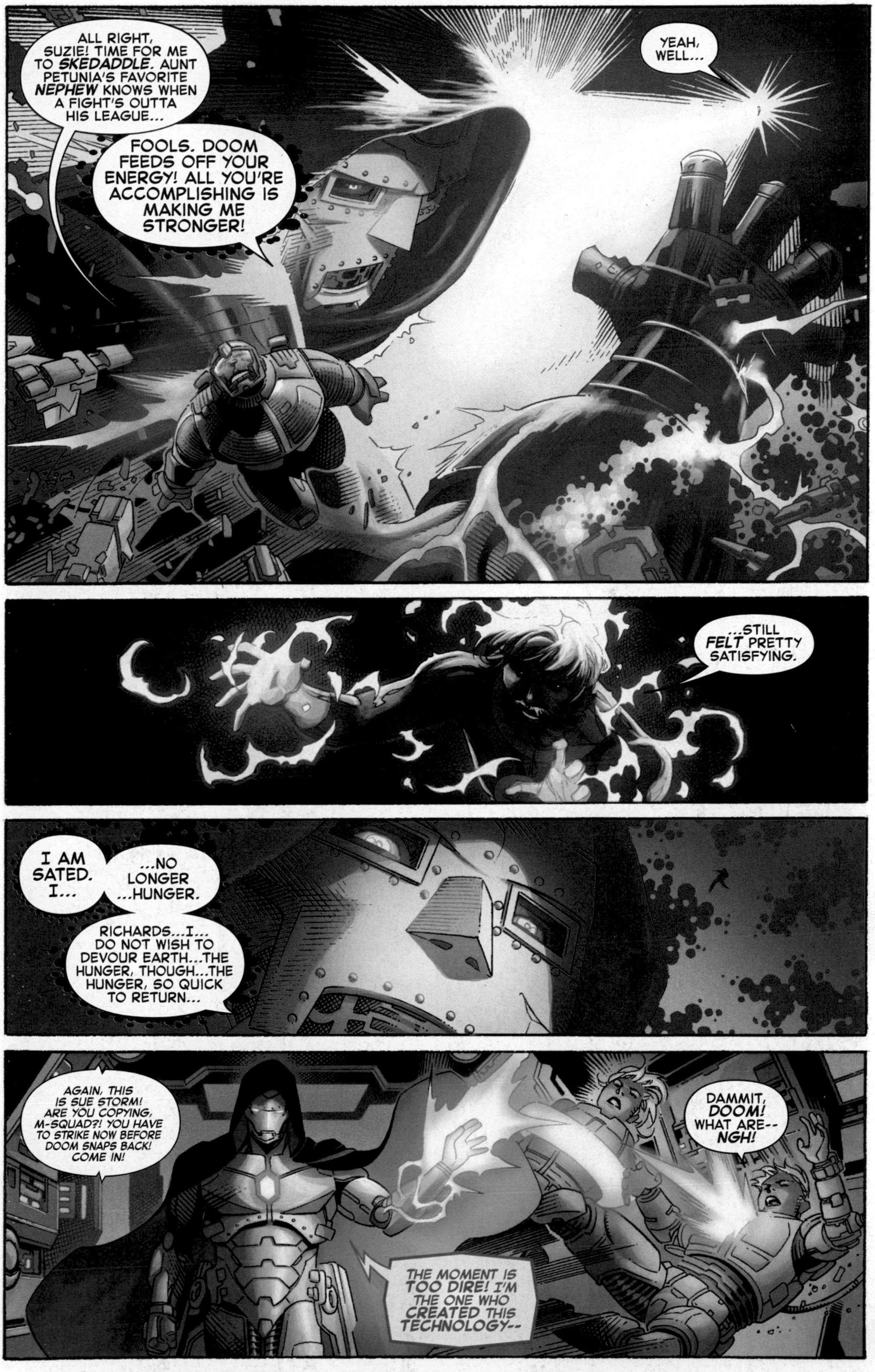

ALL RIGHT, SUZIE! TIME FOR ME TO SKEDADDLE. AUNT PETUNIA'S FAVORITE NEPHEW KNOWS WHEN A FIGHT'S OUTTA HIS LEAGUE...
FOOLS. DOOM FEEDS OFF YOUR ENERGY! ALL YOU'RE ACCOMPLISHING IS MAKING ME STRONGER!
YEAH, WELL...
...STILL FELT PRETTY SATISFYING.
I AM SATED. I...
...NO LONGER ...HUNGER.
RICHARDS...I... DO NOT WISH TO DEVOUR EARTH...THE HUNGER, THOUGH...THE HUNGER, SO QUICK TO RETURN...
AGAIN, THIS IS SUE STORM! ARE YOU COPYING, M-SQUAD?! YOU HAVE TO STRIKE NOW BEFORE DOOM SNAPS BACK! COME IN!
DAMMIT, DOOM! WHAT ARE--NGH!
THE MOMENT IS TOO DIRE! I'M THE ONE WHO CREATED THIS TECHNOLOGY--

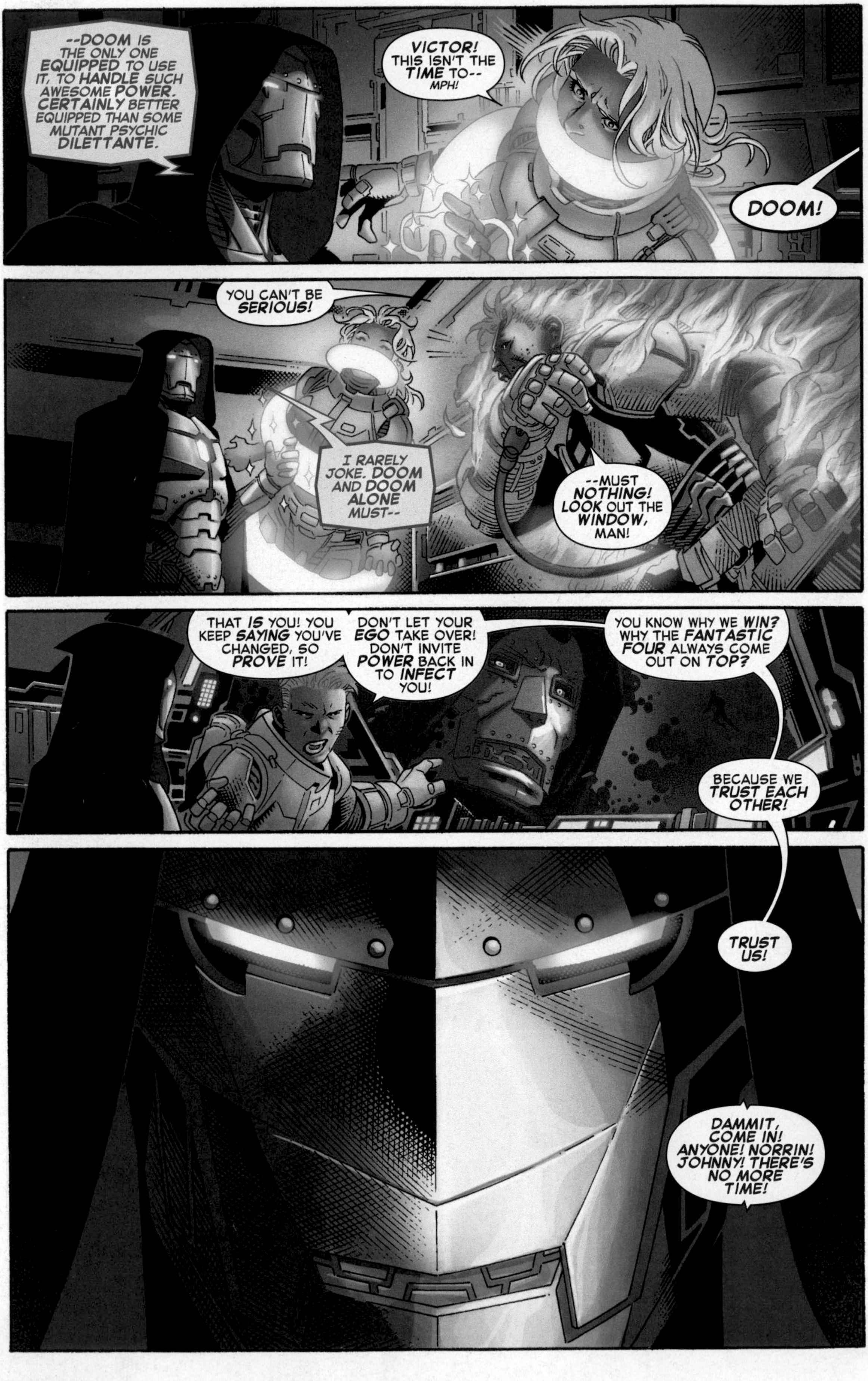
--DOOM IS THE ONLY ONE EQUIPPED TO USE IT, TO HANDLE SUCH AWESOME POWER. CERTAINLY BETTER EQUIPPED THAN SOME MUTANT PSYCHIC DILETTANTE.
VICTOR! THIS ISN'T THE TIME TO-- MPH!
DOOM!
YOU CAN'T BE SERIOUS!
I RARELY JOKE. DOOM AND DOOM ALONE MUST--
--MUST NOTHING! LOOK OUT THE WINDOW, MAN!
THAT IS YOU! YOU KEEP SAYING YOU'VE CHANGED, SO PROVE IT!
DON'T LET YOUR EGO TAKE OVER! DON'T INVITE POWER BACK IN TO INFECT YOU!
YOU KNOW WHY WE WIN? WHY THE FANTASTIC FOUR ALWAYS COME OUT ON TOP?
BECAUSE WE TRUST EACH OTHER!
TRUST US!
DAMMIT, COME IN! ANYONE! NORRIN! JOHNNY! THERE'S NO MORE TIME!

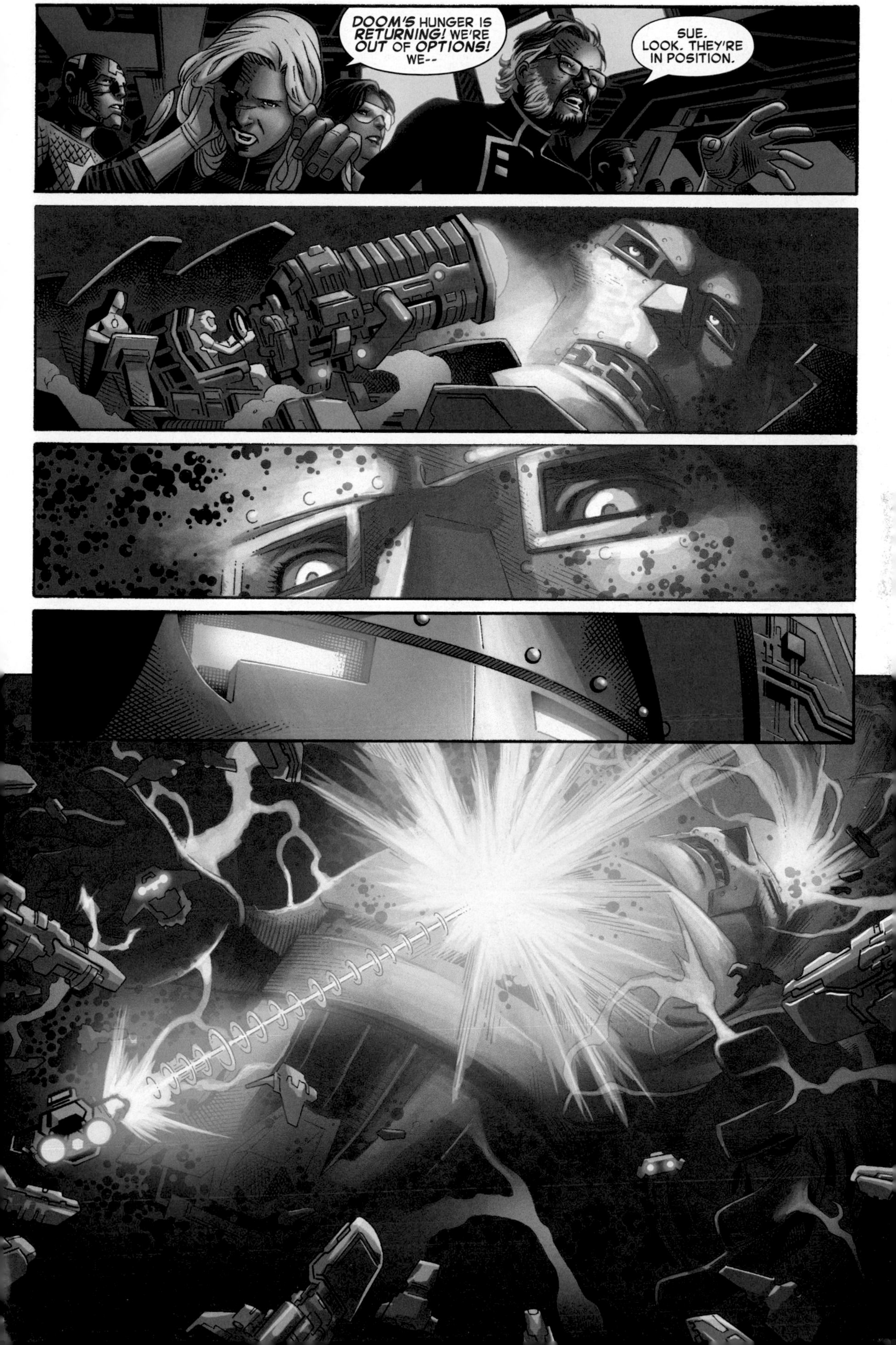
DOOM'S HUNGER IS RETURNING! WE'RE OUT OF OPTIONS! WE--
SUE. LOOK. THEY'RE IN POSITION.

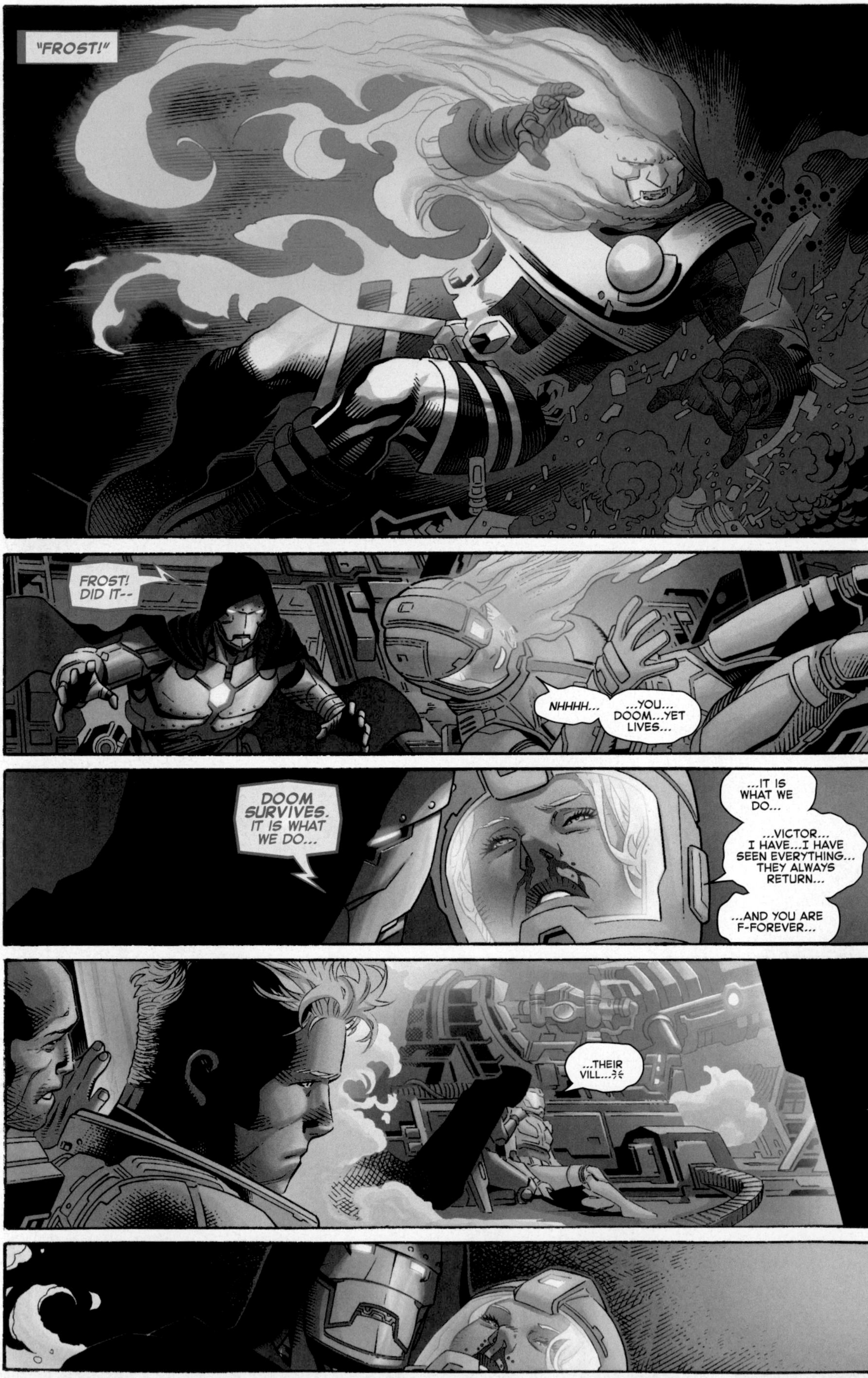
"FROST!"
FROST! DID IT--
NHHHH...
...YOU... DOOM...YET LIVES...
DOOM SURVIVES. IT IS WHAT WE DO...
...IT IS WHAT WE DO...
...VICTOR... I HAVE...I HAVE SEEN EVERYTHING... THEY ALWAYS RETURN...
...AND YOU ARE F-FOREVER...
...THEIR VILL...

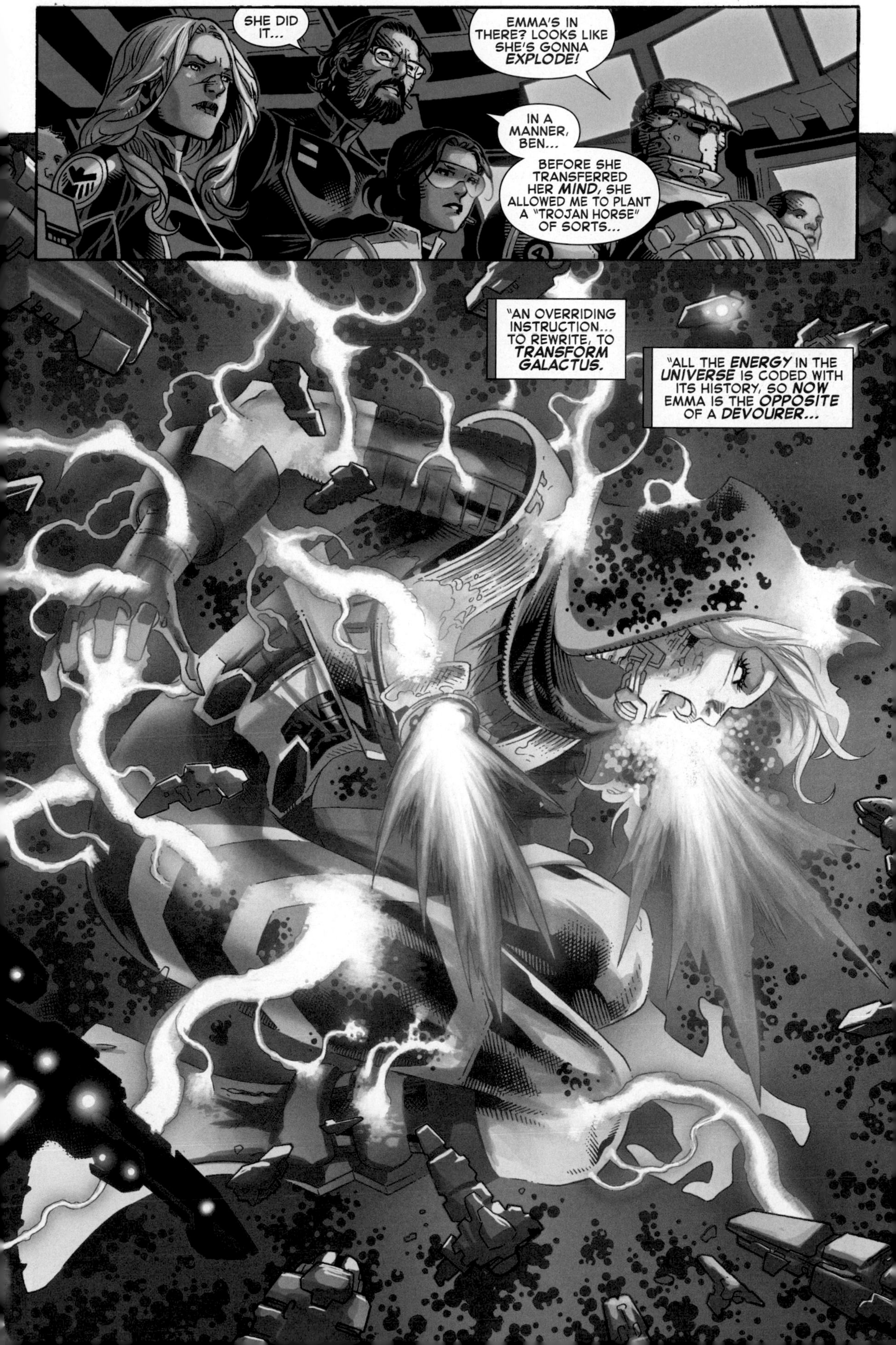
SHE DID IT...
EMMA'S IN THERE? LOOKS LIKE SHE'S GONNA EXPLODE!
IN A MANNER, BEN...
BEFORE SHE TRANSFERRED HER MIND, SHE ALLOWED ME TO PLANT A "TROJAN HORSE" OF SORTS...
"AN OVERRIDING INSTRUCTION... TO REWRITE, TO TRANSFORM GALACTUS.
"ALL THE ENERGY IN THE UNIVERSE IS CODED WITH ITS HISTORY, SO NOW EMMA IS THE OPPOSITE OF A DEVOURER...

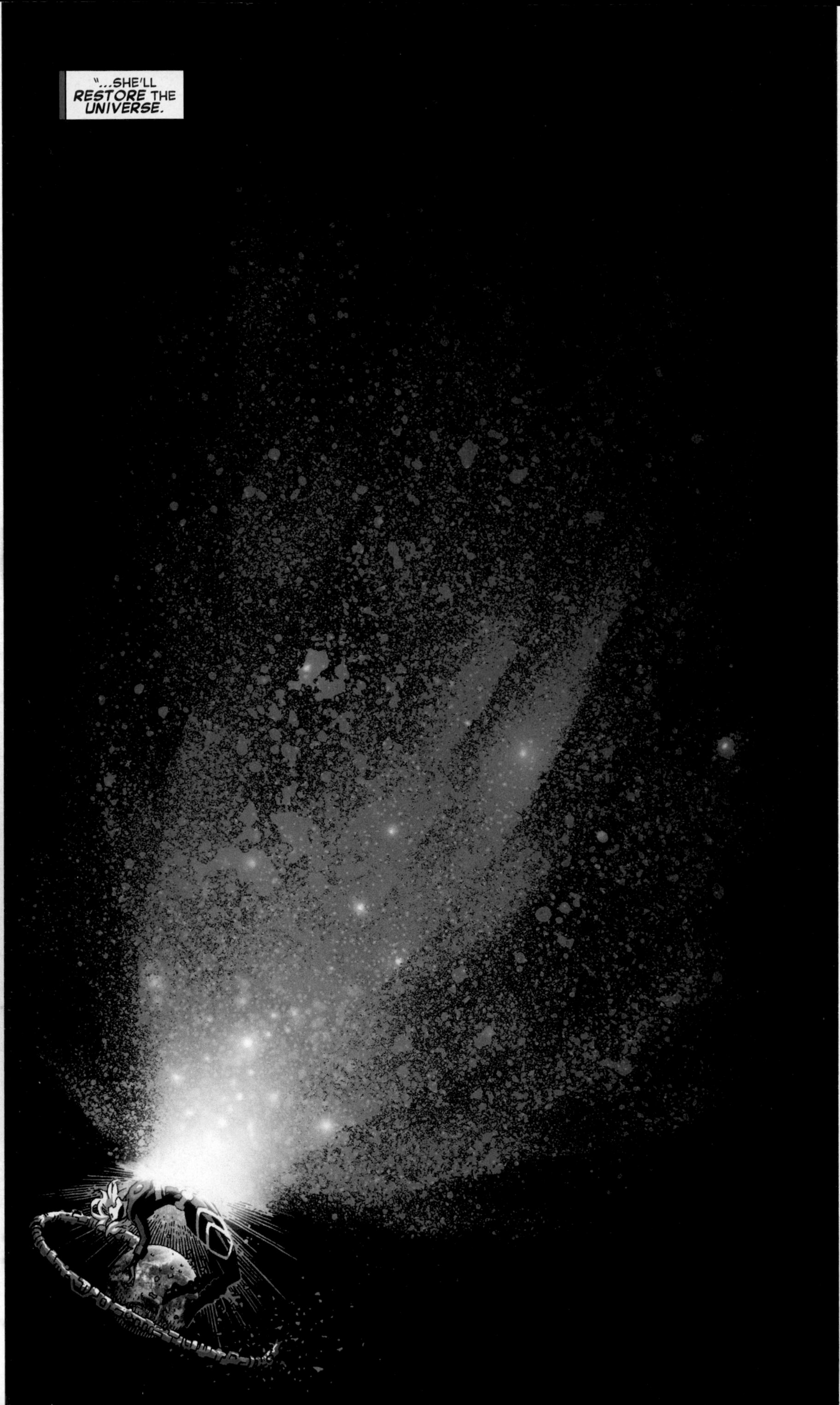
"...SHE'LL *RESTORE* THE *UNIVERSE.*

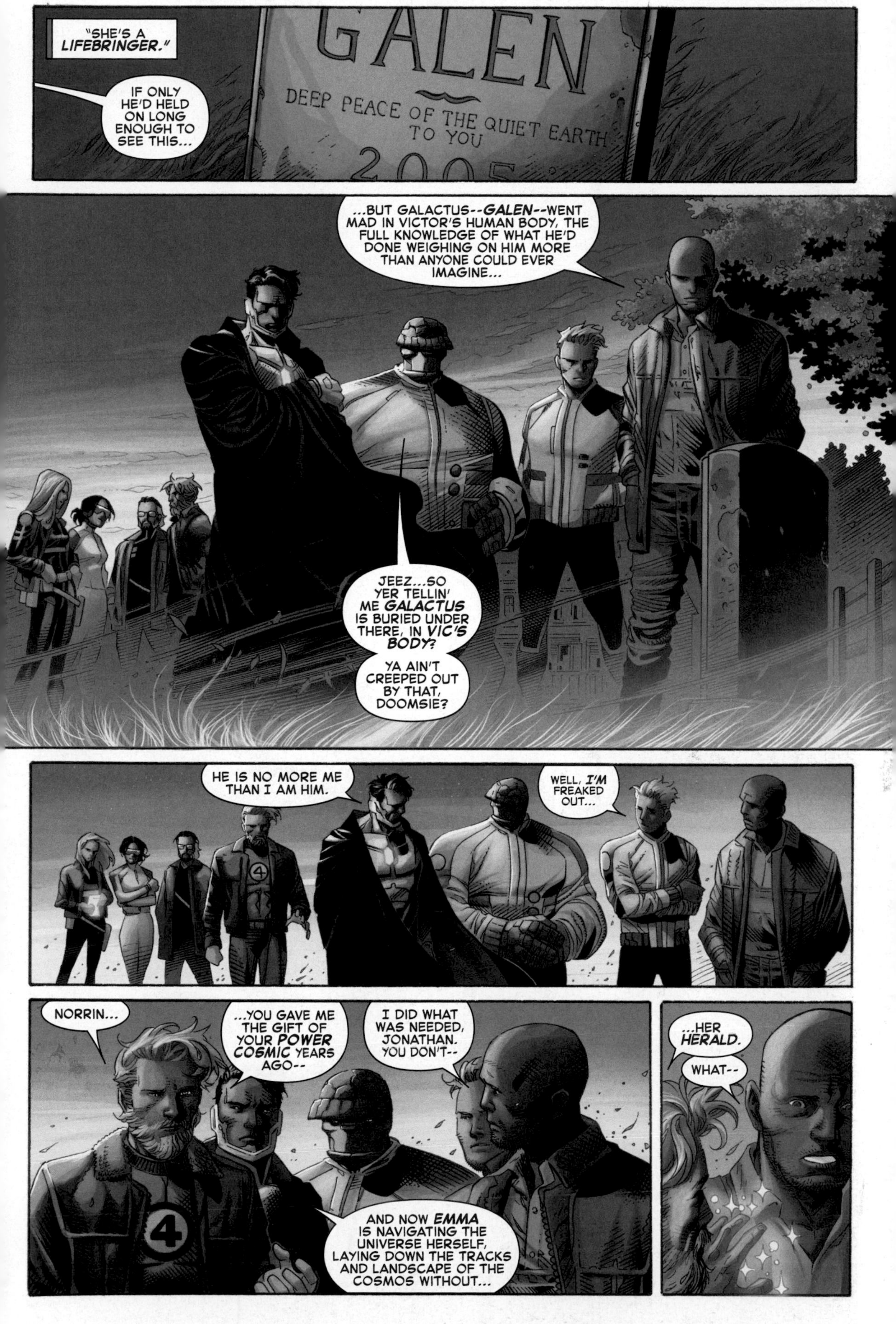
"SHE'S A LIFEBRINGER."
IF ONLY HE'D HELD ON LONG ENOUGH TO SEE THIS...
GALEN
DEEP PEACE OF THE QUIET EARTH TO YOU
...BUT GALACTUS--GALEN--WENT MAD IN VICTOR'S HUMAN BODY, THE FULL KNOWLEDGE OF WHAT HE'D DONE WEIGHING ON HIM MORE THAN ANYONE COULD EVER IMAGINE...
JEEZ...SO YER TELLIN' ME GALACTUS IS BURIED UNDER THERE, IN VIC'S BODY?
YA AIN'T CREEPED OUT BY THAT, DOOMSIE?
HE IS NO MORE ME THAN I AM HIM.
WELL, I'M FREAKED OUT...
NORRIN...
...YOU GAVE ME THE GIFT OF YOUR POWER COSMIC YEARS AGO--
I DID WHAT WAS NEEDED, JONATHAN. YOU DON'T--
AND NOW EMMA IS NAVIGATING THE UNIVERSE HERSELF, LAYING DOWN THE TRACKS AND LANDSCAPE OF THE COSMOS WITHOUT...
...HER HERALD.
WHAT--

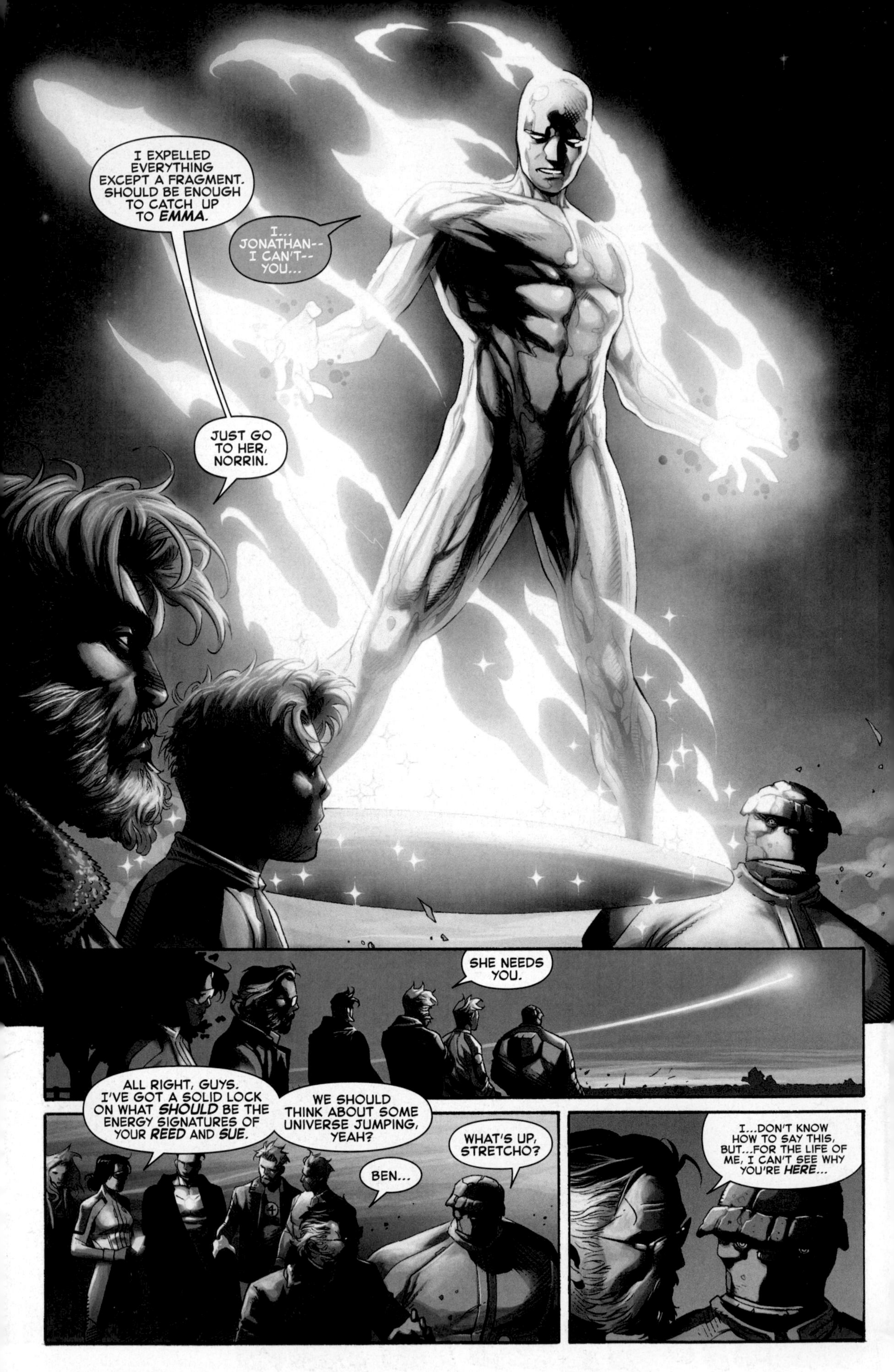
I EXPELLED EVERYTHING EXCEPT A FRAGMENT. SHOULD BE ENOUGH TO CATCH UP TO EMMA.
I... JONATHAN-- I CAN'T-- YOU...
JUST GO TO HER, NORRIN.
SHE NEEDS YOU.
ALL RIGHT, GUYS. I'VE GOT A SOLID LOCK ON WHAT SHOULD BE THE ENERGY SIGNATURES OF YOUR REED AND SUE.
WE SHOULD THINK ABOUT SOME UNIVERSE JUMPING, YEAH?
BEN...
WHAT'S UP, STRETCHO?
I...DON'T KNOW HOW TO SAY THIS, BUT...FOR THE LIFE OF ME, I CAN'T SEE WHY YOU'RE HERE...

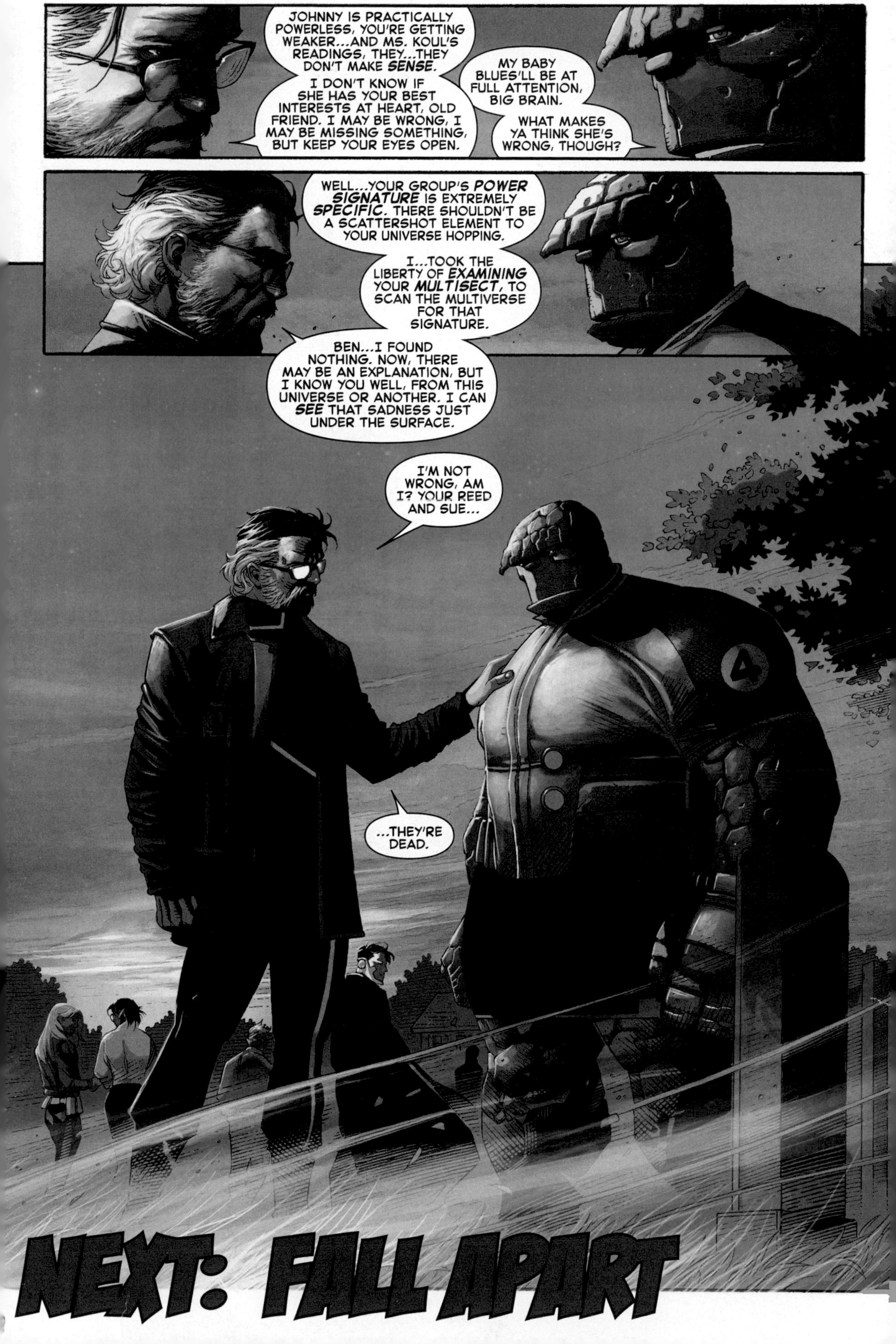
JOHNNY IS PRACTICALLY POWERLESS, YOU'RE GETTING WEAKER...AND MS. KOUL'S READINGS, THEY...THEY DON'T MAKE SENSE.
I DON'T KNOW IF SHE HAS YOUR BEST INTERESTS AT HEART, OLD FRIEND. I MAY BE WRONG, I MAY BE MISSING SOMETHING, BUT KEEP YOUR EYES OPEN.
MY BABY BLUES'LL BE AT FULL ATTENTION, BIG BRAIN.
WHAT MAKES YA THINK SHE'S WRONG, THOUGH?
WELL...YOUR GROUP'S POWER SIGNATURE IS EXTREMELY SPECIFIC. THERE SHOULDN'T BE A SCATTERSHOT ELEMENT TO YOUR UNIVERSE HOPPING.
I...TOOK THE LIBERTY OF EXAMINING YOUR MULTISECT, TO SCAN THE MULTIVERSE FOR THAT SIGNATURE.
BEN...I FOUND NOTHING. NOW, THERE MAY BE AN EXPLANATION, BUT I KNOW YOU WELL, FROM THIS UNIVERSE OR ANOTHER. I CAN SEE THAT SADNESS JUST UNDER THE SURFACE.
I'M NOT WRONG, AM I? YOUR REED AND SUE...
...THEY'RE DEAD.
NEXT: FALL APART

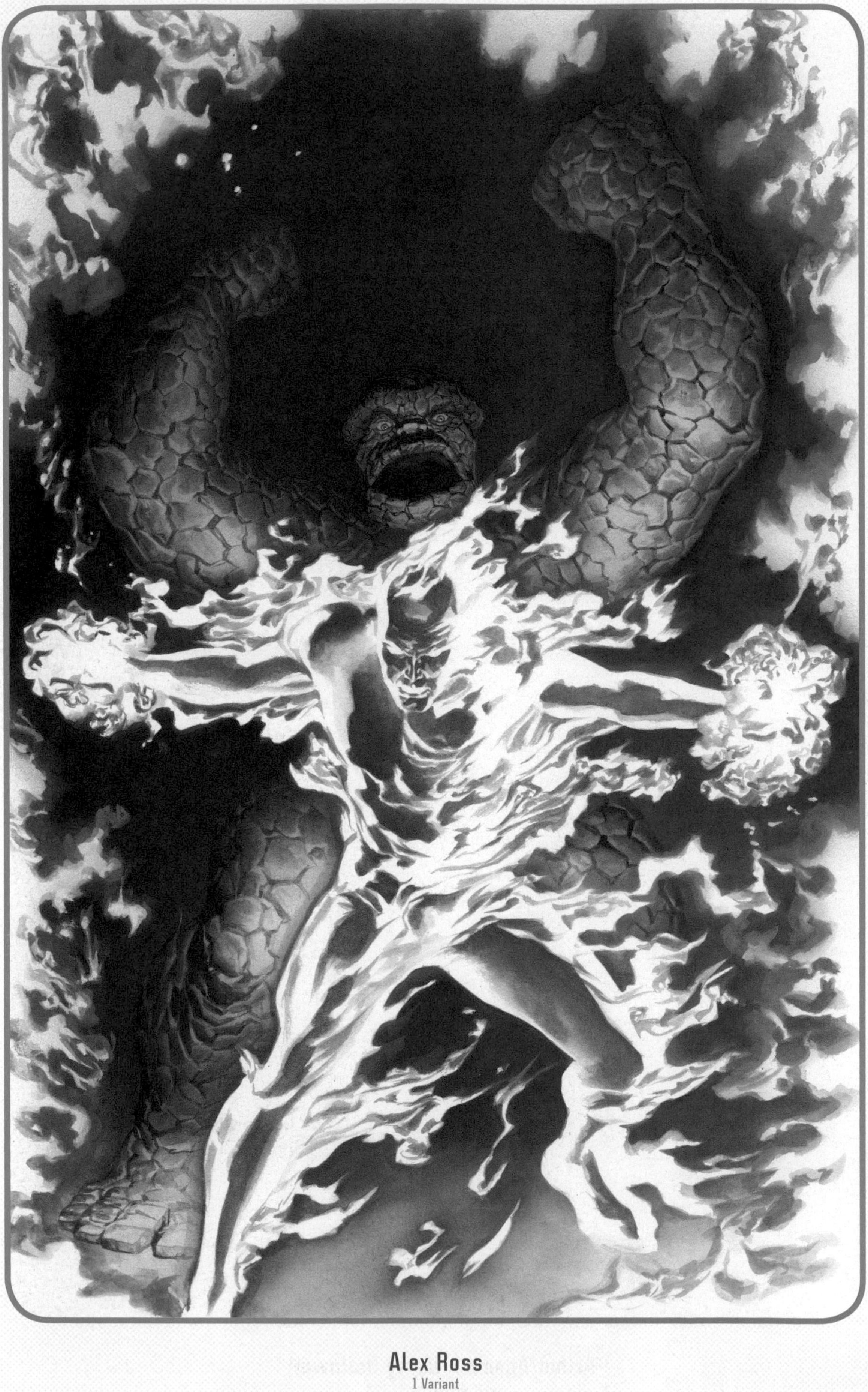

Alex Ross
1 Variant

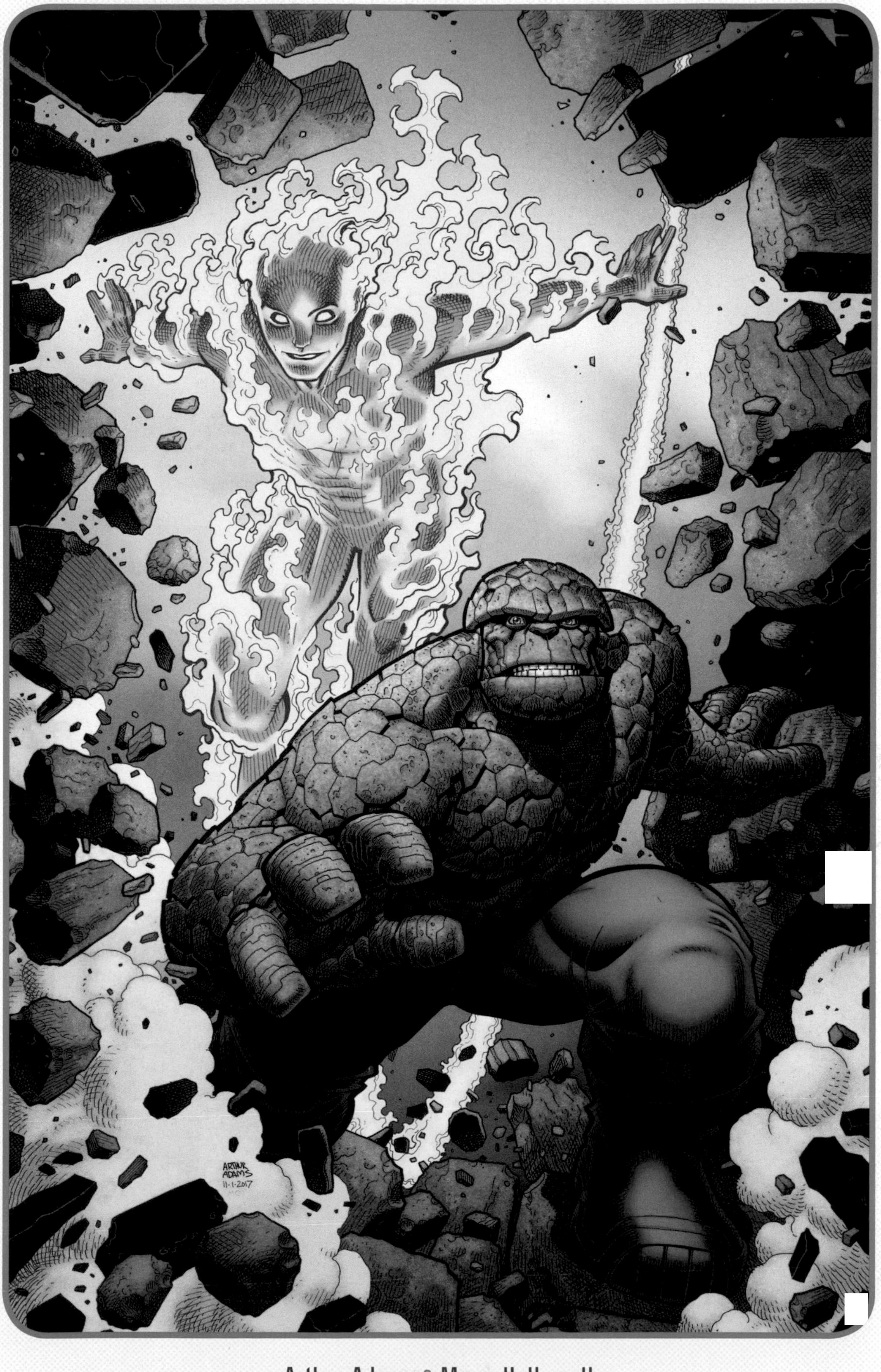
ARTHUR ADAMS
11-1-2017

Arthur Adams & Morry Hollowell
1 Variant

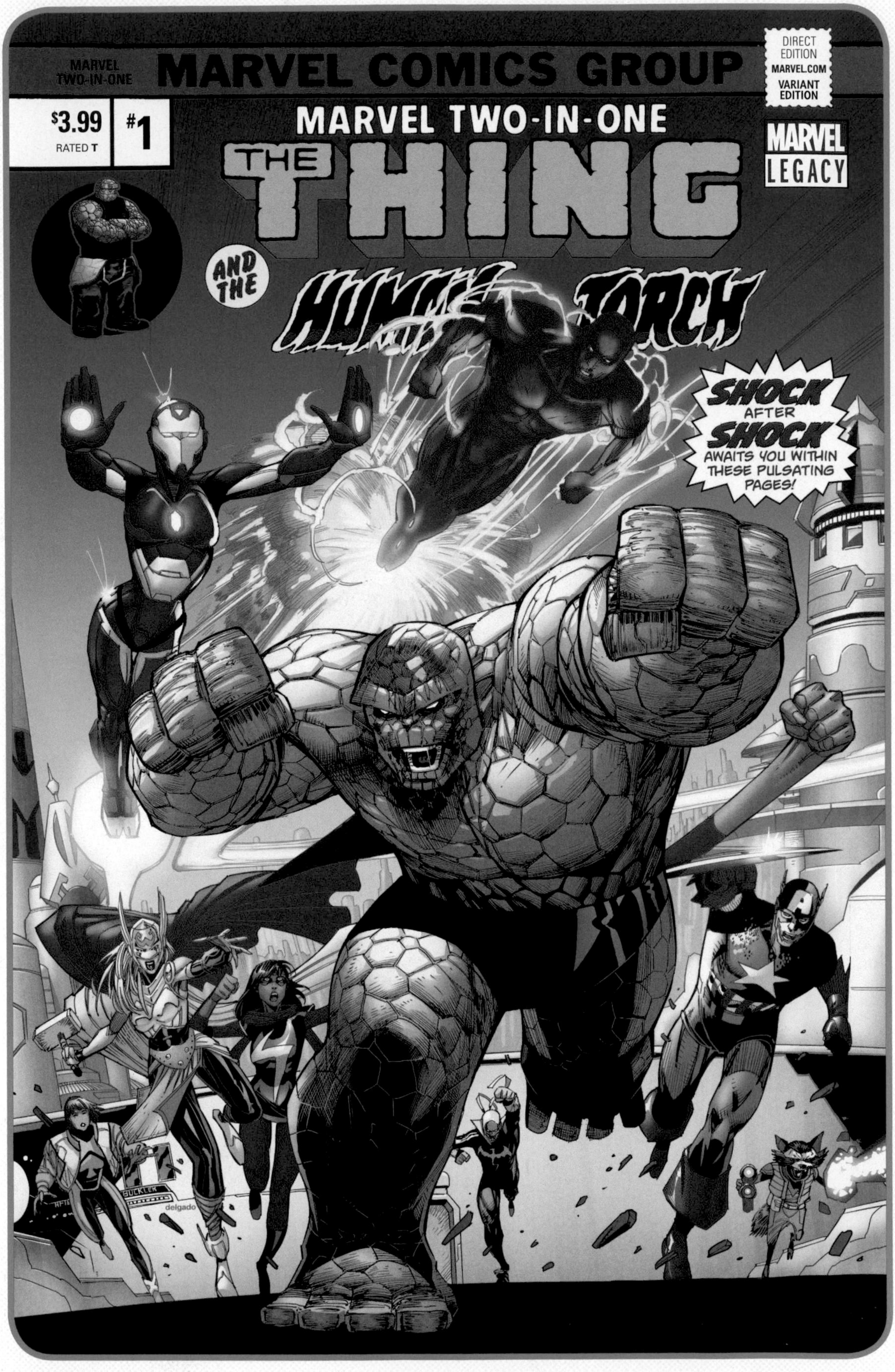
MARVEL TWO-IN-ONE
MARVEL COMICS GROUP
DIRECT EDITION MARVEL.COM
VARIANT EDITION
$3.99 RATED T
#1
MARVEL TWO-IN-ONE
THE THING
AND THE
HUMAN TORCH
MARVEL LEGACY
SHOCK AFTER SHOCK AWAITS YOU WITHIN THESE PULSATING PAGES!

Jon Malin & Edgar Delgado
1 Homage Variant

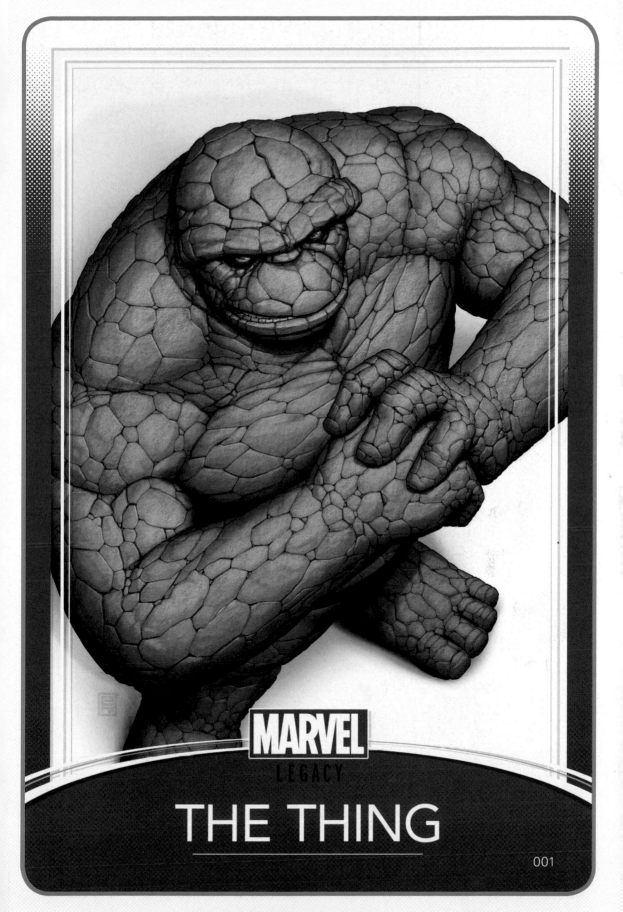

MARVEL
LEGACY

THE THING

001

John Tyler Christopher
1 Trading Card Variant

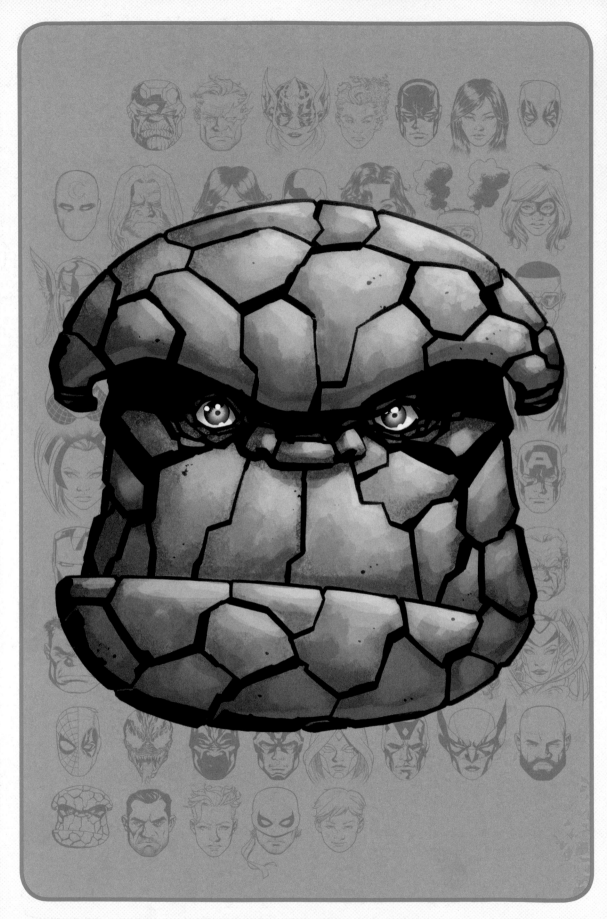

Mike McKone & Rachelle Rosenberg
1 Legacy Headshot Variant

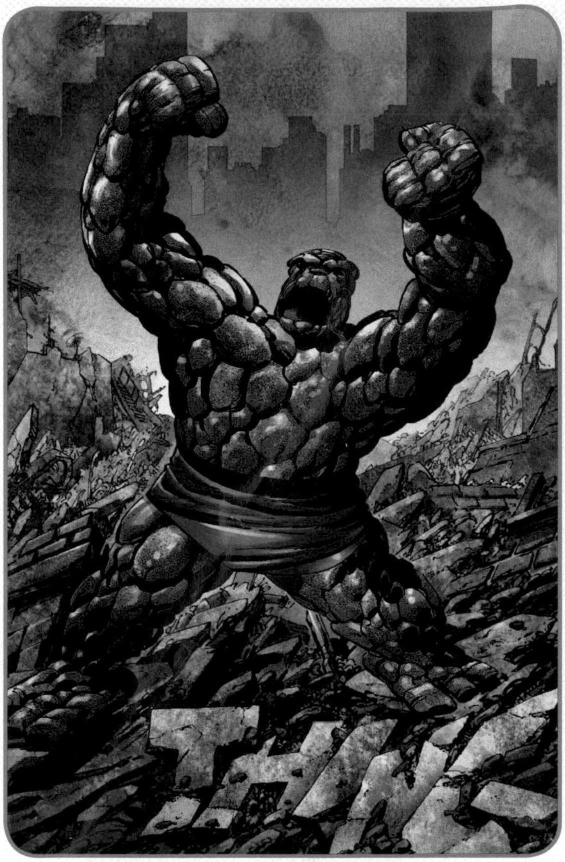

John Byrne & Paul Mounts with Joe Frontirre
1 Remastered Variant

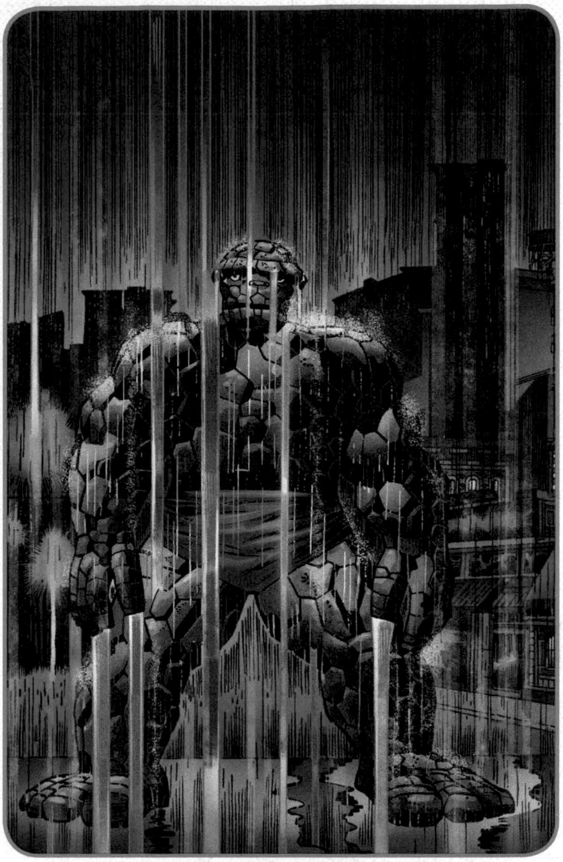

Jack Kirby & Joe Sinnott, Paul Mounts with Joe Frontirre
1 Kirby 100th Variant

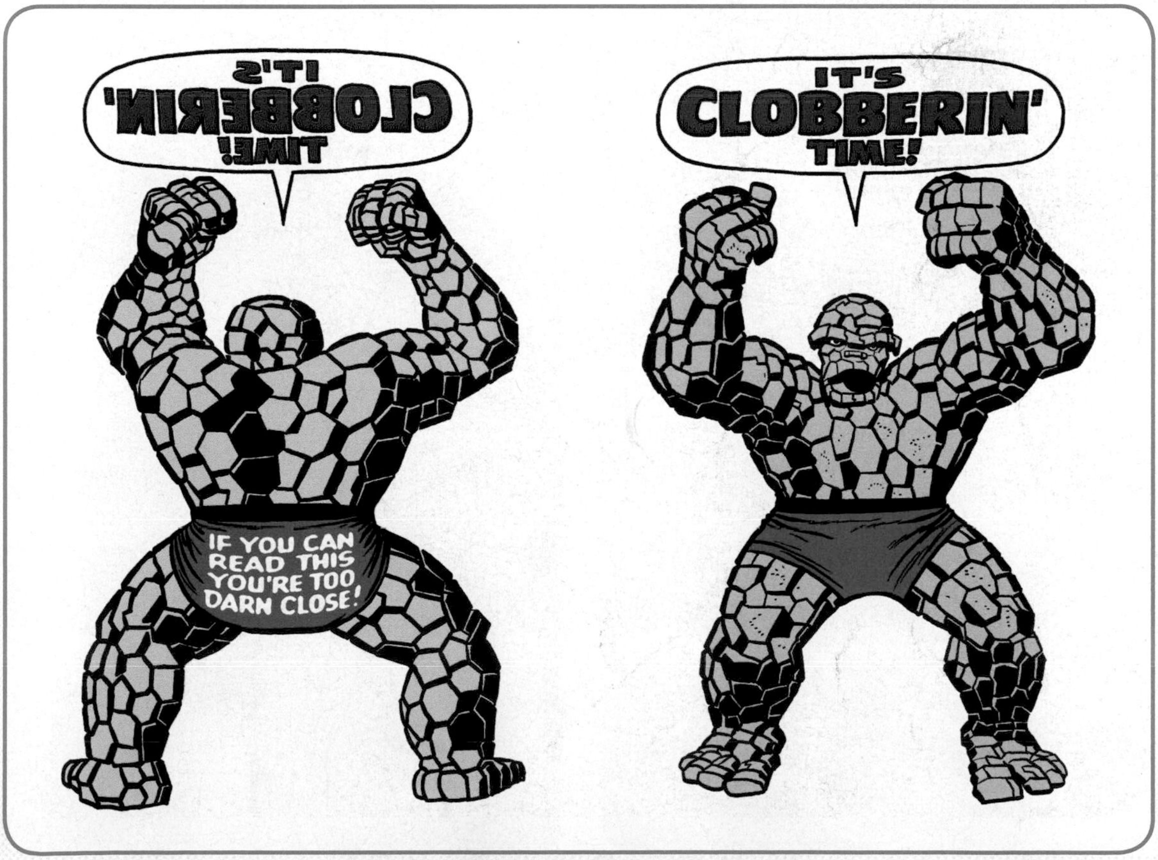
IF YOU CAN READ THIS YOU'RE TOO DARN CLOSE!
IT'S CLOBBERIN' TIME!

Jack Kirby & Joe Sinnott
1 1965 T-Shirt Variant

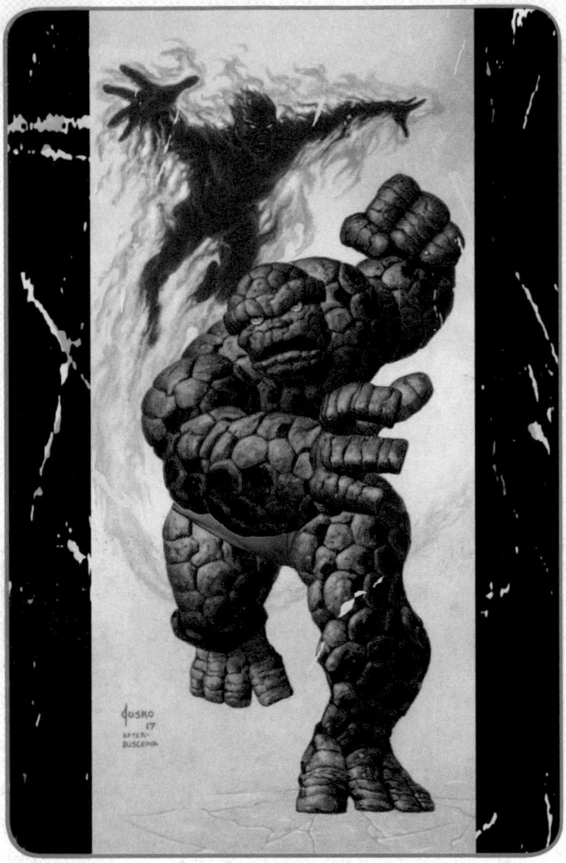

Joe Jusko
1 Variant

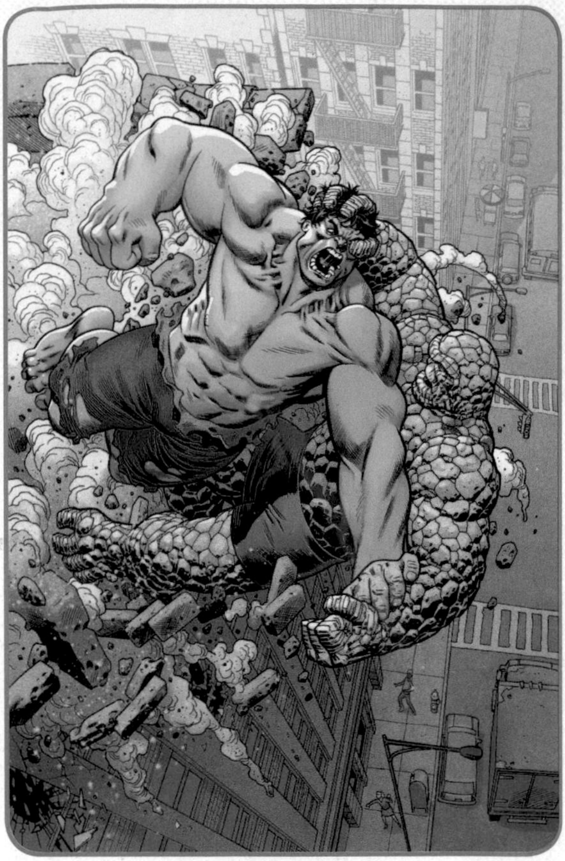

Mike Hawthorne & Nolan Woodard
3 Hulk Variant

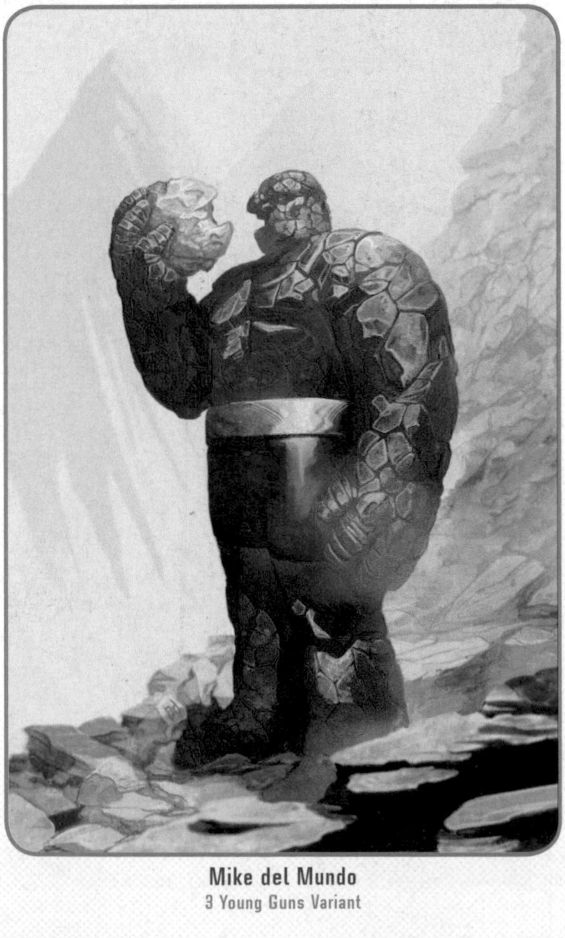

Mike del Mundo
3 Young Guns Variant

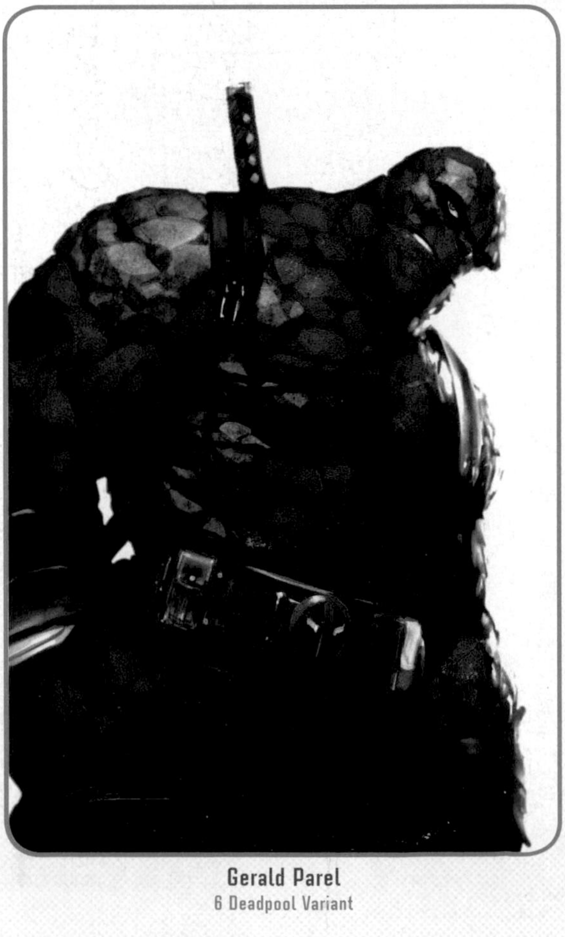

Gerald Parel
6 Deadpool Variant